I Choose Us

A Christian Perspective on Building Love Connection in Your Marriage by Breaking Harmful Cycles

John Philip Louis & Karen McDonald Louis

LCTS
Louis Counselling & Training Services Pte. Ltd.

All rights reserved. No part of this publication may be reproduced, stored in a retrieval system, electronic or transmitted, in any form or by any means, electronic, mechanical, photocopying, recording or otherwise, without the prior written consent of the publisher.

Copyright © 2010 by Louis Counselling & Training Services Pte Ltd
Website: http://www.icu.sg
Email: johnlouis@louiscts.com

All scriptures quotations, unless otherwise stated are from the Holy Bible, New International Version, copyright © 1973, 1978, 1984 by International Bible Society. Used by Permission of Zondervan Publishing House. All rights reserved.

First Edition Printed in Singapore

First Edition
National Library Board, Singapore Cataloguing-in-Publication Data

Louis, John Philip, 1963-
I choose us / John Philip Louis & Karen McDonald Louis; contributing editor, Catherine Amon. – Singapore : Louis Counselling & Training Services, c2010.
p. cm.
Includes bibliographical references and index.
ISBN-13 : 978-981-08-5597-0 (pbk.)

1. Marriage – Religious aspects – Christianity. I. Louis, Karen McDonald, 1962- II. Amon, Catherine. III. Title.

248.844 -- dc22   OCN600917008

Previous ISBN: 978-981-08-5597-0

Second Edition
Copyright © 2015 by Louis Counselling & Training Services Pte Ltd American Edition ISBN: 978-1-939086-94-5. Distributed by Illumination Publishers. Illumination Publishers, 6010 Pinecreek Ridge Court, Spring, Texas 77379
New ISBN: 978-1-939086-94-5. Available at www.ipibooks.com.

I Choose Us by John & Karen Louis
Illustrations by Sher Lee Wee
Assisted by: Tan Beng Hwa

*We lovingly dedicate this book
to the brothers and sisters
of the Central Christian Church
in Singapore.*

Preface

Why another book about marriage? This project got started because people who have attended our Movie Therapy™ Marriage Workshops over the years have been asking us to write a book to go along with it. After putting them off as long as possible, we finally started and this is it.

But once we began writing, we felt that this book really *needed* to be written. We have been married for over 23 years, and we have learned lots of lessons the hard way, so we thought it would be nice if we could help others learn things a bit sooner and easier than we did. And in our work as Christian ministers, leadership trainers, and marriage counsellors, we have done thousands of hours of reading and research on marriage. Since we know most folks don't have that kind of time, we have distilled our favourite ideas, findings, and convictions into one book. (On this note, we offer a tip—this is probably not a book to be read in one sitting, or even in one week. We hope it will be used over the years, with different sections being more pertinent to your marriage at different times.) Lastly, ever since we began combining spiritual principles with Jeffrey Young's theories of Schema Therapy, we have been able to help resolve marriage issues that in the past had us completely stumped. We are true believers of the teachings we advocate in our workshops and in this book, and we really try to practise what we preach, albeit imperfectly—once you read some of our foibles inside, you'll see what we mean! (By the way, since we are writing from Singapore, we are using British spelling.) We hope you enjoy…

John and Karen Louis
Singapore, 2010

ADDITION TO THE PREFACE FOR OUR 2015 EDITION

In our updated version, we have added new info about Core Emotional Needs, and made references to our *Good Enough Parenting* book, released in 2012. *I Choose Us* has been translated into seven languages with more in the works, and is a recommended curriculum on the website for the US Department of Health and Human Services. We began two websites of our own, www.icu.sg and www.gep.sg, and the "Good Enough Parenting Workshop" has been taught on every continent except for Antarctica! We hope you enjoy the updates.

Love in Christ and for His glory,

The Louis, 2015

Acknowledgments

To everyone who has helped us to be able to say, "I Choose Us", we say, "THANK YOU!"

Thank you to our parents, Craig & Ann McDonald, and Philip & Sosamma Louis for being great role models of staying together "till death do us part" and fulfilling their vows "to have and to hold". *We are eternally grateful to you for many things, but especially for your faithfulness to one another.*

Thank you to all the couples from churches around the world who have given us marriage counselling throughout our journey. *There are at least 34 of you, too many to name, but you know who you are!* A special thank you to our Southeast Asia Ministry Group—the Salims, the Sims, the Ngs, the Yamazakis, and the Hartonos. *You know us inside out, and never fail to intervene when our marriage gets stuck—thank you for speaking the truth in love. We hope our partnership continues for many years to come.*

We are very grateful to those who have instructed us in various aspects of counselling: First and foremost, as this book contains many principles of Schema Therapy, we would like to thank Jeffrey Young, the founder of Schema Therapy, for training John to be a Schema Therapist and for giving us permission to use some of his material. *Thank you for training us and giving us your blessing so that we could help transform marriages and families with principles from schema therapy!*

Next, we would like to give special mention to Catherine Amon, a kindred spirit, whose help on Chapters 3 and 4 was invaluable. Sadly, several years after the first printing of this book, Catherine lost her battle with cancer. Catherine was not only my (John's) supervisor when I trained to be a Schema Therapist, but she was also a dear friend and confidante to both of us. *Catherine, you will always be with us in spirit, but you are sorely missed...*

ACKNOWLEDGMENTS

We also would like to thank John Ang from the National University of Singapore. He was our first instructor in the world of parenting education and basic counselling. *You broadened our horizons, and you made room in your heart for us in the midst of your busy schedule.* And thanks to Gary Solomon, the founder of Cinematherapy, who so generously gave us his time and expertise. *There would be no Movie Therapy™ without you.*

Bouquets are also very much due to the rest of the folks who helped us write this book: Dr Catherine M Flanagan, Department of Psychiatry, Weill-Cornell University Medical College, New York, for her incredibly beneficial feedback, especially with regards to the schema cartoons; Dr Shirlena Huang, a ruthless editor and trustworthy friend; Dr Randall Janka, another ruthless editor and fellow Movie Therapy™ buff; Sher Lee Wee, our brilliant cartoonist and Tan Beng Hwa, who assisted her; numerous friends and colleagues who contributed in one way or another; and most importantly, Pat Sim, our Movie Therapy™ assistant—she gave more than 100% to help us, from formatting to meeting deadlines. *To all of you we say, "Thank you, thank you, thank you!"*

We end by saying, *"Thanks be to God,"* who saw fit to bring a Malaysian and a Texan together in the first place. To Him be the Glory forever and ever, amen.

TABLE OF CONTENTS

PREFACE ii

ACKNOWLEDGMENTS iv

TABLE OF CONTENTS vi

INTRODUCTION – WHY SHOULD I CHOOSE "US"? 1
    Marriage Affects Our Work 4
    Marriage Affects Our Health 5
    Marriage Affects Our Parenting 6
    A Qualifier for Single Parents… 13
    In Conclusion 14

CHAPTER 1: CHOOSE LOVE CONNECTION 17
    Infatuation vs. Love Connection 17
    Mutual Affection and Disintegration 26

CHAPTER 2: CHOOSE LOVE & RESPECT 33
    FOR HUSBANDS 36
    Considerate Listeners 36
    Responsible Leaders 40
    Romantic Lovers 46
    FOR WIVES 48
    Appreciate 48
    Initiate 52
    Participate 54
    Roadblocks to Love Connection and Meeting the Need
    of Love and Respect 56
    Love Connection Enhanced by Trust and Friendship 56

TABLE OF CONTENTS

CHAPTER 3: CHOOSE AWARENESS 63
    Lifetraps (Schemas) 64
    Coping Styles 68
    Understanding Our Past 75
    Identifying Our Lifetraps 77
        The Domain Of Disconnection & Rejection 78
        Mistrust / Abuse 78
        Defectiveness / Shame 83
        Emotional Deprivation 90
        Social Isolation / Alienation 95
        Emotional Inhibition 100
        Failure 105
        The Domain Of Impaired Autonomy & Performance 110
        Vulnerability To Harm Or Illness 110
        Dependence / Incompetence 115
        Enmeshment / Undeveloped Self 120
        Abandonment / Instability 125
        Subjugation 130
        Negativity / Pessimism 135
        The Domain Of Impaired Limits 139
        Entitlement / Grandiosity 140
        Insufficient Self-Control / Self-Discipline 147
        Approval-Seeking / Recognition-Seeking 152
        The Domain Of Exaggerated Expectations 157
        Unrelenting Standards / Hypercriticalness 157
        Punitiveness 162
        Self-Sacrifice 167
    Vortex of Conflict Escalation 172

CHAPTER 4: CHOOSE TO BE VULNERABLE 179
    Being Vulnerable—A Pathway to Healing 180
    How To Be Vulnerable 185

Helping Each Other Heal: A Ten Point Plan for Weakening
Lifetraps and Coping Styles 187

CHAPTER 5: CHOOSE FIDELITY 205
   Definition of An Affair 206
   Why Does Anyone Cheat? 207
   Affairs Do Not Happen Overnight 208
   What If I'm No Longer Attracted to My Spouse? 211
   If Infidelity Has Occurred, What Next? 211

CHAPTER 6: CHOOSE RECONCILIATION 217
   Defining Forgiveness 218
   Forgiveness vs. Reconciliation 221
   Process Your Anger, Guilt and Shame 224
   Steps to Help Couples Forgive Each Other 229

EPILOGUE: IN CONCLUSION 237

APPENDIX 1: DIVORCE STATISTICS 238

APPENDIX 2: DIVORCE IN SINGAPORE 240

APPENDIX 3: HOW WORK AFFECTS MARRIAGE 241

APPENDIX 4: MARRIAGE VS. COHABITATION 243

APPENDIX 5: CORE EMOTIONAL NEEDS 245

APPENDIX 6: A JOURNAL FOR YOUR LIFETRAPS & COPING STYLES 246

APPENDIX 7: HEALING IMAGERY EXERCISE 247

APPENDIX 8: EXERCISE TO DEVELOP EMPATHY 250

REFERENCES 252

INDEX 254

INTRODUCTION

WHY SHOULD I CHOOSE "US"?

For the most part, marriages that are satisfying and fulfilling today are where they are because of the choices both partners have made. While there are exceptions, generally speaking, healthy marriages do not just happen. Healthy marriages are a result of choices that people make—intentional, deliberate, and wise choices.

Divorce in many countries is reaching alarming rates. A divorce rate of 40-50% is now the norm for countries like Sweden, Russia, the US, the UK, and many other European countries.[1] (Please refer to Appendix 1, *Divorce Statistics*). Unfortunately, even countries with traditionally low divorce rates, such as Singapore where we are based, are seeing more and more marriages split up. (Please refer to Appendix 2, *Divorce in Singapore*). Suffice it to say, whether in Stockholm, Seattle, or Shanghai, many marriages are unfulfilled and people are hurting.

Remarriage is not exactly a recommended solution either—research reveals that divorces in second marriages are about the same or 10% higher.[2] So much for thinking that after making mistakes the first time around, it's easy to remarry and start afresh. What usually happens is that the same problems are brought into the new relationship, and the cycle repeats itself.

---

[1] World divorce statistics. (n.d.). *Divorce Magazine*. Retrieved January 13, 2010, from http://www.divorcemag.com/statistics/statsWorld.shtml
[2] Martin, T. C., & Bumpass, L. L. (1989). Recent trends in marital disruption. *Demography 26*(1), 37-51.

These divorce statistics may frighten you. You surely have friends, relatives and colleagues whose marriages have ended or are on the rocks. You may be separated yourself, or think that making a marriage work is too difficult, or that at best, you'll have to settle for a mediocre marital relationship. We disagree. We believe that if you and your spouse will choose to put your marriage first, and work toward what we call "Love Connection", your marriage can become healthy and vibrant. Our book, *I Choose Us*, combines biblical teaching and more than a quarter century of cross-cultural marriage experience with findings from our research and real life counselling situations to help people like you make the right choices. (We urge those reading this book who are divorced to not take these statistics on divorce personally; they are not meant in judgment, rather they are meant to persuade couples on the verge of divorce to get counselling and try one more time, and also to paint an accurate picture statistically as to the possible and often probable outcomes of divorce. If readers happen to be in a second or third marriage, it is our goal that the principles found in *I Choose Us* might offer hope this time around.)

If you are reading this book, it shows that you *are* taking your marriage seriously. We want to *reinforce* your convictions. An unhealthy or failed marriage has farther-reaching consequences than most people realise. Each divorce statistic represents a myriad of tears, anger, despair and sadness. The collective emotional impact creates a tsunami of spiritual, mental and physical damage. Our marriages affect many facets of our lives. As an introduction to our book, we would like to bring your attention to the way our marriages affect our *work*, our *health*, and our *parenting*.

Many think that we can and should separate our marriage from other aspects of our lives. For example, we often hear of bosses who say, "When you walk into this office, leave your personal problems at the door; work is work." Then when you go back home, you hear your spouse say, "When you come home, leave your office behind. Family is family, work is work." Is this really possible? Our conviction is that our marriages have an enormous impact on our lives and deserve our priority and focus.

Unfortunately, in our experience, we have found that the priorities of most men and women usually look something like this:

Although we are speaking in general terms, this is a trend we have seen. Each partner places the other last in his or her list of priorities compared to work, children, hobbies, and household chores. This gives married couples very little undivided time for each other.

Statistics from the UK reveal modern pressures leave wives with *only ten minutes a day to talk to their husbands!* They are so busy that 40% have to save the important conversations for the car.[3] (That's when traffic jams come in handy.) Further, when couples do snatch a moment, family topics dominate the conversation nine out of ten times. When do couples actually sit down and talk with each other to nurture their relationship? Even if they do, how long does this last? If couples are only talking ten minutes a day, it would take a miracle to stay married. Is it any wonder that half of all marriages end in divorce? Ten minutes a day is not enough if you want to have a vibrant marriage. Consider the following:
- What if your children only spent ten minutes a day on their homework?
- What if your local football team only practised for ten minutes a day?
- What if you only spent ten minutes a day on personal health, hygiene and grooming?
- What if you only spent ten minutes a day starting a new business?

---

[3] Massey, R. (2007, April 26). Time pressures 'leave couples only ten minutes a day to talk'. *Mail Online*. Retrieved January 13, 2010, from http://www.dailymail.co.uk/news/article-450749/

We would not get very far in life if we set aside only ten minutes a day on any of the above. We would fail our subjects, get thrashed in sports, and our new businesses would quickly go bankrupt. Why should it be any different with our marriages? Please bear with us as we shower you with statistics to make our point!

Marriage Affects Our Work

- A significant longitudinal study found that marital quality and job satisfaction are related to each other, but that of the two domains, marital quality is the more influential; the higher the marital quality, the higher the job satisfaction. The researchers interviewed 1,065 people four times over a twelve-year period. They found that marriage (and the state thereof) affects the quality of work both positively and negatively, more than the other way around.[4]
- Happily married men stay on their job longer, miss work less and are more motivated than those not happily married.[5]
- American businesses miss out on around $6 billion annually due to lost productivity arising from marriage and relationship difficulties.[6]
- Divorce can disrupt the productivity of an individual worker by three years.[7]
- In the year following divorce, employees lose an average of 168 hours of work time. This amounts to being absent for four weeks in one year, a loss of about 8% of annual working hours.[8]
- In their startling report, "Marriage & Family Wellness: Corporate America's Business?", Dr Matthew Turvey and Dr David Olson found that for every $1 companies invest in physical and relational wellness, they get returns in the range of $1.50-$6.85. They also found that unhappily married people and divorcing employees decrease profitability of a company! Long term, it is worth making the marriages of employees a priority.[9] Wall Street, are you listening? (Please refer to Appendix 3, *How Work Affects Marriage*).

---

[4] Rogers, S. J., & May, D. C. (2003). Spillover between marital quality and job satisfaction: Long-term patterns and gender differences. *Journal of Marriage and Family, 65*(2), 482-495.

[5] Corporate Resource Council. (2002). *Why promote healthy marriages?* [Brochure]. Retrieved January 13, 2010, from http://www.corporateresourcecouncil.org/brochures.html

[6] Forthofer, M. S., Markman, H. J., Cox, M., Stanley, S., & Kessler, R. C. (1996). Associations between marital distress and work loss in a national sample. *Journal of Marriage and Family, 58*, 597-605.

[7] Corporate Resource Council. (2002). *Why promote healthy marriages?* [Brochure]. Retrieved January 13, 2010, from http://www.corporateresourcecouncil.org/brochures.html

[8] Muella, R. (2005). The effect of marital dissolution on the labour supply of males and females: Evidence from Canada. *Journal of Socio-Economics, 34*, 787-809.

[9] Turvey, M. D., & Olson, D. H. (2006). *Marriage & family wellness: Corporate America's business?* Roseville, MN: Life Innovation, Inc. 11-12.

Marriage Affects Our Health

- Pienta, Hayward and Jenkins studied 9,333 people in the United States between the ages of 51 and 61 in the year 2000. Comparisons were made between the married and non-married (cohabiting, divorced, widowed and never married). Their findings document that marriage benefits health across a broad spectrum of fatal and nonfatal chronic disease conditions, functioning problems and disabilities. Moreover, benefits of marriage are widely shared across demographic groups.[10] (For more information, please refer to Appendix 4, *Marriage vs. Cohabitation*).
- The health of a happily married man is improved to the extent that he is around 18 months younger than his chronological age. For women, the benefit is six months.[11]
- Couples in failing marriages have lower immune system functioning than people in better quality marriages.[12]
- Stress from one's marriage has a direct influence on depression levels.[13]
- Young married couples consume less alcohol than singles, while those who experience divorce tend to drink more.[14]
- Poor marital quality affects the stress level of both men and women equally. A study done with 105 middle-aged civil service workers in the London area revealed that those with poor quality marriages suffered more stress and had elevated blood pressure readings during the workday. This increased risk of heart attack and stroke was the same for both men and women.[15]
- A study by the World Health Organization across 15 countries involving 34,500 people in developing and developed nations over the past decade

---

[10] Pienta, A. M., Hayward, M. D., Jenkins, K. R. (2000). Health consequences of marriage for the retirement years. *Journal of Family Issues, 21*(5), 559-586.

[11] Waite, L., & Gallagher, M. (2000). *The case for marriage: Why married people are happier, healthier, and better off financially.* New York: Doubleday. 48.

[12] Waite, L., & Gallagher, M. (2000). *The case for marriage: Why married people are happier, healthier, and better off financially.* New York: Doubleday. 57.

[13] Vermulst, A., & Dubas, J. (1999). Job stress and family functioning: The mediating role for parental depression and the explaining role of emotional stability. *Tijdschrift voor Psycholigie & Gezonheid, 27*, 96-102.

[14] Power, C., Rodgers, B., & Hope, S. (1999). Heavy alcohol consumption and marital status: Disentangling the relationship in a national study of young adults. *Addiction, 94*(10), 1477-1487; Miller-Tutzauer, C., Leonard, K. E., & Windle, M. (1991). Marriage and alcohol use: A longitudinal study of maturing out. *Journal of Studies on Alcohol, 52*, 434-440.

[15] Barnett, R. C., Steptoe, A., & Gareis, K. C. (2005). Marital-role quality and stress-related psychobiological indicators. *Annals of Behavioral Medicine, 30*, 36-43.

shows that people who are married are less likely than their unmarried counterparts to suffer from depression, anxiety, and substance abuse.[16]
- Divorcees are more than twice as likely to be suicidal than people who are married.[17]
- A good quality marital relationship improves the emotional well-being of both the husband and wife.[18]

Marriage Affects Our Parenting

We are using the term parenting to mean how we bring up our children and we are assuming that parents are mindful of their children's well-being when they go about their parenting. In that context, is it possible to separate the two—marriage and parenting? How many times have we heard parents say they do not want their divorce to hurt their children? Consider the following:
- In 2001 the *New York Times* reported that from a child's point of view, according to a growing body of social science research, the most supportive household is one with two biological parents in a low conflict marriage.[19]
- Children, on average, do best when reared by their married biological mother and father in a stable and intact family.[20] Sadly, in Singapore, a

---

[16] Marriage good for health (2009, 16 December). *The Straits Times*, A18.
[17] Johnson, G. R., Krug, E. G., & Potter, L. B. (2000). Suicide among adolescents and young adults: A cross-national comparison of 34 countries. *Suicide and Life-Threatening Behavior, 30*(1), 74-82; Lester, D. (1994). Domestic integration and suicide in 21 nations, 1950-1985. *International Journal of Comparative Sociology XXXV*(1-2), 131-137; Kessler, R. C., Borges, G., & Walters, E. E. (1999). Prevalence of and risk factors for lifetime suicide attempts in the national comorbidity survey. *Archives of General Psychiatry, 56*, 617-626.
[18] Hope, S., Power, C., & Rodgers, B. (1999). Does financial hardship account for elevated psychological distress in lone mothers? *Social Science and Medicine, 49*(12), 1637-1649; Marks, N. F., & Lambert, J. D. (1998). Marital status continuity and change among young and midlife adults: Longitudinal effects on psychological well-being. *Journal of Family Issues, 19*, 652-686; Horwitz, A. V., White, H. R., & Howell-White, S. (1996). Becoming married and mental health: A longitudinal study of a cohort of young adult. *Journal of Marriage and the Family, 58*, 895-907; Horwitz, A. V., & White, H. R. (1991). Becoming married, depression, and alcohol problems among young adults. *Journal of Health and Social Behavior, 32*, 221-237; Kessler, R. C., & Essex, M. (1982). Marital status and depression: The importance of coping resources. *Social Forces, 61*, 484-507; Deal, L., & Holt, V. (1998). Young maternal age and depressive symptoms: Results from the 1988 national maternal and infant health survey. *American Journal of Public Health, 88*(2), 266-270.
[19] Harden, B. (2001, August 12). 2-parent families rise after change in welfare laws. *The New York Times*. Retrieved on January 4, 2010, from www.nytimes.com
[20] Moore, K. A., Jekielek, S. M., & Emig, C. (2002, June). Marriage from a child's perspective: How does family structure affect children, and what can be done about it? *Child Trends Research Brief*. Washington, DC: Child Trends. 6.

INTRODUCTION

small nation with a population of only five million, almost 6,000 children suffer through their parents' divorce every year.[21]

- In the United States, thirteen highly regarded social scientists worked together in a project sponsored by the Institute for American Values. (Rebecca O'Neill wrote a UK version of this study.[22]) The US report, *Why Marriage Matters*, concludes that marriage is an important social good, associated with an impressively broad array of positive outcomes for children and adults alike.[23]

Let's look at the effect of marriage on *specific* aspects of parenting:

Relationship between Parents and Children

- Single mothers on average report twice as much upsetting behaviour from their children as do married mothers.[24] Adult children from intact marriages report being closer to their mothers than adult children of divorced parents.[25]
- Compared to 29% from non-divorced families, 65% of young adults with divorced parents have poor relationships with their fathers.[26]
- In Britain, less than half of the children in single parent families see their fathers once a week. And 20-30% of non-resident fathers see their children less than once a year.[27] In the wake of divorce, it is common for the "leaving parent"—the one not getting basic custody, usually the father—to promise the children that he will always be there for them and

---

[21] Family Policy Unit, Ministry of Community Development, Youth and Sports. (2009, October 28). *Executive summary: State of the family in Singapore.* 5. Retrieved January 4, 2010, from http://fcd.ecitizen.gov.sg/NR/rdonlyres/2BD3B979-A48F-4C45-B29E-1CA36068585E/0/ExecutiveSummary.pdf

[22] O'Neill, R. (2005). *Does marriage matter?* London: Civitas, Institute for the Study of Civil Society.

[23] Doherty, W. J., et al. (2002). *Why marriage matters: Twenty-one conclusions from the social sciences.* New York: Institute for American Values. 5. (A second edition of this study was conducted in 2005 with the same findings).

[24] Cockett, M., & Tripp, J. (1994). *The Exeter family study: Family breakdown and its impact on children.* Exeter: University of Exeter Press. 28.

[25] O'Neill, R. (2005). *Does marriage matter?* London: Civitas, Institute for the Study of Civil Society. 6.

[26] Zill, N., Morrison, D. R., & Coiro, M. J. (1993). Long-term effects of parental divorce on parent-child relationships, adjustment, and achievement in young adulthood. *Journal of Family Psychology, 7*(1), 91-103; Amato, P. R., & Booth, A. (1997). *A generation at risk: Growing up in an era of family upheaval.* Cambridge, MA: Harvard University Press.

[27] Burghes, L., Clarke, L., & Cronin, N. (1997). *Fathers and fatherhood in Britain.* London: Family Policy Studies Centre; Bradshaw, J., & Millar, J. (1991). *Lone parent families in the UK.* Department of Social Security Research Report No 6. London: HMSO.

will maintain a close relationship with them. Unfortunately, because of inconveniences arising from the divorce, and for other reasons, fathers often find it challenging to keep this promise. It should not come as a surprise that many good intentions fall through on the part of both parents after the pain of divorce, and it is not uncommon for the bond between fathers and their children to deteriorate in such cases.
- Children in single parent families receive about nine hours less from their mother per week than children from families where the parents are still married and living together.[28]

> *In our marriage, we have found that dividing responsibilities makes for healthier family life. For example, when the kids were younger, John helped the children out with their math and science, while Karen was on standby to give suggestions with regards to history and English. When it came to conflict resolution, we took turns, depending on who was the "bad cop" in the children's eyes that day. We were both there to talk to the children when they had a difficult day at school, and we tried to have "non-judgmental" discussions with our teenagers whenever possible. As a result of this team effort, we were, and still are, usually able to sort out emotional issues fairly quickly.*

Parents as Role-Models
- Children whose parents stayed married until the children became adults themselves are more likely to imitate them and have stable marriages. They are also less likely to have children out of wedlock.[29]
- For daughters, this means a decreased likelihood of early teenage pregnancy. Daughters raised outside marriage are twice as likely as their peers to have a child outside marriage and 50% more likely to get a divorce.[30]

---

[28] Waite, L., & Gallagher, M. (2000). *The case for marriage: Why married people are happier, healthier, and better off financially.* New York: Doubleday. 128.

[29] Ross, C. E., & Mirowsky, J. (1999). Parental divorce, life course disruption, and adult depression. *Journal of Marriage and the Family, 61*, 1034-1045; Amato, P. R. (1996). Explaining the intergenerational transmission of divorce. *Journal of Marriage and the Family, 58*(3), 628-640; McLeod, J. I. (1991). Childhood parental loss and adult depression. *Journal of Health and Social Behavior, 32*, 205-220; Glenn, N. D., & Kramer, K. B. (1987). The marriages and divorces of the children of divorce. *Journal of Marriage and the Family, 49*, 811-825.

[30] O'Neill, R. (2005). *Does marriage matter?* London: Civitas, Institute for the Study of Civil Society. 8.

- For sons, parental divorce doubles the odds that they will have a child outside marriage and eventually go through a divorce.[31]
- A parental divorce during childhood continues to have a negative affect even when the child moves to adulthood and is in his twenties or thirties.[32]

We know that no one sets out to get divorced; we hope if parents know the dire consequences of the alternative, they will take better care of their marriage!

Children learn from example, and imitate their parental role models more than parents realise. The lives of the parents provide a blueprint of how the children will probably lead their lives later on. As the above statistics show, the quality of the parents' marriage affects the quality of the children's relationships when they end up getting married. Our actions have consequences, the effects of which are felt in more than one generation.

Impact of Economics of Divorce on Parenting
- Single mothers are twice as likely as two-parent families to live in poverty.[33] Single mothers are also eight times as likely to be without jobs and twelve times as likely to be on some form of government support.[34]
- Divorce causes the level of income for a middle-income family to decrease by 50%.[35]
- Single parents are also twice as likely to not have any savings.[36]
- Married couples have, on average, more wealth than singles in similar settings or cohabitating couples with similar incomes.[37] Perhaps that is because, in a functional marriage, there is more prudent spending

---

[31] O'Neill, R. (2005). *Does marriage matter?* London: Civitas, Institute for the Study of Civil Society. 8.
[32] Waite, L., & Gallagher, M. (2000). *The case for marriage: Why married people are happier, healthier, and better off financially.* New York: Doubleday. 146.
[33] O'Neill, R. (2005). *Does marriage matter?* London: Civitas, Institute for the Study of Civil Society. 10.
[34] Office for National Statistics. (2001). *Work and worklessness among households.* London: The Stationery Office; Office for National Statistics. (May 2002). *Family resources survey, Great Britain, 2000-01.* London: The Stationery Office.
[35] McLanahan, S., & Sandefur, G. (1994) *Growing up with a single parent.* Cambridge, MA: President and Fellows of Harvard College. 167-168.
[36] Office for National Statistics. (2002). *Social trends 32.* London: The Stationery Office. Table 5.25, 103.
[37] Lupton, J., & Smith, J. P. (2002). Marriage, assets and savings. In Grossbard-Schectman, S. A. (Ed.), *Marriage and the economy.* Cambridge: Cambridge University Press. 129-151; Hao, L. (1996). Family structure, private transfers, and the economic well-being of families and children. *Social Forces, 75*(1), 269-292.

- and better planning, such as buying a home together and sharing their resources.
- Research conducted worldwide found that married men earn between 10% and 40% more than do single men with similar education and job history.[38]
- The earning power of married men is 10-20% higher when compared to non-married men.[39] Certainly in a functional marriage, men gain a tremendous amount of emotional support from their wives. When marriage quality improves, work productivity often improves, as mentioned earlier.

Performance at School
- A shocking report indicates that children whose fathers have died do better in school than children whose parents are divorced.[40] It is speculated that children are able to attribute a more positive meaning from a death, however painful, than when their parents go through a divorce. In the case of divorce, children have been known to blame themselves, which usually does not happen in the event of a parent's death.
- Children whose parents remarry do no better in school than children raised by single mothers.[41]
- Children of divorced parents are less likely to graduate from university. They also stand to have a higher unemployment rate and face more economic hardship.[42]

---

[38] Waite, L., & Gallagher, M. (2000). *The case for marriage: Why married people are happier, healthier, and better off financially.* New York: Doubleday. 99; Gray, J. (1997). The fall in men's return to marriage. *Journal of Human Resources, 32*(3), 481-504; Schoeni, R. F. (1995). Marital status and earnings in developed countries. *Journal of Population Economics, 8,* 351-359; Korenman, S., & Neumark, D. (1991). Does marriage really make men more productive? *Journal of Human Resources, 26*(2), 282-307.

[39] Korenman, S., & Neumark, D. (1991). Does marriage really make men more productive? *Journal of Human Resources, 26*(2), 282-307.

[40] Biblarz, T. J. (2000). Family structure and children's success: A comparison of widowed and divorced single-mother families. *Journal of Marriage and the Family, 62*(2), 533-548.

[41] Jeynes, W. H. (1999). Effects of remarriage following divorce on the academic achievement of children. *Journal of Youth and Adolescence, 28*(3), 385-393; Zill, N., Morrison, D. R., & Coiro, M. J. (1993). Long-term effects of parental divorce on parent-child relationships, adjustment, and achievement in young adulthood. *Journal of Family Psychology, 7*(1), 91-103.

[42] Ely, M., West, P., Sweeting, H., & Richards, M. (2000). Teenage family life, life chances, lifestyles and health: A comparison of two contemporary cohorts. *International Journal of Law, Policy and the Family, 14,* 1-30; Ross, C. E., & Mirowsky, J. (1999). Parental divorce, life course disruption, and adult depression. *Journal of Marriage and the Family, 61,* 1034-1045; Amato, P. R., & Booth, A. (1997). *A generation at risk: Growing up in an era of family upheaval.* Cambridge, MA: Harvard University Press. 173-175.

- The National Child Development Study followed 10,000 British children from birth through young adulthood and found that children from married families are twice as likely as children from divorced families to attain some kind of qualification by the time they reach 33 years of age.[43]

Children's Health
- Children of divorced parents have a 50% increased likelihood of health problems over children from two-parent homes.[44]
- Children in single-parent homes are 80% more likely to have health problems, such as pains, headaches, and stomach symptoms, than children from two-parent homes, even after taking into account economic hardship.[45]
- Divorce causes children to have more emotional distress and increases the risk of mental illness.[46] These symptoms do not disappear quickly.
- The psychological effect of divorce on children is dependent on the quality of the marital relationship. If the level of conflict is high between the father and mother, children do better psychologically if the parents do get divorced. If it is low, and the parents still get a divorce, the children suffer more.[47] In the UK, more and more low-level conflict marriages are ending in divorce,[48] which may mean that more children are suffering.

Juvenile Delinquency
- Boys raised in a single parent environment are twice as likely as boys from two-parent homes to commit a crime by the time they reach thirty years old.[49]

---

[43] O'Neill, R. (2005). *Does marriage matter?* London: Civitas, Institute for the Study of Civil Society. 14.

[44] Cockett, M., & Tripp, J. (1994). *The Exeter family study: Family breakdown and its impact on children.* Exeter: University of Exeter Press. 21.

[45] Cockett, M., & Tripp, J. (1994). *The Exeter family study: Family breakdown and its impact on children.* Exeter: University of Exeter Press. 21.

[46] Amato, P. R. (2000). Consequences of divorce for adults and children. *Journal of Marriage and the Family 62*, 1269-1287; Simons, R. L., Lin, K-H., Gordon, L. C., Conger, R. D., & Lorenz, F. O. (1999). Explaining the higher incidence of adjustment problems among children of divorce compared with those in two-parent families. *Journal of Marriage and the Family, 61*(4), 1020-1033.

[47] Amato, P. R., & Booth, A. (2001). Parental predivorce relations and offspring postdivorce well-being. *Journal of Marriage and the Family, 63*(1), 197-212.

[48] Amato, P. R., & Booth, A. (2001). Parental predivorce relations and offspring postdivorce well-being. *Journal of Marriage and the Family, 63*(1), 197-212.

[49] Harper, C., & McLanahan, S. (1998, August). *Father absence and youth incarceration.* Paper presented at the annual meeting of the American Sociological Association, San Francisco, CA.

- Teenagers from both single parent and remarried homes are more likely to exhibit undesirable behaviour than those from homes of parents whose marriages are intact.[50]
- Young men from single parent homes are 60% more likely to be repeat-offenders than those from homes where the parents' marriages are intact.[51]

Child Abuse
- Children who live in a house with a stepfather, or a mother's boyfriend, are more likely to be abused than those living with their father or with a mother only.[52]
- Living with a stepparent has turned out to be the most powerful predictor of severe child abuse.[53]
- Young people are five times more likely to experience abuse if they grow up in a single parent home than if they grow up with parents whose marriages are still intact, according to the National Society for the Prevention of Cruelty to Children (NSPCC).[54]

The overwhelming evidence points conclusively to the fact that the state of marriages affects parenting, and has huge ramifications on children's relationships with their parents, economic well-being, physical and psychological health, protection from domestic violence, and the likelihood that these children in turn will stay together later on in their marriages.

---

[50] Coughlin, C., & Vuchinich, S. (1996). Family experience in preadolescence and the development of male delinquency. *Journal of Marriage and the Family, 58*(2), 491-501; Sampson, R. J., & Laub, J. H. (1994). Urban poverty and the family context of delinquency: A new look at structure and process in a classic study. *Child Development, 65*, 523-540; Sampson, R. J. (1987). Urban black violence: The effect of male joblessness and family disruption. *American Journal of Sociology, 93*, 348-382.

[51] Flood-Page, C., Campbell, S., Harrington, V., & Miller, J. (2000). *Youth crime: Findings from the 1998/99 youth lifestyle survey.* London: Home Office Research, Development and Statistics Directorate, Crime and Criminal Justice Unit.

[52] O'Neill, R. (2005). *Does marriage matter?* London: Civitas, Institute for the Study of Civil Society. 27.

[53] Daly, M., & Wilson, M. (1996). Evolutionary psychology and marital conflict: The relevance of stepchildren. In Buss, D. M., & Malamuth, N. M. (Eds.), *Sex, power, conflict: Evolutionary and feminist perspectives.* Oxford: Oxford University Press. 9-28.

[54] Cawson, P. (2002). *Child maltreatment in the family.* London: NSPCC. 10.

A Qualifier for Single Parents...

Having said much about the consequences of poor marriages and the devastation of divorce, we feel that we need to give a qualifier to those who have already gone through such an ordeal. Even though the data is more negative than positive, we do not want to say that everything has to be gloom and doom for parents once they get divorced. The above are "statistics", so, statistically speaking, the odds are against someone in this situation. However, we personally know many people who have been able to tap into their resilience and develop character during this difficult chapter of their lives. Sometimes it takes a crisis for these noble qualities to surface, and for some people, that is exactly what has happened.

We know of quite a few single parents who have done extraordinarily well, rising to the occasion because they were able to draw upon their inner strength and fight against the odds. They found new energy and new ways of getting support, either from extended family or from church friends who functioned like a family. They got busy with meaningful work, created new opportunities, developed new intimate relationships, and eventually made up for what was lacking in their single parent home. They were able to overcome their pain and eventually contribute to the well-being of others. Some of them also raised children who excelled, even beyond their peers who were from non-divorced families.

We hope, if you are in such a situation, that this will be true of you. To that end, we would like to recommend a great book by E. Mavis Hetherington and John Kelly, entitled *For Better or For Worse*,[55] about the choices that divorcees can make in order to get healed and have a positive impact on their children.

---

[55] Hetherington, E. M., & Kelly, J. (2002). *For better or for worse: Divorce reconsidered.* New York: W. W. Norton & Company, Inc.

In Conclusion

As we have helped more and more couples on the brink of divorce, what has become obvious to us is that couples come for counselling way too late! The conflicts that build up along the way, combined with unmet needs, erode a marriage long before one of the spouses starts talking divorce, which is usually when couples come for counselling.

In our opinion, what is indicated here is the need for proper marriage education, starting during the engagement period (or even earlier), and continuing on after the wedding. This would help couples to be empowered to meet each other's needs and be better equipped at conflict resolution. When couples come for help only after deep emotional wounds have been inflicted, the pain makes it difficult for them to have hope that their relationship will ever get any better. We believe that early education and intervention can make the difference. The old adage is true that "an ounce of prevention is worth a pound of cure".

Good healthy marriages have far-reaching consequences. They affect not just the couple and their offspring, but also their children's children. Marriages should thrive, not just survive. Healthy marriages have untold positive consequences on the family, the society and eventually the nation.

This book, along with the corresponding "I Choose Us" Movie Therapy™ workshop, is meant to be "an ounce of prevention" for some of you, and we hope that for others, it will provide the "pound of cure" that you need. Nothing would make us happier than thinking that couples around the world are taking each other by the hand, looking each other in the eye, and saying, "I Choose Us!"

You have convinced us. We are ready to start the journey, and we want to be able to say, "I Choose Us!" So, are you going to teach us how to get that "Just Married" feeling back?

CHAPTER 1

CHOOSE LOVE CONNECTION

Infatuation vs. Love Connection

"Falling in love", like falling into a manhole, or falling off a cliff, implies an unplanned and dangerous occurrence. Well, that is sort of accurate. We would like to point out that, while relationships with our spouse usually *begin* with "falling in love", otherwise known as the Infatuation phase, they don't stay that way forever. Our first challenge for couples: Don't lament the loss of infatuation. Instead, choose LOVE CONNECTION. (Read on to find out what that means!)

Merriam-Webster defines infatuation as "foolish or extravagant love or admiration."[56] Dr Elaine Hatfield, professor of psychology at the University of Hawaii and past president of The Society for the Scientific Study of Sex, calls this initial outburst of emotion "passionate love" and defines it as follows:

> A state of intense longing for union with an other. Reciprocated love (union with the other) is associated with fulfillment and ecstasy. Unrequited love (separation) with emptiness; with anxiety or despair. A state of profound physiological arousal.[57]

The power of infatuation has been acknowledged for years. Take a look at these lines from the Old Testament, written some 3000 years ago:

> *I will get up now and go about the city, through its streets and squares; I will search for the one my heart loves. So I looked for him but did not find him.* (Song of Songs 3:2)

---

[56] Infatuation. (1533). In *Merriam-Webster's online dictionary*. Retrieved January 18, 2010, from http://www.merriam-webster.com/netdict.htm
[57] Hatfield, E., & Walster, G. W. (1978). *A new look at love.* Reading, MA: Addison-Wesley. 9.

When two people "fall in love", they enter into the Infatuation phase, and become the centre of each other's world. Think back to your first love... You daydreamed about the object of your desire (see Figure 1). You made plans around him/her, and when you thought about your love, all problems seemed to fade away. (And, unbeknownst to you, your facial expression changed!) To you, he/she was the one, and you were sure that there was no other person for you.

It is said that love is blind. Dr Helen Fisher agrees. A anthropology professor at Rutgers University and expert on human attraction, Fisher conducted a survey about the thoughts of those in a state of infatuation. Of those surveyed, 65% of men and 55% of the women asserted that their lover *"has some faults but they don't really bother me."* And 64% of men and 61% of women agreed with the statement, *"I love everything about my boyfriend/girlfriend."* [58]

Figure 1: Infatuation

As wonderful as it feels, research shows that infatuation is only temporary. Dr Hatfield wrote that the Infatuation phase lasts at most for a few years and then declines over time.[59] And The University of Pavia in Italy reported that the Infatuation phase lasts for only one year. Piergluigi Politi and his colleagues found that a chemical cocktail in the bloodstream is responsible for the sweaty palms, increased heart rate, and queasy stomach felt with the first flush of love. The Italian researchers found high levels of certain chemicals in those who had just started a relationship, but after a year, the levels were back

---

[58] Fisher, H. (2004). *Why we love: The nature and chemistry of romantic love.* New York: Henry Holt and Company, LLC. 8.
[59] Hatfield, E., & Walster, G. W. (1978). *A new look at love.* Reading, MA: Addison-Wesley. 108.

to normal. Politi concluded that the love became more stable but the acute love was gone.[60]

So what happens after this phase? A new phase, which we call the Love Connection phase, is supposed to take over. Dr Hatfield refers to it as "companionate" love and describes it as "the affection we feel for those with whom our lives are deeply intertwined."[61]

Whatever the names, experts agree that this is a commitment-based love that can last forever, and is different from short-term infatuation. Most married couples want this kind of connection, a connection that will last, a connection that will lead them to being lovers and friends...hence, Love Connection.

A major difference between the Infatuation phase and the Love Connection phase has to do with effort. When we become infatuated with someone, dopamine and a few other naturally induced "drugs" stir our emotions, which in turn affects our attitudes; our behaviour follows as a result. In other words, our behaviour towards the object of our affection is driven by our attitude, which is being fuelled by our brain chemistry! We are, in essence, on *autopilot*. There is little self-denial involved in having the kind of behaviour needed to please our beloved. Our hearts are blazing with the fire of love, and it is reflected in our actions and behaviour. We do not need reminders to write love notes to our beloved. Everything is automatic and small acts of kindness flow effortlessly.

However, the reverse takes place when we leave the Infatuation phase. This time it is our behaviour that affects our attitude, which in turn affects our feelings of love. In Love Connection, our behaviour affects our attitudes towards our spouse. **So many people are ignorant of this difference!** We repeat: *In Love Connection, our behaviour affects our attitudes towards our spouse.*

If this makes you sad, we are sorry to disappoint you, but you must accept the fact that Love Connection does not work in the same way as infatuation. In the Love Connection phase, feelings of love for our beloved will come when our behaviour and actions are in place. It is a phase that requires effort in order to be sustained, or else it will slowly die. In this phase, we are no longer

---

[60] Romantic love 'lasts just a year'. (2005, November 28). *BBC News*. Retrieved January 15, 2010, from http://news.bbc.co.uk
[61] Hatfield, E., & Walster, G. W. (1978). *A new look at love*. Reading, MA: Addison-Wesley. 9.

on autopilot. We are in "manual mode" and we have to make the effort that affects our attitude. When we do not make effort, our attitude towards our spouse changes for the worse and we no longer feel in love. Picture a bush fire or forest fire (see Figure 2). It is completely spontaneous, and it spreads without any assistance. When the dry brush is hit by lightning, and the wind is high, watch out! The fire is strong and wild and needs no maintenance. In some cases, the fire can rage out of control, destroying life and property. However, usually through the simple passage of time, the fire will lose its strength, and begin to die down. This is how we see the Infatuation phase.

Figure 2: Infatuation – the autopilot stage. The fire is strong and wild and needs no maintenance.

When we think of Love Connection, we think of a different kind of fire, similar to that in a fireplace or wood stove (see Figure 3). This fire has a steady roar that warms the house and provides a pleasant ambience. However, without continual care and the addition of more logs, even the strongest fire will be reduced to glowing embers and eventually smouldering ash. We are harping on this because we believe that a lack of understanding about the differences between these two phases is a major contributor to husbands and wives getting frustrated with themselves and their partners when they come out of the Infatuation phase.

Figure 3: Love Connection – manual mode, regular stoking / effort required. A steady glowing fire keeps the house warm and provides a pleasant ambience.

When couples do not have the same kind of feelings, they think they are no longer in love. They get confused because their actions are no longer on autopilot. They have to *plan* to be together, and schedule things in, sometimes even sex, so they worry that maybe their love is no longer from the heart. How many times have we read headlines from Hollywood: "We just weren't in love anymore"?

On the positive side, we build lots of favourable romantic memories during the Infatuation phase, so we shouldn't discount the benefits. The amount of willing self-denial and overlooking of faults that goes on during infatuation is astounding. We often reminisce about the good old days of our dating life, and humorously mock each other with those positive memories. ("You wouldn't have said that to me when we were dating…" to which the other sheepishly replies, "I'm sorry.") When we are at a marital low point after a big argument, memories like these can lift us emotionally, not to mention make us giggle. Never forget those early days of infatuation!

Think about it. Would you really want to stay in the Infatuation phase forever? The mood of people who are infatuated often depends on how their love interest feels about them. One minute they may be in the clouds, and the next minute they are singing the blues. Infatuated individuals often become extremely possessive and jealous at the slightest sign. Their concentration suffers. Picture having to contribute at work, year after year, while in the Infatuation phase. Imagine trying to bring up children! And pity the army officer trying to marshal a troop full of infatuated privates. Even Moses took this into account:

> *If a man has recently married, he must not be sent to war or have any other duty laid on him. For one year he is to be free to stay at home and bring happiness to the wife he has married.* (Deuteronomy 24:5)

As fun as those memories are, we are glad that eventually we all come out of the Infatuation phase. It is not a very rational place to live! We wouldn't be able to work, study and focus on other matters pertinent to our well-being if we were constantly daydreaming about our spouse. It is just as well that after the initial attitude-affects-behaviour phase, we enter into the behaviour-affects-attitude phase. It is a state that is a lot more practical, more rewarding and one that is able to last a lifetime.

Hopefully by now you have realised that it's normal to leave the feelings from the Infatuation phase behind. It has to happen. God designed us and He knew what He was doing—He expected us to move toward Love Connection! In fact, we believe that when God commanded husbands to love their wives in Ephesians 5, He was referring to the kind of love described beautifully in I Corinthians 13, which is said to be based not on the value of the recipient, but on the character of the giver.[62]

> *An Infatuation phase story from Karen: When we had just started dating, we were going to have our picture taken with colleagues. While getting ready, I accidentally put hair removal cream on my scalp. (I thought it was hair mousse, not hair removal mousse—the container was labelled in French!) Later that night when I discovered my mistake, I called John on the phone and, as we were speaking, I was also frantically checking the mirror to see if I was going bald. John comforted me sweetly and promised, "Don't worry sweetheart. If all your hair falls out, I'll shave my head."*

---

[62] Templeton, J. (1999). *Agape love: A tradition found in eight world religions.* Radnor, PA: Templeton Foundation Press.

So how's *your* Love Connection? Dr Robert J Sternberg is dean of the School of Arts and Sciences at Tufts University. He has authored or edited 60 books, including *The New Psychology of Love* and *Why Smart People Can Be So Stupid*. Take Dr Sternberg's questionnaire below and see how you score.[63]

Sternberg's Triangular Love Scale
To complete the following scale, fill in the blank spaces with the name of your spouse. Then rate your agreement with each of the items by using a nine-point scale in which 1 = "not at all," 5 = "moderately," and 9 = "extremely." Then consult the scoring key at the end of the scale.

Scale	Intimacy Component
	1. I am actively supportive of _____'s well-being.
	2. I have a warm relationship with _____.
	3. I am able to count on _____ in times of need.
	4. _____ is able to count on me in times of need.
	5. I am willing to share myself and my possessions with _____.
	6. I receive considerable emotional support from _____.
	7. I give considerable emotional support to _____.
	8. I communicate well with _____.
	9. I value _____ greatly in my life.
	10. I feel close to _____.
	11. I have a comfortable relationship with _____.
	12. I feel that I really understand _____.
	13. I feel that _____ really understands me.
	14. I feel that I can really trust _____.
	15. I share deeply personal information about myself with _____.

---

[63] Sternberg, R. J. (1988). *The triangle of love: Intimacy, passion, commitment.* New York: Basic Books.

Scale	Passion Component
	16. Just seeing _____ excites me.
	17. I find myself thinking about _____ frequently during the day.
	18. My relationship with _____ is very romantic.
	19. I find _____ to be very personally attractive.
	20. I idealise _____.
	21. I cannot imagine another person making me as happy as _____ does.
	22. I would rather be with _____ than with anyone else.
	23. There is nothing more important to me than my relationship with _____.
	24. I especially like physical contact with _____.
	25. There is something almost "magical" about my relationship with _____.
	26. I adore _____.
	27. I cannot imagine life without _____.
	28. My relationship with _____ is passionate.
	29. When I see romantic movies and read romantic books I think of _____.
	30. I fantasise about _____.

Scale	Commitment Component
	31. I know that I care about _____.
	32. I am committed to maintaining my relationship with _____.
	33. Because of my commitment to _____, I would not let other people come between us.
	34. I have confidence in the stability of my relationship with _____.
	35. I could not let anything get in the way of my commitment to _____.

Scale	Commitment Component
	36. I expect my love for _____ to last for the rest of my life.
	37. I will always feel a strong responsibility for _____.
	38. I view my commitment to _____ as a solid one.
	39. I cannot imagine ending my relationship with _____.
	40. I am certain of my love for _____.
	41. I view my relationship with _____ as permanent.
	42. I view my relationship with _____ as a good decision.
	43. I feel a sense of responsibility toward _____.
	44. I plan to continue my relationship with _____.
	45. Even when _____ is hard to deal with, I remain committed to our relationship.

Source: *Sternberg's Triangular Love Scale*. Reproduced with permission from Dr Robert Sternberg.

Scoring Key

Add your ratings for each of the three sections—intimacy, passion, and commitment—and write the totals in the blanks below. Divide each sub-score by 15 to get an average subscale score.

	Sub-score: add up the scores in each section	**Average Rating:** divide each sub-score by 15 (sub-score ÷15)
Intimacy		
Passion		
Commitment		

Examining your ratings for each of the three sub-scales will give you an idea of how you perceive your love relationship to be composed of various amounts of intimacy, passion, and commitment.

Sternberg's scale does not come with detailed recommendations. However, we contend that if your score on one or more of the sub-scales is low (an average of 5 or below, for example), there is a good chance that your marriage is not in the Love Connection phase. You may be in what we call the "Mutual Affection" phase, our name for the stage of the relationship between a husband and wife when their feelings of infatuation have died out, and when they have not made the effort to stoke the fire of Love Connection. (For those of you who are still in the Infatuation phase, we encourage you to try to go straight into Love Connection and avoid Mutual Affection if possible.)

Mutual Affection and Disintegration

Mutual Affection is akin to the love we have for our siblings or relatives. In a manner of speaking, we are stuck with our brothers and sisters. We don't mean this as an insult to our siblings, whom we love dearly, but are just making a comparison. They are family, and there is nothing we can do to change that fact. Whether we like them or not, we are still siblings. Even if we don't quite get along, we feel something for them because of our family identity. Unless something really bad happens, we stay with them for the long haul.

This kind of feeling for our spouse is based on commitment and shared experiences but without the connection. If you are in the Mutual Affection phase (see Figure 4), you may feel some or all of the following:
- You both do not give or receive much emotional support to or from your spouse
- You do not feel loved and respected by your spouse (see Chapter 2)
- You do not feel understood by him/her
- You do not share deep personal information with him/her
- Seeing him/her does not excite you
- Your thoughts about him/her throughout the day do not bring positive emotions
- You would rather be with close friends than with your spouse.

If you are in the Mutual Affection category, then it is time to get help. The flames of love in your marriage are not strong. Just as a fire can grow again when we stoke it with more wood, so your Love Connection can grow if nurtured with effort.

Figure 4: Mutual Affection – The flames are not strong, and without further stoking they will die out.

If your score on Sternberg's scale is extremely low, say 2 or below for each component, your relationship is breaking down. Perhaps your marriage is on the rocks where you do not even like being with each other very much. You feel better being alone than with your spouse, and you are considering divorce. We call this the Disintegration phase. There are virtually no flames here, only smoke and ashes (see Figure 5). Your marriage needs immediate intervention. You need to hit the brakes in your life and get help immediately if your relationship is to have any hope of getting to Love Connection.

In summary, we believe that the following scores from Sternberg's scale will generally reflect the phase that your marriage is in:

>   1 – 2   Disintegration
>   3 – 5   Mutual Affection
>   6 or above Love Connection

Most of us begin our relationships in the Infatuation phase. Then we decline into the Mutual Affection phase. In some cases, with further neglect, the marriage plunges into the Disintegration phase. To slip from the Infatuation phase into the Mutual Affection or Disintegration phases may take only a few years.

Figure 5: Disintegration — There are virtually no flames here, only smoke and ashes.

After the initial 1-3 years of infatuation, couples will usually still try and persevere for a little longer before pulling the plug. At least in Singapore, slightly more than half of the divorces in 2007 occurred in marriages that had lasted less than 10 years, with about one third of the divorces occurring within 5-9 years of marriage.[64] However, couples can't rest on their laurels just because they get past the first ten years. Many couples put up with being stuck in the Mutual Affection and Disintegration phases for "the sake of the children" or because of other influences. In a noteworthy study, Dr Paulin Straughan, working on Singapore divorce figures from 1995 to 2001, found that the proportion of marriages of twenty years ending in divorce is around 18.3%.[65]

If nothing else, statistics like these underline the fact that marriages need consistent lifelong effort. We should never think that we have crossed an imaginary "safe line" and take our marriages for granted. It is not like nursing a wound and then being able to leave it unattended after it is healed. On

---

[64] Straughan, Paulin Tay. (2009). *Marriage dissolution in Singapore: Revisiting family values and ideology in marriage.* Leiden, the Netherlands: Koninklikje Brill NV. 17.
[65] Straughan, Paulin Tay. (2009). *Marriage dissolution in Singapore: Revisiting family values and ideology in marriage.* Leiden, the Netherlands: Koninklikje Brill NV. 17.

the contrary, our emotional needs do not dissipate with time. For as long as we are alive, whether we know it or not, we desire Love Connection. At any point, if we don't make effort and if we stop giving attention to it, our marriage will start to regress. We have to feed the flames to keep the fire burning steadily. So, only with effort will we be able to reverse the unhealthy trend in our marriage and enter into the Love Connection phase. In some cases, the process of Reconciliation may be needed, which will be discussed at length in Chapter 6 (see Figure 6).

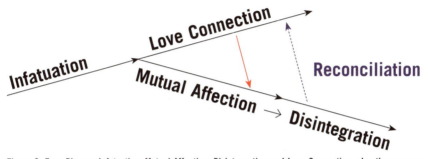

Figure 6: Four Phases: Infatuation, Mutual Affection, Disintegration and Love Connection, plus the process of Reconciliation.

In the words of Dr John Gottman, arguably the foremost marriage research scientist in the world:

> To maintain a balanced emotional ecology you need to make an effort—think about your spouse during the day, think about how to make a good thing even better, and act.[66]

So, even if you feel frustrated, angry and lost, don't despair. It shows that you have a desire for things to be different. This desire to change is the most important ingredient. It is so much easier to work with people in this situation, despite the volatility of emotions, than with couples where one of them has given up hope but is being polite. It is the desire to change that will foster cooperation and that will lead to Love Connection. Therefore, if you are angry, confused, and frustrated, please keep your desire to change and learn new things about each other and yourself. This is an important starting point.

---

[66] Gottman, J. M. (1994). *Why marriages succeed or fail*. New York: Simon & Schuster. 61. You can catch Dr. Gottman's TV program called The Love Lab.

Some will wonder, "If we are in the Mutual Affection or Disintegration phase, are you sure that it's even *possible* to enter into the Love Connection phase?" The answer is absolutely yes. And it won't take forever. A study from Stonybrook University in New York found that some couples in long-term relationships were able to sustain high levels of dopamine (one of the "love drugs" from the Infatuation phase). According to anthropologist Helen Fisher:

> This is the real difference between early-stage and late-stage romantic love: You feel that deep attachment and (desire) to be with the person, but you don't have that early, manic obsession of when you first fall in love (where) if you don't hear from the person you cry.[67]

We believe that this research proves our claim: Husbands and wives who choose to leave behind the autopilot mentality of the Infatuation phase and embrace the idea of making the effort outlined in the rest of this book will stoke the fires of their relationship and have Love Connection.

We close this chapter with an Infatuation phase exercise... enjoy!

---

[67] Lite, J. (2009, January 6). This is your brain on love: Lasting romance makes an impression--literally. *Scientific American*. Retrieved January 18, 2010, from http://www.scientificamerican.com

Favourite Infatuation Memories

Approximate Date	Nature of Event	Story

Hold hands, look each other in the eye, and share one by one.

*All right, we're relieved that long-term marital love is not meant to be the same as the Infatuation phase. We have also experienced Mutual Affection in the past, and we don't want to settle for that— we want to stoke the fires of Love Connection!
So where do we start?*

CHAPTER 2

CHOOSE LOVE & RESPECT

When we are helping others to build Love Connection, we start with love and respect. Most of us are familiar with the apostle Paul's teaching about *wives respecting their husbands* and *husbands loving their wives*. However, Paul also instructed the young evangelist Titus to make sure that wives were being taught to *love their husbands,* and the apostle Peter, a wise old married man, told husbands to *treat their wives with respect!* Let's have a look:

> [25]**Husbands, love your wives,** just as Christ loved the church and gave himself up for her [26]to make her holy, cleansing her by the washing with water through the word, [27]and to present her to himself as a radiant church, without stain or wrinkle or any other blemish, but holy and blameless. [28]In this same way, husbands ought to love their wives as their own bodies. He who loves his wife loves himself. [29]After all, no one ever hated his own body, but he feeds and cares for it, just as Christ does the church— [30]for we are members of his body. [31]"For this reason a man will leave his father and mother and be united to his wife, and the two will become one flesh." [32]This is a profound mystery—but I am talking about Christ and the church. [33]However, each one of you also must love his wife as he loves himself, and **the wife must respect her husband**. (Ephesians 5:25-33; emphasis added)

> Then they can **train the younger women to love their husbands** and children, to be self-controlled and pure, to be busy at home, to be kind, and to be subject to their husbands, so that no one will malign the word of God. (Titus 2:4-5; emphasis added)

> **Husbands,** *in the same way be considerate as you live with your wives, and* **treat them with respect** *as the weaker partner and as heirs with you of the gracious gift of life, so that nothing will hinder your prayers.* (I Peter 3:7; emphasis added)

Looks like our Creator knew that both husbands and wives would need the same thing, perhaps packaged a bit differently.

Fast-forward a couple of millennia to Dr Gottman. Not surprisingly, his twenty years of study have concluded that the two most basic ingredients for a healthy marriage are love and respect! Says Gottman:

> In our study of long-term marriages we recruited couples from a wide range of backgrounds who had been married twenty to forty years to the same partner. Despite the wide differences in occupations, lifestyles, and the details of their day-to-day lives, I sense a remarkable similarity in the tone of their conversations. No matter what style of marriage they have adopted, their discussions, for the most part, are carried along by a strong undercurrent of two basic ingredients: love and respect.[68]

It always puts a smile on our face when 21st century research confirms biblical wisdom.

In our experience, the hopes, desires, and expectations we are about to discuss apply most of the time—after conducting marriage seminars around Asia, Europe, and the US, we strongly feel that these principles cut across all cultures. (We are speaking in general terms. Since we are all unique individuals, it is impossible to accurately say, "All husbands need _____" or "All wives want _____." Our suggestions are not research-based, nor are they rigidly gender-specific. Rather, they are related to our needs of Love and Respect, gained from our experiences as counsellors, both in a pastoral as well as in a secular setting. We have met couples in which the wife can identify more with the needs of the husband and vice versa. We have categorised them in the above pattern because most folks tend to favour the needs as we have outlined below.)

---

[68] Gottman, J. M. (1994). *Why marriages succeed or fail.* New York: Simon & Schuster. 61.

For the remainder of this chapter, we will give specific practical suggestions that will enable both husbands and wives to better grasp how to make their spouses feel loved and respected.

> When we got married back in 1987, we were blessed to receive some very helpful counselling in the weeks running up to our wedding. The people who advised us were neither seminary-trained scholars nor professional counsellors, but their teaching provided an unshakable foundation. (We left our home congregation to lead a mission team after only two months of marriage, so it was a good thing we had a foundation!) Our counselling consisted of four lessons:
>
> **Lesson One:** "Leave, Cleave, and Weave" from Genesis 2:24 and Ephesians 5:31 about husbands and wives separating from their parents, becoming their own family and building a life together.
>
> **Lesson Two:** "Roles and Communication" from Ephesians 5:22-33, quite a bit of which is included in this chapter, along with some healthy warnings against harshness and nagging from Proverbs.
>
> **Lesson Three:** "How To Fight Fairly" on incorporating one another Christianity, including praying together, with the basic do's & don'ts of early married life. Contact albaird@laicc.net for more information.
>
> **Lesson Four:** "More on Weaving" is about the sexual relationship from I Corinthians 7:3-5 and Song of Songs. Our advisors also gave us each a copy of Tim LaHaye's *The Act of Marriage*[69] and encouraged us to cherish each other, be patient, have fun and enjoy.
>
> (For a more helpful and in-depth look at pre-marriage counselling, see the new book by Randall Alexander from Illumination Publishers called, *Learning to Live as One: A Workbook for Engaged Couples.*[70])

---

[69] Lahaye, T., & Lahaye, B. (1976). *The act of marriage.* Grand Rapids, MI: Zondervan.
[70] Alexander, R. (2010). *Learning to live as one: A workbook for engaged couples.* Spring Hill, TN: DPI.

FOR HUSBANDS
Considerate Listeners

Husbands help their wives to feel loved and respected by being Considerate Listeners.

When husbands are considerate of their wives, and take time to listen to them, it is amazing how loved and respected their wives will feel. Some husbands think that their only duty is to "bring home the bacon", even when their wives are bringing home the bacon as well! Financial responsibility is crucial (and will be addressed under the next heading), but when it comes to knowing the importance of being considerate and listening to their wives, some husbands are completely in a fog.

Husbands, consideration can take many forms, depending on your wife. There is no "one size fits all" when it comes to being considerate to your spouse. You have to "consider her", i.e., think about her, do your homework, and then act on it. The New Testament writer of the book of Hebrews urged Christians to "consider how to spur one another on to love and good deeds" (Hebrews 10:24).

For some women, that might mean helping out with chores. For others, it might mean letting her choose the movie, surprising her with a night away, or just keeping the atmosphere at home happy and free from conflict. It might mean making sure that you spend time every day talking about life, like you did when you were dating. Some women just want their husbands to ask how their day was. This lets the wife know that the husband thinks she is worthy of his attention. It makes her feel she is still special to him. This in turn will draw her to him and voilà—you have the beginnings of Love Connection! (You may have already read Gary Chapman's book, *The Five Love Languages*.[71] We have found his principles helpful.)

It shouldn't be embarrassing to admit that you need training in being considerate. We all need help when changing things that don't come naturally. Some guys are only considerate during the infatuation period, but some men are not even that considerate when dating! (Sometimes the

---

[71] Chapman, G. D. (1992). *The five love languages: The secret to love that lasts.* Chicago, IL: Northfield Publishing.

wife-to-be assumes being married will change him.) Some men are brought up around violence or rough language, and are not trained to think about others' needs. Some are over-indulged by their mothers or older sisters, and don't learn to be "giving". However, if husbands do not become considerate listeners, there is little chance that their wives will feel loved and respected, and consequently there is little hope for Love Connection. If you need to grow in this area, ask an older man whose marriage you respect to help you. Tell him that you want to learn to encourage your wife, to be more considerate, and to listen better.

> *John: I thought that I was pretty good at being a considerate husband, mostly because I write expressive cards for special occasions and readily splurge on my wife whenever she needs something. However, after we had been married for ten years, Karen began to bring things up more and more. At first, I was frustrated, and wondered, "What's wrong with her? Where's my happy wife?" Then several older brothers in the Lord taught me that I needed to learn to listen to my wife. It was hard for me, especially when I found out that she had been writing things down in a journal! I had to listen for several days! I realised that in the early years of our marriage I had not allowed her to influence me, especially in the areas of her strengths. That was the beginning of a new maturity in our marriage, and we were able to get to a deeper level of Love Connection. And my happy wife was back!*

As for improving in your listening, most wives want to be able to talk to their husbands about a problem without the husbands trying to solve it in the first five minutes. In our marriage, we are both working on listening with love and respect, hearing the message behind the words better, and using our listening as a way to build Love Connection.

Here are two questions for the husbands striving to show love and respect to their wives—Would it be easy for someone else to show your wife more consideration than you do? If that were to happen, what would that do to your marriage? Perhaps you could start with spending more time with your wife—few acts touch a wife's heart more than her husband setting a consistent time to be with her. Most wives want to feel that their husband enjoys being with them as a friend. (The complaint we often hear is that husbands generally talk only when they have an agenda.)

Husbands whose marriages are in the Mutual Affection phase spend time with their wives when there is a need, when she is ill or is going through a difficult time, or when something needs to get done. Husbands whose marriages are in the Love Connection phase spend time with their wives because of a deep bond of friendship, and because they cherish their wives' companionship. *They like to be with their wives.* They think about their wives and make it a priority to be together. They give off vibes that, while work is important, it is not anywhere nearly as important as the marriage.

(Speaking of spending time together, in Singapore, according to the Singapore Employment Act,[72] regular office hours for a full-time employee are 44 hours per week. In fact, on 12 August, 2004, the Prime Minister endorsed a 5-day work week to boost the quality of family life.[73] The effects of this initiative may have helped some employees get Saturdays off, which is an improvement, but in our experience, patterns of overtime work during the week have only continued. It seems to be the norm for employees to get a "dirty look" when they leave for their homes at 6pm, even after pouring nine hours into their work that day. Though research shows that employers who are sensitive to and support their employees' family lives and allow greater work flexibility eventually see encouraging returns in productivity, by and large this proven principle has yet to take root in the Asian culture. The constant push to deliver results has caused emotional damage in many marriages.)

A poll was conducted in which 1,315 people were asked whether or not their spouse's working hours contributed to unhappiness in their marriages. A whopping 30.8% of divorced people said yes, compared to only 9.5% in the married group.[74] Clearly the commitment that these spouses had for work took its toll on their marriages. In our introduction, we revealed that a poor quality marriage does affect one's work, which begs the question: *After all this commitment to work, and after a divorce, was the job worth it?*

---

[72] Singapore Attorney General. *Employment Act (Chapter 91), Part IV, Section 38(1).* Retrieved May 2, 2010, from Singapore Statutes Online: http://statutes.agc.gov.sg

[73] Prime Minister Lee Hsien Loong's National Day rally speech, Sunday 22 August 2004, at the University Cultural Centre, NUS - Our future of opportunity and promise. (2004, 22 August). *National Archives of Singapore.* Retrieved May 2, 2010, from http://stars.nhb.gov.sg/stars/public/viewHTML.jsp?pdfno=2004083101

[74] Straughan, Paulin Tay. (2009). *Marriage dissolution in Singapore: Revisiting family values and ideology in marriage.* Leiden, the Netherlands: Koninklikje Brill NV. 90.

Behind every divorce statistic is an ocean of tears and emotional pain, not only for the couple, but also for their children and for those closest to them. Spending time investing in your marriage is the best thing you can do for yourself, your spouse, your children, and society.

Personally, we recommend that all spouses spend at least *eight hours of undivided attention per week* with each other. This translates to roughly one hour a day for five days plus a weekly three-hour-long date. (We left one day out for unanticipated and unexpected interruptions.) Undivided attention means being with each other, talking, sharing, perhaps a bit of romantic intimacy. This does not include silently watching TV, constantly checking the computer or phone, or hanging out with the kids. We try to shoot for approximately an hour a day most days and then one date night per week. This is only achievable when we prioritise our marriages and, for husbands, become considerate listeners.

Exercise on Being A Considerate Listener
Using a scale of 1-5, put a numerical value in the blank next to each statement, with 1 meaning not at all, and 5 meaning very much so. If desired, fill in the extra boxes with your own ideas.

Scale	Your Definition of a Considerate Listener
	My husband listens to me and responds with a respectful tone even when we disagree with each other or when he gets triggered.
	My husband is patient and listens well to me when I am troubled, have an opinon or when my narration is lengthy.
	My husband takes the trouble to find out my plans for the day.
	My husband shares the housework with me.
	My husband's responsiveness to helping with the children is more than satisfactory.
	My husband allows me at times to influence him and doesn't have to win every argument.
	My husband takes his personal time with me seriously and is consistent about it.
	My husband rarely gets distracted when we are having conversations.

Scale	Your Definition of a Considerate Listener
	My husband takes the trouble to probe into my problems respectfully even when I am reluctant to bring them out.
	My husband usually gives me the benefit of the doubt and trusts that my motives are reasonable.
	My husband helps me when I am sick.
	My husband is more dedicated to our marriage than to his work.
	My husband projects to me, through his verbal and non-verbal communication, that he likes me as a best friend and life partner and really enjoys spending time with me.
	My husband enjoys learning about my past, as well as getting to know my preferences, likes, dislikes, and aspirations.

Responsible Leaders

Husbands help their wives to feel loved and respected by being Responsible Leaders.

Love Connection will start to grow if the husband loves and respects his wife by being a considerate listener, but just as importantly, he needs to be a responsible leader. It's not fair for wives to expect their husbands to be good at everything. (Do we hear an "Amen"?) And wives need to be responsible in certain areas as well. But husbands, if you want your wives to feel loved and respected, work on being responsible in these key areas: Doing your part supporting the family, taking an active role in family life, and having integrity.

Supporting The Family Financially
In today's fast-paced world, most homes have two breadwinners. When a husband is not able to keep a steady job, the onus to make ends meet may fall on the wife, which usually adds to the burden she already feels regarding running the household and caring for children. If, because of illness or a disability, the husband is not able to work, that is a different matter. Perhaps the husband has recently lost his job—that is discouraging for the husband and he needs to be emotionally supported. However, we are talking about

during normal times. When all is said and done, it is hard for a wife to feel Love Connection for a husband who does not help out to support the family.

Most husbands feel guilty if the wife is the sole source of support financially, but some men are content to let their wives bear the entire load. We are not trying to imply that women should never work. (Karen finds great satisfaction in her work and feels fortunate to have a job with flexible hours.) The problem we are talking about here is not whether or not the wife should work or even how much, but whether or not the husband is doing his part.

Some men do work, but their wives have been devastated because of the irresponsible way their husbands handle money. Some wives resent their spouses for relying on the wife's financial contribution and caring of the children while the husbands do minimal work, waiting for the "right job" or not being able to keep a job. Many wives have come to us for counselling, bitter that they have less time to care for their children and everything else because their husbands are irresponsible. Such behaviour causes heartaches and resentment.

Husbands, you will go a long way in helping your wife feel loved and respected if you are a responsible leader in the area of supporting your family financially.

Taking An Active Role in Family Life
Some men are very responsible at work, but not at home. Wives get a real thrill when they see their husbands having fun and playing with the children. It helps wives feel loved and respected, and gets them more emotionally connected to their husbands. Women are drawn to their husbands when there is adequate involvement between father and offspring, not to mention the aphrodisiacal properties that have been linked to the amount of time husbands spend vacuuming and washing dishes!

Many husbands' minds are still in the office when they come home. They end up not giving much attention to their children or anything else. They do not make time for things like:
- Parent-teacher meetings or helping with homework
- Children's performances or athletic events
- Talking with their children and getting involved in their lives
- Checking up on elderly parents and in-laws
- Helping out with household chores
- Having meals as a family during the week.

One study found that family meals were inversely associated with tobacco, alcohol and low grades. In other words, the more a family spends time sitting at the table and eating together, the less likely it is that the children will get involved in substance abuse, experience mood disorders, or perform poorly at school.[75] When husbands are not active in family life, their wives will have a hard time feeling loved and respected. Instead, they will feel burdened, and this burden interferes with Love Connection.

Having Integrity (No Hidden Life)
When a wife discovers that her husband is involved in illicit activities, such as Internet pornography, cybersex, or even having an affair, the couple can pretty much kiss Love Connection goodbye! When a husband's behaviour is dishonest, the wife will inevitably feel insecure in the marriage.

Ruth Houston, who hosts a much-visited website containing information about men cheating on their wives, reports the following:

> Infidelity is now so common that it is hard to pinpoint exactly how widespread it is. Though statistics vary, the most widely accepted figures indicate that between 50% and 70% of all married men have cheated on their wives. A study conducted by the psychology department of the University of Michigan puts that estimate as high as 75%. Other studies reveal that as many as 84% of American men cheat. So we can conservatively say that roughly 3 out of every 4 men cheat on their wives.[76]

This is staggering. It should also remind us of how strong the pull is from the world to cheat. Dr Gary Neuman, one of the most respected couples' therapists in the United States and author of *The Truth about Cheating*, wrote that 69% of the men who cheated never considered it a possibility until it happened, and a mere 7% told their wives that they had cheated.[77] So, based on the above statistics, we can at least draw the conclusion that the majority of men will be dishonest with their wives. Everyone knows that

---

[75] Eisenberg, M. E., Olson, R. E., Neumark-Sztainer, D., Story, M., & Bearinger, L. H. (2004). Correlations between family meals and psychosocial well-being among adolescents. *Archives of Pediatrics & Adolescent Medicine, 158*(8), 792-796.
[76] Houston, R. (2002). *Is he cheating on you? 829 telltale signs.* New York: Lifestyle Publications. 24.
[77] Neuman, G. (2008). *The truth about cheating: Why men stray and what you can do to prevent it.* Hoboken, NJ: John Wiley & Sons, Inc. 4.

lying is wrong. We teach this to our children. Yet, these statistics reveal that it is common for men to lie to their wives, to their close friends who could help them, and even to counsellors.

Having integrity is not just about owning up to a potential or proven affair (see Chapter 5, *Choose Fidelity*). It is about being honest and respectful in other matters, such as:

Finances – Husbands need to disclose everything about their finances, including information about side businesses, investments, and personal loans. Too many times, wives are left in the dark about accumulating debts until they receive a phone call from the bank or inadvertently open a credit card bill. Needless to say, when that happens, it's "goodbye, Love Connection".

Hobbies and interests – There is a saying, "As we get older our toys gets more expensive". Sometimes men put money away for a hobby or an interest that their wife knows nothing about. Large expenses should be discussed and agreed upon, with both sides being willing to bend a bit.

Personal communication – When a wife sees her husband taking private calls in his bedroom, with the door locked, it is hard for her to feel loved and respected. The same goes for emails, text messages, and social media. We believe that both husband and wife should have access to each other's personal communication.

Internet history – The sin of viewing pornography and addiction to pornography is hurting many marriages today. While a detailed discussion of this is beyond the scope of this book, it is sufficient to note that when a wife catches her husband surfing porn, they will both probably suffer from lack of Love Connection!

Lies and deceit in a relationship will sow seeds of mistrust and this will eventually build a wall between a husband and a wife. Coming clean and admitting to everything will pave the way for Love Connection, because your spouse will feel loved and respected when you care enough to be honest. If you feel too nervous to be open, get advice from a trusted professional.

We suggest that husbands update their wives regularly about all sorts of issues:
- How was work? What is going well, and what is not?
- Is anything bothering him? What is making him sad or happy?
- How is he feeling about his home?
- How is he feeling about his children?

All of this makes for excellent conversation. Taking a walk together or holding hands while discussing these things will bring you even closer, and you will certainly feel more connected than when sitting behind a computer or watching TV. Spending time together is a huge part of how we come out of the Mutual Affection phase or the Disintegration phase and restore Love Connection.

Most wives love it when their husbands talk with them about their deepest thoughts. Many husbands keep such matters too close to their chest. Their wives are left guessing all the time. This does not help wives to feel loved and respected, but rather creates feelings of insecurity and instability. When you are a responsible leader in the areas we have mentioned, you will not end up leading separate lives. Rather, as you share and plan, your Love Connection will deepen.

> *John: There have been times over the years when I have struggled with lust. I am grateful for friends who hold me accountable, and with whom I have been open when I haven't been as righteous as I should have. I need people in my life who will ask me about how I am doing. Confessing one's sins is challenging, but I make it a point to have at last two people who know the dark side of my life, and who care about my well-being; with these brothers, I can emerge victorious. Without my best friends, I would not have made it. Surely Satan prowls around like a roaring lion, and I don't want my marriage to get devoured!*

CHOOSE LOVE & RESPECT

Exercise on Being a Responsible Leader

Using a scale of 1-5, put a numerical value in the blank next to each statement, with 1 meaning not at all, and 5 meaning very much so. If desired, fill in the extra boxes with your own ideas.

Scale	Your Definition of a Responsible Leader
	My husband is honest about _____ (work, finance, relationships with other women, financial debts, his parents).
	My husband honours our agreed plans when it comes to dinner times at home. (If you do not have one, discuss and make one.)
	I am not worried that my husband is flirting or having an affair.
	My husband sets aside time to be together with me and with the family during the week.
	My husband is an excellent provider.
	My husband and I share many similar values related to how we spend our income.
	My husband does not make significant purchases without discussing them with me first.
	My husband is generous with me and with the family.
	My husband sets aside money for our family to be able to go on holidays.
	My husband does not allow other aspects of his life (work, hobbies, friends) to take priority over our family.
	My husband is not in the practice of socialising with irresponsible people.

Romantic Lovers

Husbands help their wives to feel loved and respected by being Romantic Lovers.

Many men are responsible and honest, and some are good at being considerate, because they are just that kind of guy. In fact, they treat everyone with consideration. But a wife doesn't want to be like everyone else—she wants to be special to her man. Wives want to feel like their husbands are still in love with them. (This is partly why it is hard for women to take criticism from their husbands—they are afraid that the husband will no longer be attracted to them when they have noticed their flaws.) What helps women feel that way? When their husbands are romantic!

Opinions about what is romantic differ between each wife. Some women love dressing up, having a candlelit dinner, and getting flowers. Most women that we know are understanding of financial limitations—there is nothing wrong with getting dressed up and lighting candles for a picnic with canned beans and sausages! The specifics may differ, but it's the effort and planning and thought that counts!

Some women want physical affection from their husbands that is not necessarily sexual in nature. When a husband is affectionate, he communicates to his wife that he still loves her, and that he finds her attractive. Kissing and touching each other during the day does wonders for most women's moods, and helps them to feel confident that their husbands love and respect them. Gentle caresses, lightly touching the cheek, loving looks (as well as playful glances)—these acts of affection feel romantic to a woman. We've heard men say that they are not the affectionate type. However, when they were dating, they *loved* walking arm and arm, or holding hands with their girlfriend! What happened?

Sam Laing,[78] parenting expert and well-loved speaker, once commented that his daughter told him she wanted her future husband to look at her the way that her father looked at her mother. Now *that* is romantic!

Husbands, don't even try to be romantic if you have been speaking to your wives harshly or impatiently. What a turn off! Most wives don't want to spend

---

[78] Laing, S. Retrieved May 2, 2010, from http://www.SamandGeriLaing.com

time alone with someone who brings more conflict into their already hectic lives. This is an important part of being a romantic lover—you don't speak to someone harshly when you are flirting with them! If you make her feel like your queen, she just might treat you like a king!

Some men are only affectionate when they want sex. The wives get wise to this, and when "hubby starts getting cuddly", they get very put off. At best, they may grudgingly "have sex", as opposed to "make love", just to get it over and done with.

Showing affection is not just something husbands should do at night because they want sex. Husbands should show affection, physically and verbally, throughout the day. This cannot be faked. If you are being inconsiderate, but saying nice words, your wife will figure it out. When husbands show their wives love and respect in the ways we have discussed, the wives are usually more attracted to their husbands, and all the more eager to make love. As a result, the sexual relationship becomes that much more fulfilling for both!

Some women have trouble experiencing sexual pleasure as easily as their husbands. We think that God made us differently so that husbands have to take the time to learn to give sexual pleasure to their wives. We have found that when husbands are romantic lovers during the day, and when there is an atmosphere of love and respect in the home, it helps women to enjoy the sexual relationship in the way that God intended.

> *John: The upside of loving my job is work satisfaction. The downside is that sometimes I neglect the more important things in life, like remembering to romance my wife! There was one point in our marriage when I must confess that I was really giving Karen my "leftovers". I forgot appointments we had scheduled together, I didn't arrange special nights out, we weren't praying together, and I only spent time with her when we were with our children. As I began to feel more and more frustrated and disconnected, I realised that I was reaping what I had sown, so I decided to make my marriage my utmost priority (outside of my relationship with God). Our marriage is now approaching the three-decade-mark; we are having fun new adventures and looking forward to hopefully many more years of romance.*

Exercise on being A Romantic Lover

Using a scale of 1-5, please put a numerical value in the blank next to each statement, with 1 meaning not at all, and 5 meaning very much so. If desired, fill in the extra boxes with your own ideas.

Scale	Your Definition of a Romantic Lover
	My husband often displays his affection by touching and kissing me during the day.
	My husband likes to be with me.
	My husband meets my sexual needs regularly.
	My husband finds me attractive.
	My husband frequently tells me he loves me.
	My husband encourages me often without a hidden agenda.
	My husband likes to wind down with me at the end of the day.
	My husband is my best friend, or one of my best friends.
	My husband takes me out on a date regularly.
	When we are out together we never run out of things to talk about.
	My husband remembers our special times with fondness.
	My husband makes me feel that his life will turn upside down for the worse without me.

FOR WIVES

Appreciate

Husbands will feel loved and respected when their wives appreciate and admire them.

In just the same way that some men are not good at being considerate, some women are not very good at showing appreciation and admiration to their husbands. These women feel that if they were to do so, it would go to their husbands' heads and puff them up—another example of the male ego. But that's the wrong way to look at it. We believe that men have a need for appreciation and admiration just like women need men to be considerate and romantic. When a man feels appreciated and admired by his wife, when she makes him feel like he is her hero, he will feel very loved and respected, and experiencing Love Connection will almost be a given.

In his book *The Truth about Cheating*,[79] Dr Neuman reveals that the number one reason men have affairs is because of emotional dissatisfaction. It's not about sex! Of the men he interviewed who had been unfaithful, only 8% said sexual dissatisfaction outweighed emotional dissatisfaction! Further, only 12% said that the other woman was more attractive. The participants in his study repeatedly cited a lack of appreciation for things they were doing well as husbands is what caused them to feel emotionally distant and ruin their Love Connection. Of course, this in no way justifies any man cheating on his wife or being unfaithful to his wife in any way. We are using these statistics to support the need for appreciation, not to give an excuse for extra-marital mess-ups!

In one of our marriage seminars, we asked the following question to 300 men participants, "What need would you rank as being more important?" Our findings mirrored Neuman's—feeling appreciated and admired came out on top, even above sex.

Some men do not provide for their family, which we addressed earlier. However, the majority of men are trying, and when they do not feel appreciated for the things they are already doing right, they do not feel loved or respected, and this erodes their Love Connection. Without this, consciously or not, they look for it elsewhere.

If men are shown more appreciation and admiration at work than by their wives at home, what will eventually happen? Imagine the following scenario: a man who gets little encouragement at home, and feels nagged and belittled by his wife, receives admiration from his secretary for a presentation. How would this make him feel? Imagine if constant encouragement pours in from her week after week, while he gets criticised at home. Before he knows it, his emotional needs are being met by another woman. Lack of Love Connection breeds further disconnection, and the marriage is in danger. At best the couple

---

[79] Neuman, G. (2008). *The truth about cheating: Why men stray and what you can do to prevent it.* Hoboken, NJ: John Wiley & Sons, Inc.

will be stuck in Mutual Affection, possibly degrading to Disintegration. There is no excuse for cheating, regardless of how a man's wife is treating him. Infidelity is always wrong. However, as wives, when we build Love Connection by showing appreciation to our husbands, we decrease the chance that they will seek connection elsewhere.

Wives, ask yourselves if you are truly showing appreciation and admiration for your husbands:

- Do you communicate gratitude for his strengths more often than criticism?
- Do you listen without being judgemental when he complains about tension with his boss or colleagues?
- Do you call him from time to time to say how much you appreciate him (not just on his birthday)?
- Do you encourage him when he makes a godly decision?
- Do you appreciate when he plays with the children or helps them with their homework?

Here is a question for wives who want to show love and respect to their husbands—If someone else were to show your husband more appreciation and admiration than you do, what would that do to your marriage?

> *Karen: Amidst my many weaknesses, I know that one of my strengths is being encouraging to others, so I never dreamt that John wouldn't feel that from me. However, after many years of marriage, I realised that I had come to expect quite a bit from my husband. He is spiritual, very hardworking, extremely financially responsible, and spends loads of time with the children, and I was taking him for granted. Learning to specifically show appreciation to John for what he had been doing well for years (and for what I ungraciously felt he was supposed to be doing anyway) went a long way in helping John feel loved and respected by me. I am still working on this, but the better I get at it, the deeper our Love Connection becomes.*

CHOOSE LOVE & RESPECT

Exercise for Appreciate

Using a scale of 1-5, please put a numerical value in the blank next to each statement, with 1 meaning not at all, and 5 meaning very much so. If desired, fill in the extra boxes with your own ideas.

Scale	Define What Makes You Feel Appreciated & Admired
✱ 5	My wife shows me appreciation for what I am doing well.
✱ 5	My wife often says how much she admires my achievements and accomplishments.
5	I can list three things that my wife appreciates about me.
✱ 5	My wife often calls or texts me to tell me how much she appreciates me.
5	My wife is understanding when I have had a hard day.
5	My wife listens to my side of the story when I tell her about my relationship problems with others.
5	My wife does not "put me down" in front of others.
5	My wife (sincerely) boasts about me when we are with others.
4	My wife does not discuss our disagreements in front of the children.
4	My wife values my opinions about the children's affairs.
5	My wife values my opinions, and solicits them before making any major household decisions.
5	My wife often encourages me.
3	My wife appreciates my leadership in the family.
4	My wife usually gives me the benefit of the doubt and trusts that my motives are reasonable.

Initiate

Husbands will feel loved and respected when their wives initiate to enter into their world.

All men are different, but most men feel loved and respected when their wives take an interest in things they like. This may not be as big of a need as appreciation or sexual fulfilment, but husbands often say they lack Love Connection with their wives because they have stopped doing fun things together, or their wives don't care about their work. When life gets hectic, and it often does, both husbands and wives need time and space for their interests. The problem is when they go separately too often, it is harder to maintain Love Connection. After all, we only have so much free time. When wives initiate and enter their husband's world, it helps the husband to feel loved and respected.

Sometimes due to age or illness or other constraints, a wife might not be able to (or want to) take part in a husband's interest. However, initiating and entering his world can actually be a spectator sport—it's the desire and effort that count, not how well you swing a golf club or hammer a tent peg. Learning more about your husband's work, hobbies or interests conveys the message that you care about him. While it is not helpful for men to make their wives feel like "sports widows", it wouldn't be a bad idea to try to know the names of the top players on your husband's favourite team. (And getting your husband tickets for a big game might do wonders for your Love Connection!)

One mistake that some wives make is to look down on the interests of their husbands. Some wives think that after having children, all their husband's hobbies should be thrown out of the window. Having said that, if both the husband and wife work outside the home, then it does seem unreasonable to expect the wife to give him unlimited space while she is occupied with the lion's share of the housework and looking after the kids. This is when it is extremely crucial for them to sit down together, divide the responsibilities, and have clear expectations.

It is not throwing off the gains that women have made over the years to learn to cook your husband's favourite food or make him feel special in his own home. Wives shouldn't do this because they are trapped in a social institution and have no way out—they should do it because they want their husbands to feel loved and respected.

Anthropologist Helen Fisher reports that dopamine, one of those crazy love chemicals found in the brain of couples in the Infatuation phase, actually gets released when couples take risks or try something new:

> I'm not just talking about novelty in the bedroom (although that would be a good start). You can get the same effect from sampling a new type of cuisine together or riding the roller coaster at an amusement park.[80]

So, wives, we can literally feel more in love with our husbands, and help them feel more in love with us by taking initiative, entering their world, and even trying new things with them.

On the downside, when husbands don't feel that their wives appreciate them, or that their wives care enough to enter into their world, resentment builds up, bitterness sets in and the marriage may enter into the Disintegration phase. Let's make sure this doesn't happen. Show love and respect by initiating and entering his world—then watch your Love Connection grow.

> *Karen: Having grown up in an active family, I loved every kind of sport. For years, I followed professional and college level American football, basketball and tennis. However, I was completely unprepared for John's favourite sport – badminton! Not the dinky kind that children play in the backyard, but the ruthless racquet game that happens to be one of the most competitive sports in Southeast Asia. I was insensitive at the beginning of our marriage, but I finally "repented" and got interested in the game. Now I know the names of the top players (any surprise that the current World #1 is a Malaysian?) and am excited that my son excels in the sport as well. I get tickets for my husband to attend championship tournaments, and make sure to record the matches that he misses on television. John is happy with my level of interest, and he said that it has helped him to feel loved and respected.*

---

[80] Fisher, H. (2009, December 17). Real aphrodisiacs to boost desire. *O, The Oprah Magazine*. Retrieved January 18, 2010, from http://www.oprah.com/relationships/Real-Aphrodisiacs-to-Boost-Desire

Exercise for Initiate

Using a scale of 1-5, please put a numerical value in the blank next to each statement, with 1 meaning not at all, and 5 meaning very much so. If desired, fill in the extra boxes with your own ideas.

Scale	Define How You Want Your Wife to Initiate & Enter Your World
	My wife knows my major burdens in life.
	My wife knows my aspirations in life.
	My wife emotionally supports my aspirations.
	My wife takes an interest in what I like: Sports, favourite teams, hobbies.
	My wife does not get bored when I talk to her about my interests.
	My wife does not prioritise the children over me.
	My wife enjoys joining me in some of my interests.
	My wife likes to talk to me on issues other than the children, finances and her work.
	My wife knows a lot about my childhood.
	I don't feel lonely in this marriage.

Participate

Husbands will feel loved and respected when their wives participate in the bedroom.

Wives may be expressive about how much they appreciate their husbands, and they may take an interest in their husband's lives, but if they are not meeting their husbands' needs in the sexual relationship, their husbands may not feel loved and respected. Wives are helped in this department when the husbands are being romantic (remember the earlier section?) and some wives have a stronger sex drive than their husbands, but in general, at least in our experience, this is an area where many husbands wish their wives participated at least a bit more.

Many women do not realise that their husband's sexual desires are as strong as their own desire for emotional connection. There is a reason that the Bible says we are not to deprive each other sexually (I Corinthians 7:3-5). Most women we know don't want to be deprived of sexual pleasure, but for men, the feeling is sometimes even stronger and contributes heavily to their feeling of Love Connection. Depriving your husband of sex would be as frustrating for him as if he had not spoken to you for that same length of time. Wives, how would that make you feel?

On the extreme side, some women "use" sex as a way to reward their husband for changing, and they withhold sexual favours until they feel he deserves them. While a husband needs to make every effort to work on his issues, using his sexual desires as ammunition will only make matters worse. (Wives who refuse to meet their husband's sexual needs and then are surprised when their husbands struggle with lust are in "la la land".)

In our counselling, we have found that some husbands feel their wives look down upon them for having an active sex drive. As a result, husbands can feel ashamed and some resort to unhealthy ways to have their needs met. Because of shame or fear, they do not get vulnerable with their wives about their sexual desires. This hurts both of them. Wives need to understand and show love and respect for their husbands in this area. God gave the sexual relationship to husbands and wives as a blessing for both. We should enjoy the ways that it brings Love Connection to the marriage.

Gary Neuman says that when a wife initiates in the bedroom, it makes the husband feel like a winner. (And we all know how much men like to win!) He also said that when husbands initiate lovemaking, wives should, rather than focusing on how tired they feel, take it as their husbands saying, "I adore you, I care about you, I want to do something nice for you."[81]

As we said earlier in the section on romance, we are not saying that women do not need sexual fulfilment as well. In fact, sexual fulfilment in marriage cannot be properly achieved until both sides have their needs met. If husbands are serious about bringing pleasure to their wives, then their wives will probably

---

[81] Neuman, G. (2009, February 12). Why Men Cheat. *The Oprah Winfrey Show*. (O. Winfrey, Interviewer). Retrieved January 16, 2010, from http://www.oprah.com/relationships/Why-Men-Cheat_2/slide_number/10#slide

be much more motivated to participate in the bedroom; there will be giving and receiving on both sides. Good sex starts outside the bedroom. It is this emotional component for the woman that makes the sexual relationship much more fulfilling for her, and as a result, for him.

Speaking of women and sex, Dr Helen Fisher also did research on female sex drive: Women with low libido can get a prescription for testosterone, but they can also increase their levels without medication. Playing competitive sports has been shown to trigger testosterone production; making love can also create the same effect. Studies have suggested that sex raises testosterone levels, so the more sex you have, the more sex you desire.[82]

The bottom line is that both husbands and wives need to communicate their desires, expectations, and preferences to each other sensitively and respectfully. Both sides need to make the effort to meet each other's needs. When sex is just "one way", it makes the entire encounter unpleasant. Many women are not even aware of their own needs in this area. For more information, please see Tim LaHaye's *The Act of Marriage*.[83]

Wives, when you show love and respect for your husbands by lovingly and willingly participating in the bedroom, you will see your Love Connection growing year by year.

> *Karen: After developing food allergies and psoriasis, an unsightly skin condition, I struggled with our physical relationship. This definitely took its toll on our marriage. Fortunately, the things we learned while studying counselling helped us, and we were finally able to be vulnerable with each other. Eventually my health improved and I am still improving as the years go by. And we learned to take this part of our Love Connection seriously.*

---

[82] Fisher, H. (2009, December 17). Real aphrodisiacs to boost desire. *O, The Oprah Magazine.* Retrieved January 18, 2010, from http://www.oprah.com/Real-Aphrodisiacs-to-Boost-Desire
[83] Lahaye, T., & Lahaye, B. (1976). *The act of marriage.* Grand Rapids, MI: Zondervan.

CHOOSE LOVE & RESPECT

Exercise for Participate

Using a scale of 1-5, please put a numerical value in the blank next to each statement, with 1 meaning not at all, and 5 meaning very much so. If desired, fill in the extra boxes with your own ideas.

Scale	Define Participation in the Bedroom
	My wife does not give off signs that sex is a burden to her.
	My wife enjoys making love.
	I do not consider our sex life boring.
	My wife satisfies me sexually.
	My wife experiences orgasms frequently.
	My wife does not refuse to meet my sexual needs.
	My wife does not think that my sex drive is too high—in fact, she appreciates it.
	My wife knows how to initiate sex and turn me on.
	My wife meets my needs when I am spontaneous.
	My wife makes the atmosphere of the bedroom romantic.
	I am satisfied with the frequency of our sexual intercourse.

Roadblocks to Love Connection and Meeting the Need of Love and Respect

In our experience, many couples who come to us for counselling or who attend our marriage workshop agree at the outset to spending eight hours a week, but when the rubber meets the road, they falter in the first week! They come back discouraged and feel that this is just not achievable. Here are some of the most common roadblocks:

- Not Putting Young Children To Bed Early – in *Good Enough Parenting*, we underscored the importance of children getting enough sleep. Unfortunately, it is all too common to see young children inadvertently preventing their parents from spending time with each other; this is what happens when little ones are not taught to stay in bed, and wander into their parent's bedroom, sometimes even sleeping in their parent's bed. This does not help children because they are not learning healthy and reasonable limits; the parents are unintentionally allowing the children to control them when it should be the other way round. Parents should take control of the situation and establish Reasonable Limits (see *Good Enough Parenting*).[84] More and more research has surfaced linking mental health problems with lack of sleep for both adults and children. Few parents are aware of the harm caused by lack of sleep, be it mental health, cognitive function, or the workings of the immune system.[85] When children are not in bed at a reasonable time, the parents are too tired to give to each other and eventually they lose motivation. It is important for the benefit of the children as well as the parents to put children to bed "early" (young children need 10-12 hours per day; 7-12 years old need 10-11 hours per day).[86]

---

[84] Louis, J. P., & Louis, K. M. (2012). *Good enough parenting: A Christian perspective on meeting core emotional needs and avoiding exasperation*. Singapore: Louis Counselling & Training Services.

[85] Swaminathan, N. (2007, October 23). Can a lack of sleep cause psychiatric disorders? *Scientific American*. Retrieved January 31, 2015 from http://www.scientificamerican.com/article/can-a-lack-of-sleep-cause/.

[86] WebMD. (n.d.) *How much sleep do children need?* Retrieved January 31, 2015 from http://www.webmd.com/parenting/guide/sleep-children.

- Not Prioritising Marriage Over Work – spouses who put their jobs above their marriage will convey the message that something else comes first. While it is understandable if work issues come up occasionally, it should not be a lifestyle.
- Not Prioritising Marriage Over Screen Time – a great friendship and closeness with our spouse brings energy and vitality to life, but by the times couples realise this, it is often too late. Watching hours of TV, surfing the Internet or being sucked into other gadgets is a poor substitute for a real relationship, yet many spouses gravitate to the virtual world and give their spouses leftovers. A marriage cannot move to Love Connection when such activities are habitual.
- Not Helping Each Other Be Emotionally Healthy – when a marriage is at the Mutual Affection or Disintegration stage, it is easy for one spouse to get sarcastic, make unhelpful remarks or allow past resentments to interfere with the promised time together. (Please see Chapter 3 for details about schemas and coping styles.) Arguments set in and conflict ensues. Sometimes couples even give each other the cold shoulder and stop spending time together. Our advice is that they should push themselves to work on being friends, no matter what. It is possible to get to Love Connection, but it takes effort and sometimes self-denial. When husbands and wives make it a goal to refresh their spouse, as the Proverbs teach us, they themselves will be refreshed (Proverbs 11:25). If resentment is deep, couples should go through Chapter 6 and work towards forgiving each other. This help provide motivation for those who might feel that there has been "too much water under the bridge".

Love Connection Enhanced by Trust and Friendship

What does consistent time together do for our marriage? We believe that it restores *trust* and *friendship* which sometimes gets lost along the way. It is the loss of trust and friendship that results in the relationship slipping into the Mutual Affection phase or Disintegration phase. We believe couples can rekindle their trust and friendship provided they make the most of their eight hours a week.

One way to tell when trust is low is when we often impugn our spouse's motives. This happens when we are not in the Love Connection phase. Many of us have had unbringings where we were abused or witnessed abuse; we are easily triggered, developing mistrust towards our spouse. The best antidote to mistrust and lack of friendship is spending consistent time together, not in destructive conflict with each other, but when we are in dialogue as friends and partners. A healthy amount of trust and friendship does not develop by simply living under one roof. We have to make effort by setting time consistently in our weekly schedules. Many partners rely on their holiday to play catch up but this rarely works since feelings of hurt and resentment are built up by then. A steady consistent pace of spending time together to build trust and friendship is the best prescription to getting into Love Connection.

> *John: I grew up seeing and experiencing a lot of abuse, both verbal and physical; mistrust is a weakness of mine. Over the years, I have come to realise that when I don't spend consistent time with Karen, my trust towards her erodes. For example, when I get into "workaholic mode" and forget to put my own advice into practice (i.e., I don't spend eight hours a week with my wife!), it is easy for me to be negative and misinterpret Karen's behaviour: when she disagrees with me in front of others, I will be tempted to think she is intentionally putting me down and making herself look good; when she makes an innocent comment about something, I will impugn her motives and assume she was being disrespectful. When I took the trouble to clarify, I realised my wife simply wanted to express an opinion but had no intention to promote herself or put me down. When my trust level is high, I will think, does she not have the right to express her opinion like I do mine? When I trust her motives, I am better able to handle her responses (even though she sometimes could have said it in a nicer way). But when I suspect her motives, I get really hurt as I believe in my distorted lifetraps and then get into a counterattacking mode. Love Connection means that we trust each other. Love "always protects, always trusts, always hopes, always perseveres (I Cor 13:7).*

Gary Neuman recommends that when couples have their weekly date, they avoid talking about *work*, *finances*, and the *children*.[87] His point is that during courtship, these subjects were probably not discussed much if at all; rather there was a lot of friendship and time spent getting to know one another. We support his advice and encourage couples to enhance their Love Connection / trust and friendship by doing any or all of the following:

- Play "Love Maps". This can be purchased as a smart phone app or found in Gottman's book, *The Seven Principles for Making Marriage Work*.[88] We recommend couples play this during their time together, to help get them talking if they have not been in the habit of doing so for a long time.
- Give each other a short massage. If this leads to intimacy, go for it! Otherwise just enjoy giving to each other.
- Talk about each other's life – highs and lows, aspirations, plans, but avoid getting into a destructive conflict.
- Play a sport or take up a hobby.
- Go for walks in a beautiful garden or park.
- Go to a favourite café.

---

[87] Neuman, G. (2012, February 29). Saving your marriage after financial hardship. Huffpost Weddings. Retrieved January 31, 2015 from http://www.huffingtonpost.com/m-gary-neuman/saving-your-marriage-financial-hardship_b_1307224.html

[88] Gottman, J. M., & Silver, N. (1999). *The seven principles for making marriage work*. New York: Three Rivers Press; The Gottman Institute. *Love Maps*. Retrieved from https://itunes.apple.com/us/app/love-maps/id389288067?mt=8.

We agree with your points—and we have been trying to practise some of those things for years! But we keep getting stuck on the same old things! What's wrong?

CHAPTER 3

CHOOSE AWARENESS

Even after being Christians for years, we are sometimes at a loss as to why we behave the way we do. Developing awareness is not a very comfortable or popular activity. As Solomon said, "The purposes of a man's heart are deep waters, but a man of understanding draws them out" (Proverbs 20:5). This chapter will help us draw out the deep waters of our hearts and our spouse's hearts, and when we say deep waters, we mean it! In fact, we'll need to put on our "spiritual wading boots", because this chapter, written with the help of Catherine Amon, a senior Schema Therapist, will take us into new, deep, and exciting territory. If we persevere, we will gain awareness about the way we come across to other people, especially in marriage. This growth will take time and effort, but we will be rewarded with insights about the ways our marriages get stuck, and we will be able to make real progress in our Love Connection.

The previous chapter examined the importance of building Love Connection by starting with love and respect. In this chapter, we will reveal the habitual and harmful thinking patterns that trigger negative cycles in our relationship with our spouse. Choosing to grow in awareness will free us to explore new ways of thinking and behaving, help us to better empathise with our spouse, and hopefully trigger them less often. Understanding what triggers us will help us make better sense of our own reactions, rather than focusing on what our spouse is doing "wrong".

We know this is easier said than done. If it were easy to do this, we would not be seeing such high divorce rates worldwide. Some counsellors give struggling couples advice about stopping annoying behaviour. Obviously, breaking negative behavioural patterns is something that we all should work towards. However, is it as simple as just "stopping the bad behaviour?" Doesn't the negative behaviour raise its head over and over again in different situations? Just when we think we have conquered it in one area, it shows up somewhere else.

The solution: *Get to the root.* In other words, figure out where the negative thoughts come from in the first place and how to get rid of them, along with the beliefs that bring about the negative behaviour. If we focus only on the behaviour, we may just be treating the symptoms. Getting to the root will produce long-lasting change.

Lifetraps (Schemas)

Think of lifetraps like this: during childhood, we develop certain thinking patterns. For example, the first born child in a family where the breadwinner is struggling to make ends meet might develop a greater sense of responsibility than the last born in a family of four with an upper middle class income. In the same way, a child who has been brought up in a neighbourhood which values athletic achievement might develop differently if he moves to a city that places a premium on academic performance.

Unfortunately, influences on a child are not always so benign. A child who is sexually molested by a relative might think that he cannot trust any authority figure. A child who is bullied at school might begin to think she is unlovable. A child who is berated by his parents might begin to think he is worthless or that he will never measure up. These toxic experiences lead to the development of negative patterns of thinking, feeling and behaving, of conscious and nonconscious painful memories, and of negative beliefs about ourselves and others that carry over into our adulthood, into our marriage and into our parenting! These thoughts and beliefs are *distorted*. The *stronger* our lifetraps, or "schemas,"[89] the more *distorted* our view (see Figure 7).

We all develop lifetraps in childhood, partly due to inborn temperament, and partly due to environment. *However, the number (and strength) of our lifetraps increases to the extent that our core emotional needs are not met.*

---

[89] Young, J. E., & Klosko, J. S. (1994). *Reinventing your life.* New York: Plume.

Figure 7: Schema / Lifetrap

(Please refer to Appendix 5, *Core Emotional Needs*). Perhaps we tried gaining attention or love from our caregivers. Perhaps our number one goal was to avoid being shamed. Perhaps we had an early sexual experience or were held to an unrealistically high standard. If we were abused, abandoned, shamed, or deprived of love by our parents, siblings, authority figures or peers, we almost certainly would have developed some corresponding active lifetraps.

As children, we were not able to look at our parents (or others in authority) and think, "They had a rotten childhood, so I am sure they don't really mean what they say." We could not help but take their words (or lack of words) personally. We internalised their messages, so much so that those messages became part of our makeup. We formed views about ourselves and others, and we acted on them. We heard a voice in our head, though there was little or no truth in it, that said:

- "People I love will eventually leave me."
- "If they really knew me, they would know that I am worthless."
- "People cannot be trusted."
- "Something bad is bound to happen."
- "I just can't get close to other people."
- "Dad was right—I'll never amount to anything."
- "Showing emotions is weak."
- "I should be punished."

For many of us, this voice stayed with us into adulthood and is still so strong it has power over our behaviour and decision making process even now.

The more we counsel people, the more we have come to realise the power of our childhood. We have seen the immense correlation between early experiences and current unhealthy behaviour and thinking. For some of us, our lifetraps are so prevalent and strong, they have become a roadblock to us becoming healthier adults and a barrier in our relationships with others. *In the context of marriage, our lifetraps prevent us from getting to Love Connection.*

We do not believe that this means we should blame our parents for our problems as adults. For one thing, in some cases, the harm wasn't caused by our parents anyway, but by others, such as teachers, siblings, neighbours, classmates, etc. However, in the situations where our parents did hurt us either by their actions or lack of action, for *most* parents, the harm they caused was unintentional and was largely based on ignorance.

At the same time, it is important to realise that when harm is done to children, the children are not at fault. They have little or no choice. However, in order to become healthy emotionally, adults must accept personal responsibility for themselves. Coming to terms with our lifetraps is a combination of acceptance and resolve. Acceptance helps us to understand ourselves and give ourselves (and our spouse) grace. Resolve says, "Just because I have a certain makeup as a result of my childhood does not mean that I am not able to break away from it." We believe that people can change. We believe in breaking unhealthy cycles but we accept that no matter how much we change, our childhood will always be a part of us. Appreciating and understanding that will greatly improve the state of our marriages.

People get so tangled up in their lifetraps that they end up sending messages that are completely counter-productive. Their lifetraps cause them to misinterpret what their spouse says, and then they end up in an argument, which either escalates into hurtful words or bitter isolation. Eventually needs are not met and the couple drifts apart. Unable to build Love Connection, the couple stays in the "Mutual Affection" phase or moves into the "Disintegration" phase.

Why are lifetraps so strong? One possible answer is that we get drawn more to what is *familiar* than to what is *healthy.* Because we have had these lifetraps since childhood, they, in a strange way, make us feel at home and we become familiar with them.[90] There is some kind of predictability and comfort that gets generated when we are with the familiar old self. Of course, logically, changing into something healthier is better, but change is unfamiliar and frightening. The pull towards the familiar, though destructive, is more powerful than the pull towards the healthy. That is why we end up imitating what is unhealthy from our parents and the dysfunction gets passed down. (Gary Solomon,[91] founder of Cinematherapy, likes to say, "Dysfunction is the gift that keeps on giving.")

---

[90] Young, J. E., & Klosko, J. S. (1994). *Reinventing your life.* New York: Plume. 6.
[91] Solomon, G. Retrieved May 2, 2010, from http://www.cinema-therapy.com

Coping Styles

Part of the dysfunction is the lifetrap. The other part of the dysfunction is the way we cope when these lifetraps are triggered. Before we take a look at each of the 18 lifetraps, we will turn our attention to our coping styles—the way we react when one of our lifetraps gets triggered. When our core emotional needs are not met as children, we get exasperated and subconsciously develop a way to cope with the pain of the unmet need. The way that we cope (e.g. to run away or fight back) has a lot to do with our temperament. We bring these coping styles into our adult life; they may appear to lessen the pain in the moment, but invariably they perpetuate or intensify the lifetrap in the long run and leave our deeper needs unmet. When our lifetraps are triggered, we cope in one of three ways: surrender, avoidance, or overcompensation, (also known as counterattacking).[92] Sometimes we accidentally imitate these coping styles from our parents. Others of us go in the opposite direction and develop a different coping style. Usually our temperaments push us toward a certain style. (Eighty years ago, Walter Cannon first identified fight and flight as common responses to stress; combined with fright, these correlate to the three coping styles.[93])

Surrender (Fright)

The surrender coping style is based on a fear of what we believe is the truth the lifetrap tells about us. We react from a negative and fearful place where the lifetrap is in control of what happens to us. The message, or underlying belief, of this coping style is, *"What my lifetrap is telling me about myself is true and I am powerless to change it."*

People with the surrender coping style believe in their own distorted view of themselves. They then act in ways to confirm this distorted view. If the husband says something rude, for example, that the wife is ugly or stupid, the wife agrees with him in her heart—she really believes that she is ugly or stupid. People with this coping style have a low opinion of themselves. This causes them to have a distorted view of others, and a distorted notion of how others view them, especially their spouse. They tend to blame themselves,

---

[92] Young, J. E., & Klosko, J. S. (1994). *Reinventing your life.* New York: Plume. 36.
[93] Stress: The fight or flight response. (n.d.). *Psychologist World.* Retrieved May 2, 2010, from http://www.psychologistworld.com

CHOOSE AWARENESS

Figure 8: Surrender (Fright) Coping Style

comply and give in when something goes wrong in the marriage. The voice in their heads says, "It is my fault." Surrender types (see Figure 8) tend to:
- Feel inferior to others
- Think others are better
- Accept all criticism
- Expect people to be critical
- Look for events to confirm that "it is their fault"
- Put the needs of others before their own.

Examples of "surrender behaviour" associated with criticism and blame:
- Giving in to others during arguments
- Being overly apologetic
- Keeping rules compliantly
- Being drawn to others who are more confident.

Avoidance (Flight)

The avoidance coping style is based on flight from the pain associated with the lifetrap. We react by avoiding situations and interactions that lead to the lifetrap being triggered. The message, or underlying belief, of this coping style is, *"It is too painful and uncomfortable to hear or feel my lifetrap. I must keep myself separate and distracted so I am not aware of this painful truth about myself."*

When their needs are not met or when their lifetraps are triggered, people with this coping style will do almost anything to escape feelings of disappointment and pain. They bypass situations that could be painful and trigger their lifetrap. Sometimes, feeling powerless, they come up with ways to delay thinking about the situation. They circumvent getting triggered by conflict and intimacy by distracting themselves. Avoiders are prone to addiction, and often try to forget their pain by drinking excessively, taking drugs, being involved in promiscuous sex, overeating, or other self-destructive behavior. Some will choose instead to immerse themselves in work or a hobby. They usually do not like to talk about their issues and will make excuses for not doing so. The voice in their head says, "I will avoid emotional pain at all costs." Sometimes they are not able to remember much from the past, and draw a blank when the past is questioned or explored because it hurts too much to remember. Those with the avoidance coping style often struggle

Figure 9: Avoidance (Flight) Coping Style

with being deceitful, and are sometimes uncomfortable with eye contact. Avoiders (see Figure 9) tend to:

- Be out of touch with their own feelings
- Dampen their feelings with substances (food, alcohol, drugs) or activities (gambling, sex, shopping workaholism)
- Act like they do not have a problem
- Avoid intimate relationships
- Walk around numb
- Avoid confronting problems.

Those who cope by avoiding often spend an inordinate amount of time engaged in the following activities:

- Reading newspapers and magazines
- Surfing the net, shopping online
- Cleaning their room
- Checking social media
- Monitoring their favourite sport or team
- Running or playing a team sport
- Watching television
- Drinking alcohol, smoking, or overeating
- Talking on the phone or texting.

Overcompensation (Fight)

The overcompensation or counterattacking coping style stems from the desire or need to fight what we believe is the underlying truth the lifetrap holds about us. We react by behaving in a way designed to create the opposite effect of the lifetrap. The message, or underlying belief, associated with this coping style is, *"I must fight as hard as I can to think and act as though what my lifetrap says about me is not true."*

When their lifetraps get triggered, people with this coping style will feel attacked, and they will attack back in order to prove that the negative feeling they have about themselves is not true. They will also lash out in anger and attack the source of the negative vibe. If they feel abused, they will abuse others. If they feel put down, they will put the other person down. Those who have been deprived of love and affection will convince themselves and those around them that they are tough and don't need anyone.

Figure 10: Overcompensation or Counterattacking (Fight) Coping Style

Overcompensation can take many forms, depending upon what painful message and/or experience the individual is fighting against. Those with this coping style often overreact to small slights or disappointments and can come across as rude, insensitive, and demanding or aloof and above it all. Someone who is overcompensating (see Figure 10) may:
- View disagreements as a threat, so they go out of their way to prove that others are wrong
- View feedback as criticism, so they go out of their way to prove that the opposite is true
- Appear strong, but actually they are fragile
- Not care who gets hurt in the process of proving themselves to be right
- Isolate themselves and not be intimate
- Prioritise protecting their image over intimacy
- Put their own needs first over the needs of others.

Examples of counterattacking behaviour:
- Constantly bringing up their unhappiness about others' annoying traits while acting as if they themselves are perfect
- Not waiting for a suitable time to talk; wanting it done there and then
- Throwing tantrums and abusing others with name-calling
- Making unhealthy comparisons with others during quarrels
- Criticising and having no qualms about getting involved in long, drawn out fights
- Becoming an over-achiever and unusually driven in work or projects.

Understanding our coping style leads to self-awareness, which in turn helps us to have more empathy on our spouse and be better equipped to meet their core emotional needs. Understanding ourselves better leads to understanding others better.

Anyone who knows us knows that John is an overcompensator, while Karen is an avoider. Now that we understand coping styles, we have figured out why we "fight" differently and are working on being sensitive to each other's style. In the section on the "Vortex of Conflict Escalation", we will explain more in detail about how our coping styles sometimes create havoc in our marriages.

Understanding Our Past

In order to identify our lifetraps, each of us needs to understand our past.[94] We have realised that while we are not able to *change* what happened to us previously, comprehending how our childhood has affected our thinking is very helpful. Understanding our past has given us better clarity and helped us develop awareness of our inclinations, patterns, and things about which we are sensitive. We cannot change our past but we can change the meaning we give to experiences in our own personal history.

Similarly, understanding our spouses and their pasts will help us to know their issues a lot better. We are better able to accept them for who they *are*, not for who we think they *should be*. We can understand that their reactions are not really so much about us, but about the way our behaviour reminds them of old hurts that turned into lifetraps.

> *John: I used to distance myself from people who emphasised the need to gain insights from the past. I often felt that this was a needless exercise with little benefit, and time consuming on top of that! Trained as an engineer, I prided myself on being a pragmatic individual. I loved solutions and did not like getting bogged down with issues and problems from the past. "What matters is the present. I am better off closing the door on the past simply because there is nothing I can do to change it. I just need to forgive and forget and move on, else I might allow my past to determine my destiny." Experience plus learning has changed my mind on this.*

When reading through the different lifetraps below, some of them will hit home. In fact, if we are honest, everyone has one or two lifetraps, most of us have several, and some of us quite a few. There is no way to completely eradicate them, because they have become a part of the way we interpret what is happening to us, a part of our memory. However, the good news is that we are able to *weaken* these lifetraps. So the gauge of a person's emotional health is not necessarily how many lifetraps he/she may have, but how strong or harmful they are.

---

[94] Young, J. E., Klosko, J. S., & Weishaar, M. E. (2003). *Schema therapy: A practitioner's guide.* New York: The Guilford Press.

At the end of this section, we will find means and ways to weaken our lifetraps by increasing the strength of our healthy side. The stronger our healthy side is, the more it will be able to combat our lifetraps and the weaker they will become. As a result, the better we will be able to build Love Connection. Do not look at this as you vs. your spouse. It is not helpful to search for who is really the culprit or who has more lifetraps. It is not about giving up responsibility for your actions and blaming your spouse's response on his/her lifetraps. It is about the two of you (with help from safe friends) working together to break the dysfunctional cycle, and become healthier. In the end, being healthier comes down to the following:

- Weakening each other's lifetraps
- Maturing in our unhealthy coping styles
- Meeting each other's needs—For the purpose of this book on marriage, these needs fall under the category of love and respect (see Chapter 2).

Being healthy is about strengthening our healthy spiritual side and weakening our unhealthy or sinful side. Paul writes in Romans 7:14-25 about our two sides:

> *[14]We know that the law is spiritual; but I am unspiritual, sold as a slave to sin. [15]I do not understand what I do. For what I want to do I do not do, but what I hate I do. [16]And if I do what I do not want to do, I agree that the law is good. [17]As it is, it is no longer I myself who do it, but it is sin living in me. [18]I know that nothing good lives in me, that is, in my sinful nature. For I have the desire to do what is good, but I cannot carry it out. [19]For what I do is not the good I want to do; no, the evil I do not want to do—this I keep on doing. [20]Now if I do what I do not want to do, it is no longer I who do it, but it is sin living in me that does it. [21]So I find this law at work: When I want to do good, evil is right there with me. [22]For in my inner being I delight in God's law; [23]but I see another law at work in the members of my body, waging war against the law of my mind and making me a prisoner of the law of sin at work within my members. [24]What a wretched man I am! Who will rescue me from this body of death? [25]Thanks be to God—through Jesus Christ our Lord! So then, I myself in my mind am a slave to God's law, but in the sinful nature a slave to the law of sin.*

When our healthy and spiritual side is weak, we will give into our sinful side, controlled by our lifetraps. If we do not weaken our lifetraps, then, like Paul wrote in Romans 7:19, we will become a slave to them and do what we know is wrong and unhealthy.

When we feed our healthy side by depending on God through diligent Bible study and prayer, seeking out feedback from others, and reflecting on our past, our lifetraps become weaker. From Proverbs 2:1-5 we learn:

> [1]My son, if you accept my words
> and store up my commands within you,
> [2]turning your ear to wisdom
> and applying your heart to understanding,
> [3]and if you call out for insight
> and cry aloud for understanding,
> [4]and if you look for it as for silver
> and search for it as for hidden treasure,
> [5]then you will understand the fear of the LORD
> and find the knowledge of God.

Here, the advice is that if we look out for insights, we will find them. Strange as it may sound, valuable insights into our character can deepen our relationship with God. Now that we understand what lifetraps are, and have a grasp of the different coping styles, we will examine each lifetrap one by one.

Identifying Our Lifetraps

There are 18 different lifetraps, grouped into four domains.[95] We will give a brief explanation of each lifetrap, along with how it can manifest with the different coping styles (because three individuals with the same lifetrap may have three different ways to cope with the same lifetrap). We will discuss what possible early family environment may have unintentionally facilitated the development of the lifetrap. Next, we will provide a questionnaire that can be used to measure the strength of each lifetrap. We will also illustrate each lifetrap with a cartoon, a case study, and a focus of change. Finally, we will recommend some Scriptures that can help to weaken each lifetrap.

---

[95] While empirical research on the clustering of schemas (lifetraps) over the years has at times revealed three domains, the majority of the research indicates four domains. For more details, please go to www.gep.sg.

Note to readers: All case studies in this book are based on our real counselling cases; therefore, the names and some details have been altered to protect confidentiality.

THE DOMAIN OF DISCONNECTION & REJECTION
Mistrust / Abuse

The core message of the mistrust lifetrap is, *"I cannot expect others to treat me in a fair, considerate or just manner. I should expect to be hurt (emotionally or even physically), lied to, taken advantage of, and manipulated. Others always have their own agenda."*

People with this lifetrap find it hard to trust others. They feel that people are out to take advantage of them or cause them harm. In marriage, this can cause quite a few problems. For example, if you have this lifetrap, and your partner is nice to you, you might suspect that he/she has a hidden agenda. You are constantly on the alert. You suspect that your spouse wants something from you. You make a series of tests in your head, without your spouse knowing, and if your spouse fails the test, then you decide that indeed he/she is untrustworthy. You test almost everyone, not just your spouse, and most people will fail your tests. (And they don't even know that they have taken a test!)

In one way or another, these instances take us back to when we were children. For some of us, the abuse was very intense, full of pain, verbally, physically and/or sexually. We carry the pain and mistrust into our marriage, and we frequently misconstrue the words of our spouse. We do not give them the benefit of the doubt, and we accuse them of not caring for us when that is not the case.

People with the mistrust lifetrap often label others. For example, they might think a certain way about *all* men or *all* women, or *all* people from a particular ethnic group, religion or race. They often try to expose others' duplicity, even though there may not be any. They sometimes do not have a good opinion of loving and caring people.

How the lifetrap of mistrust is manifested in the three coping styles, particularly in marriage...

Surrender – Individuals with this coping style surrender to their belief that they will be mistreated by others. Acting in a way that makes their negative belief seem true, they are unusually (and unhealthily) tolerant of uncaring or abusive behaviour. They tend to pick partners who are abusive, deceitful and uncaring. They expect to be mistreated, as this is a familiar and predictable pattern for them (see Figure 11).

Figure 11: Mistrust Lifetrap

Avoidance – Individuals with this coping style tend to avoid relationships or they do not allow themselves to be close to their spouse. They are in flight from what they believe to be inevitable—their partner will hurt them. They can be secretive. They are uncomfortable talking about their hurts and being intimate. They take a long time to open up and fear that their partners will eventually use this information to hurt them.

Overcompensation – Individuals with this lifetrap who counterattack will usually have anger issues. They may be abusive themselves, operating from the attitude "I better get you before you get me" as they fight against the belief they will be mistreated or abused in their close relationships. They blow up at the slightest hint that someone might take advantage of them. Because they expect to be mistreated, put down, and abused, they humiliate the supposed abuser first. They often engage in name-calling. Their spouses will drift away from them. In extreme cases, overcompensators with the mistrust lifetrap may enjoy seeing others hurt. They may imitate the way they were abused, using the same words and methods. What they inherit, they pass down.

Possible Early Family Environment
- You were abused verbally, physically and/or sexually, by a parent, a relative, a teacher, a classmate, or any combination of the above. (If you have never discussed your past abuse with your spouse, it will be very painful when you choose to open up. And if your spouse needs to talk about early abuse, be patient and understanding. Give them time to talk through it all, and do not hurry them.)
- Your siblings fought with you constantly and your parents allowed it and did not protect you.
- There was a lot of tension in your home—you witnessed your dad abusing your mother.
- You grew up in an environment where abuse was not done to you directly, but to others, and you observed the abuse. For example, perhaps a sibling was ill-treated, or you knew that one of your friends was being abused, or you saw peers in school being abused by teachers.

THE MISTRUST / ABUSE QUESTIONNAIRE

This questionnaire will measure the strength of your mistrust lifetrap. Please read each statement and decide how well it describes you and/or your beliefs. When you are not sure, base your answer on what you emotionally **feel**, not on what you **think** to be true. If you desire, reword the statement so that the statement would be even more accurate in describing you (but do not change the basic meaning of the question). Then choose the **highest rating from 1 to 6** that describes you (including your revisions), and write the number in the space before the statement.

RATING SCALE:
1 = Completely untrue of me
2 = Mostly untrue of me
3 = Slightly more true than untrue
4 = Moderately true of me
5 = Mostly true of me
6 = Describes me perfectly

Score	Description
	1. I often feel that I have to protect myself from other people.
	2. If someone acts nicely towards me, I assume that he/she must be after something.
	3. Most people only think about themselves.
	4. I have a great deal of difficulty trusting people.
	5. I am quite suspicious of other people's motives.
	6. Other people are rarely honest; they are usually not what they appear.
Your Total Score (Add your scores together for questions 1-6. Maximum Score: 36)	

Interpreting Your Mistrust Score

6-11: Very low. This lifetrap does not apply to you.
12-17: Fairly low. This lifetrap is very weak in your life.
18-23: Moderate. This lifetrap is weak in your life.
24-29: High. This lifetrap is a fairly strong in your life.
30-36: Very high. This lifetrap is very strong in your life.

This is a limited questionnaire taken from Young Schema Questionnaire, 3rd Edition (YSQ-L3). Used with permission.[96]

---

[96] Copyright © 2005, Jeffrey Young, Ph.D. Unauthorised reproduction without written consent of the authors is prohibited. You may order/purchase the complete version of the questionnaire at www.schematherapy.com, or write to: Cognitive Therapy Center of New York, 130 West 42nd St., Suite 501, New York, NY 10036.

Case Study: Mistrust

Sam and his wife, Julie, have been married for 14 years. Sam has a hard time trusting his wife, and admits to making extreme accusations and being very controlling in the marriage. Given the opportunity, he says he monitors her every move. Both Sam and Julie came for therapy. She said their most recent argument happened because Sam felt she was flirting with her colleague.

Julie: *I do not know what his problem is. Last Thursday, I got a lift home from my male colleague—we teach in the same university and he lives nearby. When Sam phoned home later in the day, he became enraged when he found out about it. When he came home, he questioned me again and again. I do not have any feelings whatsoever for this colleague, or anyone else for that matter, but Sam does not trust me at all.*

Sam: *Well, why should she take a lift from him? Perhaps he is after my wife. I will tell him to lay off or I'll go after him.*

Sam is completely mistrusting of his wife. He is meticulous about what she wears, not wanting her to draw attention to herself. He is sure she will flirt with other men. He does not trust how she spends money. He constantly questions her and they have frequent fights about finances. Julie feels as if she is always walking on eggshells when they talk. On several occasions, Sam became abusive towards his wife. He chased her with a knife and threw her belongings out of the house in a rage. Fearing for her daughter's safety, and her own, Julie made him move out, but they continued therapy. Eventually Sam shared about his abusive childhood, especially about his father.

Therapist: *What are your memories of your own childhood?*

Sam: *My father would not allow me to play much when I was young. So I lied to him and told him that I wanted to study in the library when in fact I wanted to play. Once he caught me. He threw me, along with all my clothes, out of the house and locked me outside until my grandparents came to my aid. He constantly lectured me to trust no one, not business partners, not family members. I guess in hindsight it isn't hard to understand why it is so difficult for me to trust people...*

The origins of Sam's inability to trust, and of his abusive behaviour, are in his childhood. A parent is someone that a child is supposed to be able to trust the most. If a parent betrays that trust, the child wonders, "Who can I trust?" Sam's father's treatment left lasting injuries. People who are abused often end up in relationships with people who abuse them, or, like Sam, they become the abusers. The dysfunction of Sam's father was passed down to Sam, his son.

Focus of Change
People with the lifetrap of mistrust normally see everything in black and white. The aim of treatment is for them to start seeing that people do not just fall into the two categories of those who can be trusted and those who cannot. Rather, people's motives lie somewhere in a range.

For someone like Sam, a counterattacker, he has to not lump his wife into the untrustworthy category. By constantly giving her new tests, he reinforces his lifetrap, because at some point she will definitely fail one of the tests. While Julie is not perfect, and also has things to improve, she is trustworthy. Sam has to learn that people can be trustworthy and still make mistakes. He needs to be vulnerable with his wife and not attack when his lifetraps are triggered.

◁ SCRIPTURES FOR MEDITATION ▷

• Matthew 10:16   • I Corinthians 13:6-7   • I Peter 4:8

Defectiveness / Shame

The core message of the defectiveness lifetrap is, *"I am not good enough. I am inherently flawed. Anyone who truly knows me could not love me."*

Do you know smart people who don't think they're smart, and attractive people who don't think they're attractive? This lifetrap is about feeling shame. People with this lifetrap feel that something inside is wrong with them—that they are strange, stupid, short, fat, etc. They do not accept compliments easily. They feel they do not deserve praise. They get jealous and competitive and feel insecure around those who they perceive as being better than they are. They make a lot of comparisons, even in common interactions. If the lifetrap is strong, they become consumed with status and position, and they overvalue successes, such as excelling academically or athletic achievement.

Because they feel defective, they are rarely satisfied with their present state of affairs. Nothing they accomplish makes them feel good enough. They push themselves all the time, to the point that their closest relationships get hurt along the way. They become more consumed about not being defective than they are about meeting the core needs of their spouse. They also fear that their defectiveness will get exposed and that they will be shamed. The feeling of defectiveness may be based on something tangible, or invisible, which makes it difficult to detect.

How the lifetrap of defectiveness is manifested in the three coping styles, particularly in marriage…

Surrender – Individuals with this coping style will believe that they are truly flawed and will surrender to the "truth" of their defectiveness, acting as though there is nothing good about them. They react to the world around them from a place of fear, frozen in the false reality that they are not good enough. When they do not get their needs met, or when there is a problem in the marriage, they believe it is because something is wrong with them. They hide themselves and have trouble sharing their innermost thoughts, feelings, and struggles as they believe they will be rejected if they let anyone really know them. They feel that they are not deserving of love from their spouse. They have a hard time accepting praise or encouragement from their spouse (see Figure 12).

Avoidance – Individuals with this coping style try to avoid situations in which their defectiveness would be triggered. They are in flight mode from their core belief, which is that they are unlovable and not good enough, so they often underachieve or fail to try at all. If avoidant types feel that their defectiveness is being exposed, they will find ways to get distracted, rather than face up to their weaknesses (real or imagined). The pain of defectiveness is too great so avoiders create a means by which to escape, but in so doing, cut themselves off from intimacy in their marriage. They feel powerless over (what they believe is) the truth of the lifetrap, and see no option other than escape. What they are avoiding is the bad feeling that they are defective, but to the spouse it comes across as avoiding being in the marriage.

Figure 12: Defectiveness Lifetrap

Overcompensation – People with the defectiveness lifetrap and a counterattacking coping style act superior and are very demanding both of themselves and of others. (This often produces a secondary lifetrap—unrelenting standards—which will be discussed later.) They operate from the fight mode, attacking the belief that they are fundamentally flawed by requiring themselves to be perfect. They act against the lifetrap. While deep down they believe they are defective, they demand perfection of themselves and often of those around them as well. But since they do not believe they are good enough, nothing is ever good enough for them! Since they believe they are fundamentally unlovable, they may demand love from their spouse, but nothing will ever be enough—they cannot trust that the love is real!

When their defectiveness makes them feel that their spouse does not like them, overcompensators communicate the same thing to their spouse. If they feel defective, they will want to make others feel defective. Spouses caught in this situation will get hurt from the explosive anger of the counterattacker, and will then not be drawn to them, and as a result, no one's needs would be met.

When given constructive criticism, overcompensators with defectiveness don't just feel that they are getting feedback—they interpret it as an attack. Feeling put down, they will then put the other person down. Since overcompensators often come across in a confident manner, their spouses, friends and co-workers might not suspect that they have this lifetrap. They are good at hiding their defectiveness—with some "defective" counterattackers portraying just the opposite, that they are better than others.

Possible Early Family Environment
- You were compared to others (siblings, relatives, and peers) and felt that your parents were disappointed with you.
- You were unfairly blamed for wrongs growing up.
- You were criticised by at least one of your parents for being useless, slow, dumb, clumsy, ugly, stupid, etc.
- You were not favoured in the family.
- Your parents would constantly talk about their definition of a successful person and you did not make the cut.
- You always felt that you did not quite measure up (not good enough in studies, or in sports, or not pretty or talented enough, and so forth).

THE DEFECTIVENESS / SHAME QUESTIONNAIRE

This questionnaire will measure the strength of your defectiveness lifetrap. Please read each statement and decide how well it describes you and/or your beliefs. When you are not sure, base your answer on what you emotionally **feel**, not on what you **think** to be true. If you desire, reword the statement so that the statement would be even more accurate in describing you (but do not change the basic meaning of the question). Then choose the **highest rating from 1 to 6** that describes you (including your revisions), and write the number in the space before the statement.

RATING SCALE:

1 = Completely untrue of me   4 = Moderately true of me
2 = Mostly untrue of me   5 = Mostly true of me
3 = Slightly more true than untrue 6 = Describes me perfectly

Score	Description
	1. No one I desire would want to stay close to me if he/she knew the real me.
	2. No matter how hard I try, I feel that I won't be able to get a significant man/woman to respect me or feel that I am worthwhile.
	3. I feel that I'm not lovable.
	4. I am too unacceptable in very basic ways to reveal myself to other people.
	5. If others found out about my basic defects, I could not face them.
	6. When people like me, I feel I am fooling them.
	Your Total Score (Add your scores together for questions 1-6. Maximum Score: 36)

Interpreting Your Defectiveness Score	
6-11:	Very low. This lifetrap does not apply to you.
12-17:	Fairly low. This lifetrap is very weak in your life.
18-23:	Moderate. This lifetrap is weak in your life.
24-29:	High. This lifetrap is a fairly strong in your life.
30-36:	Very high. This lifetrap is very strong in your life.

This is a limited questionnaire taken from Young Schema Questionnaire, 3rd Edition (YSQ-L3). Used with permission.[97]

---

[97] Copyright © 2005, Jeffrey Young, Ph.D. Unauthorised reproduction without written consent of the authors is prohibited. You may order/purchase the complete version of the questionnaire at www.schematherapy.com, or write to: Cognitive Therapy Center of New York, 130 West 42nd St., Suite 501, New York, NY 10036.

Case Study: Defectiveness

Jennifer works as a professional athlete, is well paid and very respected by her colleagues and employees. Although successful in her career, and possessing what comes across as a huge amount of self-confidence, deep down she feels lousy about herself, and fears that any minute she will be exposed as a fraud. Jennifer and her husband, Thomas, have been married for ten years. On the outside, they look very together, but she takes everything he says personally. The slightest look can trigger her defectiveness, and send her into a downward spiral. It has become so bad that she is convinced her husband married the wrong person. She hates herself for being negative, and she hates him for causing it. Eventually, they sought therapy in order to break their cycle of fighting.

Thomas shared his feelings of frustration.

Thomas: *I love Jennifer and want us to have a great marriage. I want our sons to love their mother, too. But she really flies off the handle at the slightest provocation, and now that our boys are older, she is starting to go after them as well. I am worried about the atmosphere at home.*

Jennifer: *He is always at work. He does well there but does little at home. I work hard at my job and then come home and do all the work. Instead of complimenting me and being grateful, Thomas criticises me and tells me what I am not doing or how I could do things better. If he is such an expert on how to speak with my sponsors, why doesn't he do it? If he thinks he is better at negotiating with my agent than I am, let him try! And he could support me when I am upset that the boys are not helping around the house, rather than constantly telling me that I am too hard on them. It feels like whatever I do, I am just not good enough for him.*

Jennifer is a counterattacker, who will put people down if she feels put down. She frequently feels put down, so she has lots of run-ins with people at work and also in her extended family. Her husband says he tries to smooth things over, but she usually doesn't take it well. In subsequent sessions, Jennifer recalled her childhood.

Jennifer: *When I was young, I constantly heard my mother putting other people down. In her eyes, most people were useless. I never got the feeling that anyone outside of our family was good enough. However, she also criticised me and compared me unfavourably with my siblings. When I was accepted into a good school, she was down on me for not getting into a better one. I fought with her, but maybe I felt like she was right. This voice saying that I am not good enough is still in my head. And when my husband criticises me, I get really mad and I am determined to prove that it is not true.*

Therapist: *How did you fight your way against this voice and do so well at work?*

Jennifer: *I love sports—it is my passion. By excelling in sports, I always feel that I am able to prove myself. So now, after many years, I guess you can say that I am confident at work, but at home, with my husband criticising me, I still feel like a stupid little kid. I feel defective and down on myself. So of course, I immerse myself even more in work. I eventually saw that it was ruining my marriage, so that is why I came for counselling.*

Focus of Change
People with the lifetrap of defectiveness feel useless, ugly, stupid, clumsy, inept or just plain lousy about themselves. They are over-sensitive to their weaknesses, and they have an unjustified fear of exposing themselves to others. Even though they may be highly successful in their lives, they feel deep down that they are not quite good enough. The aim here is to help Jennifer see the distorted view of her lifetrap. While successful at work, she feels defective and put down by her husband. Being a counterattacker, she puts her husband down when she feels that he triggers her. This has affected the level of intimacy in their marriage since Thomas feels that she must not love him if she is able to speak so hurtfully to him. Both Jennifer and Thomas need to see that everyone has weaknesses, and that "to err is human". They need to accept each other and celebrate their strengths and accomplishments. (This is why we enjoy the grace of God who helps us through our weaknesses.)

SCRIPTURES FOR MEDITATION

- Psalm 139:13-16   • Luke 15:20   • Romans 5:6-8

Emotional Deprivation

The core message of the emotional deprivation lifetrap is, *"I cannot expect others to be supportive of me and care about what I need."* Emotional deprivation is about insufficient **empathy**, **nurturing**, and/or not receiving **guidance and direction**.

People with the emotional deprivation lifetrap did not feel emotionally close to one or both of their parents when they were growing up. They may or may not have been physically separated from their parents, but they were distant emotionally. In some cases, they were left to themselves, and they may have felt empty in their formative years. As adults, they still have the same feeling—that people will never love them enough. They feel that they are neither understood nor loved. They seem to have a bottomless pit—no matter how much love is shown to them, it is still not sufficient to satisfy them. Even in marriage, people with this lifetrap frequently feel lonely and feel that no one is there to give them care and concern. They might not feel a deep friendship with people even though the other parties feel close.

How the lifetrap of emotional deprivation is manifested in the three coping styles, particularly in marriage...

Surrender – People with this lifetrap who have the surrender coping style fear that no one will meet their emotional needs, so they settle for relationships that give hardly anything back to them. They give in to their thinking that what they need is not important. Their behaviour makes their fears come true. They are often in one-way relationships. It is hard for their partner to get connected to them because they have little expectation that they will be loved to their satisfaction. They have accepted as fact the idea that no relationship will meet their level of satisfaction. This prevents them from being disappointed with their spouse and others. They do not express their needs, as they have no expectation their needs will be met (see Figure 13).

Avoidance – Avoiders with emotional deprivation shy away from getting too close in relationships. They flee the pain of their belief that their needs will not be met in relationships. They are often alone. They bury themselves in their work or hobbies or addictive behaviours. They make it difficult for their partner to get close to them and they sometimes avoid being romantic.

CHOOSE AWARENESS

Overcompensation – Counterattackers with this lifetrap become very demanding and have high expectations in relation to getting their needs met. They fight their belief that their needs will not be seen as important and taken into consideration. They complain that people neither understand them nor know how to meet their needs. When their needs are not met to

Figure 13: Emotional Deprivation Lifetrap

their satisfaction, they get angry and lash out at their spouse, sometimes becoming hostile. They have both sadness and resentment towards their spouse. (Counterattackers with the emotional deprivation lifetrap can develop entitlement as a secondary lifetrap.)

Possible Early Family Environment
- You did not have loving and nurturing parents; there were not many kisses, hugs or physical touch. Although your parents were *physically* there, no one was that warm to you.
- Your parents were emotionally absent and may have had someone else raise you. You seldom went to them for love and affection, or if you tried, it didn't go well.
- Your *mother* had a busy schedule (this lifetrap may have more to do with lack of maternal closeness, rather than paternal), and was focused on her own career or social life and did not have time for you. She may have been ill and not able to meet your needs for a legitimate reason.
- Even when you did talk to your parents, they did not know how to empathise with you, so you grew up feeling like your feelings were not important or understood.
- You were given material things and vacations, perhaps even spoiled, but little interest was expressed in you and what was going on in your life.
- When you had problems, your parents were not there to listen and advise you.

THE EMOTIONAL DEPRIVATION QUESTIONNAIRE

This questionnaire will measure the strength of your emotional deprivation lifetrap. Please read each statement and decide how well it describes you and/or your beliefs. When you are not sure, base your answer on what you emotionally **feel**, not on what you **think** to be true. If you desire, reword the statement so that the statement would be even more accurate in describing you (but do not change the basic meaning of the question). Then choose the **highest rating from 1 to 6** that describes you (including your revisions), and write the number in the space before the statement.

RATING SCALE:
1 = Completely untrue of me
2 = Mostly untrue of me
3 = Slightly more true than untrue
4 = Moderately true of me
5 = Mostly true of me
6 = Describes me perfectly

Score	Description
	1. People have not been there to meet my emotional needs.
	2. I haven't gotten love and attention.
	3. For much of my life, I haven't had someone who wanted to get close to me and spend a lot of time with me.
	4. For much of my life, I haven't felt that I am special to someone.
	5. I have rarely had a person give me sound advice or direction when I'm not sure what to do.
	Your Total Score (Add your scores together for questions 1-5. Maximum Score: 30)

Interpreting Your Emotional Deprivation Score

- 5-9: Very low. This lifetrap does not apply to you.
- 10-14: Fairly low. This lifetrap is very weak in your life.
- 15-19: Moderate. This lifetrap is weak in your life.
- 20-24: High. This lifetrap is fairly strong in your life.
- 25-30: Very high. This lifetrap is very strong in your life.

This is a limited questionnaire taken from Young Schema Questionnaire, 3rd Edition (YSQ-L3). Used with permission.[98]

Case Study: Emotional Deprivation

Patrick and Marilyn have been married for eight years. Not long after their daughter was born, Marilyn became depressed. She frequently fought with her husband and accused him of not being there for her. Both Marilyn and Patrick felt they were at the end of their rope and came for therapy.

Marilyn: *We constantly fight. He loves his work more than me. I do not know when he'll come home. When he comes home, he does not talk.*

Patrick: *My work is very demanding. I like coming home, but when she accuses me of things, I shut down and avoid her by doing something else. I am tired of her telling me what to do.*

While Marilyn accused Patrick of all sorts of possible misdeeds, what she wanted was for him to show his love for her. She felt that throughout the day

---

[98] Copyright © 2005, Jeffrey Young, Ph.D. Unauthorised reproduction without written consent of the authors is prohibited. You may order/purchase the complete version of the questionnaire at www.schematherapy.com, or write to: Cognitive Therapy Center of New York, 130 West 42nd St., Suite 501, New York, NY 10036.

she was giving of herself to others at work, and at home to her family, but she longed to feel secure in Patrick's love for her. She realised that during her childhood, she had been emotionally deprived.

Marilyn: *When I was a child, my mother contracted debilitating arthritis. Not only could she not take care of me properly, I had to constantly take care of her! One of my aunts looked after us, but she was demanding and negative. I feel that I never got the love I wanted. No one had any energy for what I needed. Now I am upset because I feel that this is being repeated in my marriage. I don't want this to carry on. I am especially hurt when my husband avoids me and does not get intimate in our conversations. I cry and feel sad a lot.*

Focus of Change
People with the lifetrap of emotional deprivation yearn to feel loved. The aim for people with this lifetrap is to see that it is right for their needs to be met, but that they should express their needs appropriately, by being open and vulnerable. When we are deprived of love during childhood, we become angry and lonely. Marilyn has unresolved anger towards her mum for not loving her adequately, and now struggles to feel loved by her husband.

Marilyn is a counterattacker, and by putting her husband down for not meeting her needs, she is driving him away. Marilyn lumps everyone in the same category—"If they don't meet my needs a certain way, then they don't love me, and if they really loved me, they would know how to meet my needs!" This carries over into Marilyn's other relationships. When she tries getting close to other people, at the slightest sense that they are about to let her down in some way, she counterattacks them, which comes across as entitled behaviour.

By being vulnerable with Patrick, and holding back from counterattacking, Marilyn is starting to have her need for emotional connection met. She is also trying to not label her husband as being inept in meeting her needs when he makes a mistake.

SCRIPTURES FOR MEDITATION
- Psalms 56:3-4, 8 • Isaiah 49:15-16a • Romans 8:31-39

Social Isolation / Alienation

The core message of the social isolation lifetrap is, *"I am different from other people and do not fit in."* The feelings of isolation and being alone stem from feeling apart from any group or community, and too different to belong.

People who have this lifetrap feel different from other people, that they do not fit in. This feeling began in childhood, when they felt they did not fit in with the circle of people around them. People with this lifetrap often avoid social gatherings, because they do not like to mix with others, and they feel out of place when they are there. They feel singled out because they *feel* that they are different and not part of the group. What makes them feel different is not necessarily negative—they may be smarter, have more money, or come from a family with fame or power. Ultimately, when they look at those around them, they feel they don't belong to any one group. They are the odd one out. People with this lifetrap focus more on what makes them different and set apart from others than on what they have in common. Although it is related to the lifetrap of defectiveness, it is different from defectiveness. Someone with defectiveness feels inferior inside; people with the social isolation lifetrap feel out of place because of external factors, but it is possible to have both. People with this lifetrap often avoid social functions and feel lonely.

How the lifetrap of social isolation is manifested in the three coping styles, particularly in marriage...

Surrender – People with this lifetrap who tend to be surrendered believe that they do not fit into any social group. They give in to the fright of their belief that they are different and will never fit in. Their focus is so much on what sets them apart that they fail to notice what they do have in common with others! As a result they stand outside the circle. Conversations with friends are superficial because in their heart, they feel tremendous loneliness. Since they feel they do not fit in, they will also feel this way with their spouse and family, and think that they are the odd one out (see Figure 14). They may develop imaginary friends or resort to fantasising, as their real life is terribly lonely. However, their spouse may not detect this and will be at a loss to know how to help them. If they do not feel alienated from their spouse, they may become over-reliant on that relationship, since they feel separate and too different to be part of other relationships. This may put pressure on the marriage which becomes suffocating.

Avoidance – People with this lifetrap who tend to be avoiders will shy away from social functions and let their spouse attend alone. They will generally want to be alone. As a result, loneliness will be an issue. They flee the discomfort they experience when they are in a group. This may also create pressure in the marriage. If they do have any friends, it would usually be the friends of their spouse. Their spouse may perceive them as being unfriendly and shy.

Figure 14: Social Isolation Lifetrap

Overcompensation – Overcompensators with this lifetrap will fight the belief they are different and try to prove they fit in after all by acting superficially. Because they do not believe they can be themselves and fit in, they change who they appear to be to meet whatever criteria they think they need to meet in order to fit in. This creates an artificial personality that can be confusing and hard for their spouse to understand.

Possible Early Family Environment
- As a child you felt different from others and felt that you did not fit in.
- Perhaps your friends were of a different race, spoke a different language, or were perceived as being more intelligent than you.
- Perhaps, on the other hand, your friends may have been way behind you in school or sports or in some talent—this still may have given you the feeling that you were different from the rest.
- You felt that your family was strange or unusual, and in your heart you felt that something was wrong. This could result from problems in your family, or other factors, such as having more power, fame or fortune.
- Your parents were divorced, but your friends' parents were not. Or your school friends lived in a nice neighbourhood, but you did not, or the other way round.
- One of your parent's jobs resulted in you having to move a lot, so you felt different from everyone wherever you went.

THE SOCIAL ISOLATION / ALIENATION QUESTIONNAIRE

This questionnaire will measure the strength of your social isolation lifetrap. Please read each statement and decide how well it describes you and/or your beliefs. When you are not sure, base your answer on what you emotionally **feel**, not on what you **think** to be true. If you desire, reword the statement so that the statement would be even more accurate in describing you (but do not change the basic meaning of the question). Then choose the **highest rating from 1 to 6** that describes you (including your revisions), and write the number in the space before the statement.

RATING SCALE:
1 = Completely untrue of me
2 = Mostly untrue of me
3 = Slightly more true than untrue
4 = Moderately true of me
5 = Mostly true of me
6 = Describes me perfectly

Score	Description
	1. I feel alienated from other people.
	2. I feel isolated and alone.
	3. No one really understands me.
	4. I sometimes feel as if I'm an alien.
	5. If I disappeared tomorrow, no one would notice.
	Your Total Score (Add your scores together for questions 1-5. Maximum Score: 30)

Interpreting Your Social Isolation Score	
5-9:	Very low. This lifetrap does not apply to you.
10-14:	Fairly low. This lifetrap is very weak in your life.
15-19:	Moderate. This lifetrap is weak in your life.
20-24:	High. This lifetrap is fairly strong in your life.
25-30:	Very high. This lifetrap is very strong in your life.

This is a limited questionnaire taken from Young Schema Questionnaire, 3rd Edition (YSQ-L3). Used with permission.[99]

Case Study: Social Isolation

Sarah and Scott have been married for 16 years. Sarah came on her own for counselling—she feels she does not fit in anywhere, even in her own family. She avoids being with others, and is not emotionally close to her husband, Scott.

Sarah has a great job working as an accountant. She has two daughters and often feels burdened for their future. She has had suicidal thoughts from time to time and eventually had the courage to come for therapy.

Sarah: *I feel very out of place. I feel that everybody is better than me, and that I don't fit in.*

When asked about her childhood, she said the following:

Sarah: *As a child I felt I was different from others. My family lived on a farm, and there were no neighbours. I felt different from my friends at school. I*

---

[99] Copyright © 2005, Jeffrey Young, Ph.D. Unauthorised reproduction without written consent of the authors is prohibited. You may order/purchase the complete version of the questionnaire at www.schematherapy.com, or write to: Cognitive Therapy Center of New York, 130 West 42nd St., Suite 501, New York, NY 10036.

was never close to anyone growing up. I remember that whenever I would make a friend, that friend would leave. I always felt like I was the odd one out. Even in my family now, I feel that I don't fit in and perhaps they would be better off without me. Then I retreat and communicate with my imaginary friends in my room alone. I feel that they are the only ones who could connect with me.

Eventually, her husband accompanied her to counselling and began to take responsibility for his part in the marriage.

Scott: *I am surprised that my wife was seeking solace from imaginary friends all these years. I had no idea. I see the need to pull her in by being more accepting, not brushing her aside like I have done in the past.*

Sarah is a surrendered individual. She believes that she does not fit in. She avoids being with people in general. Sometimes she seems to be having a good time, but she says she fakes having fun. In reality, she would rather be alone. She takes a long time to warm up to people, although she will gladly talk to people she knows well.

Focus of Change
People with the lifetrap of social isolation feel that they just don't fit in, and Sarah has felt that way for almost her whole life. The aim of helping Sarah is for her to see that the differences she imagines between herself and others are exaggerated. Rather, she should focus on what she has in common with her friends and family, and not focus on the differences.

For Sarah, talking with imaginary friends was a safe and easy way to feel like she was connecting with others. Sarah is now getting close to a group of friends at church and hopes that frequent group interactions will help to weaken this lifetrap. She has become vulnerable with her husband, who no longer ignores her, but is more considerate, and values her as his wife, as well as the mother of their children.

SCRIPTURES FOR MEDITATION

- Romans 12:5 • I Corinthians 12:14-26 • Ephesians 4:14-16

Emotional Inhibition

The core message of the emotional inhibition lifetrap is, *"I should not express myself or show my emotions. I should always be in control."*

People with this lifetrap are often seen by others as being without emotions. They value being rational as a superior disposition. They do not like anything too loud, too spontaneous, too noisy, though it may not be perceived as such by their spouses or other people. Such behaviour is seen as being ill-mannered and inappropriate.

In some cases, people from upper middle class backgrounds have been brought up to think this way. In other cases, it may be a cultural issue, associated with ethnicity. Certain groups tend to feel that emotions should be contained. They are not to be shown. This becomes damaging because even intimacy has to be appropriate. Anything forthcoming is viewed as being too aggressive. People with this lifetrap do not know how to get intimate. They feel that sharing heartfelt feelings is difficult. What lurks beneath the surface is fear of shame if they were to let out their true feelings or emotions. If they are not married to someone with the same lifetrap, their spouses end up feeling like they live with Mr. Spock from *Star Trek*.

How the lifetrap of emotional inhibition is manifested in the three coping styles, particularly in marriage…

Surrender – The surrendered types will not show their emotions much, so their spouses will feel like they are facing a wall. All emotions are controlled, and there is little spontaneity; the relationship can seem boring to the spouse. Spouses may then resort to other sources of fun, and spend more time with friends who are not emotionally inhibited. Conversation at home is monotone. A good laugh or a good cry would be seen as inappropriate. They will be unable to feel empathy for others, especially their spouse (see Figure 15).

Avoidance – Avoiders stay away from situations and people which might encourage a display of emotions. They avoid intimacy even though their spouse longs to be free to be romantic, creative, and spontaneous. They dislike undertakings that involve being slightly extroverted and avoid such activities. This makes for an uninteresting dynamic in the marriage.

Figure 15: Emotional Inhibition Lifetrap

Overcompensation – Individuals who fight against their inhibited emotions may seem very awkward trying to express their feelings, trying to be emotional, but it comes across fake, like telling a joke that is not funny. Perhaps he/she has felt shut down for a long time and wants to cut loose. The superficiality and the shallowness of this behaviour may put off the partner.

Possible Early Family Environment
- One of your parents looked down on you or your siblings for displaying emotions.
- Your parents believed in the old sayings "children are to be seen and not heard" and "big boys don't cry".
- You were prevented from being a child. You had to temper your excitement about normal things and control your emotions so as to not bother father, or mother.
- Being loud, excited, and making noise were all viewed as unacceptable behaviour.
- You had to walk on eggshells when you were in the home. Loud conversations were viewed as shouting.

THE EMOTIONAL INHIBITION QUESTIONNAIRE

This questionnaire will measure the strength of your emotional inhibition lifetrap. Please read each statement and decide how well it describes you and/or your beliefs. When you are not sure, base your answer on what you emotionally **feel**, not on what you **think** to be true. If you desire, reword the statement so that the statement would be even more accurate in describing you (but do not change the basic meaning of the question). Then choose the **highest rating from 1 to 6** that describes you (including your revisions), and write the number in the space before the statement.

RATING SCALE:
1 = Completely untrue of me
2 = Mostly untrue of me
3 = Slightly more true than untrue
4 = Moderately true of me
5 = Mostly true of me
6 = Describes me perfectly

Score	Description
	1. I feel that I must control my emotions and impulses, or something bad is likely to happen.
	2. A lot of anger and resentment build up inside of me that I don't express.
	3. I am too self-conscious to show positive feelings to others (e.g., affection, showing I care).
	4. I find it embarrassing to express my feelings to others.

Score	Description
	5. I find it hard to be warm and spontaneous.
	6. I control myself so much that people think I am unemotional.
	Your Total Score (Add your scores together for questions 1-6. Maximum Score: 36)

	Interpreting Your Emotional Inhibition Score
6-11:	Very low. This lifetrap does not apply to you.
12-17:	Fairly low. This lifetrap is very weak in your life.
18-23:	Moderate. This lifetrap is weak in your life.
24-29:	High. This lifetrap is a fairly strong in your life.
30-36:	Very high. This lifetrap is very strong in your life.

This is a limited questionnaire taken from Young Schema Questionnaire, 3rd Edition (YSQ-L3). Used with permission.[100]

Case Study: Emotional Inhibition

Bill has a hard time getting intimate with his wife of eleven years, who is frustrated with his shallowness. When they came for marriage counselling, Bill's wife, Adriane, was unhappy. Among the many reasons she gave, one that stood out was her husband's shallowness and lack of intimacy.

Adriane: *When we get together, he is quiet. Usually he only talks when he wants something. When I try to get deep, he gets irritated. I feel that our relationship is not based on genuineness and depth. I am frustrated about it. Further, he is like this with our young son. Bill doesn't express himself at all, so our son does not even want to be with his father. He clings to me and thinks his dad is weird.*

Therapist: *Did you know him to be like this all along, even when you were going out before getting married?*

Adriane: *When we were dating, I thought he was cool. The fact is, I was the bubbly person with all the emotions, and I thought he would balance me perfectly. He appeared to me then as a calm and intellectual person.*

---

[100] Copyright © 2005, Jeffrey Young, Ph.D. Unauthorised reproduction without written consent of the authors is prohibited. You may order/purchase the complete version of the questionnaire at www.schematherapy.com, or write to: Cognitive Therapy Center of New York, 130 West 42nd St., Suite 501, New York, NY 10036.

Bill talked about his past.

Bill: *I don't feel comfortable sharing my inner thoughts. I have a hard time feeling for people. I don't talk much, I just do my work.*

Therapist: *What was your home environment like when you were growing up?*

Bill: *Well, my father left us when we were young. My mother was a task-oriented person. We hardly spoke a word when we were all together. Even with my own sister, I have no relationship with her at all. We never talk. We just existed, and did our work separately. There was so little connection. In my heart, I care for my mum, but sometimes I wonder how many people care about me. I guess this is how I am now with my wife and with my son.*

Bill grew up in an environment where there was a void of intimacy between him and his mother. They spoke very little. He tends to have the avoidance coping style. There was not much expression and dialogue in his home. He imitated his mother; her lifetrap "passed down" to him. Bill struggles to express himself. Even saying, "I love you" to his wife and son is difficult. He provides for them well materially, but has developed a way of coping by being "into himself" all these years.

Focus of Change
People with the lifetrap of emotional inhibition are tempted to think that it is weird to laugh loudly, to cry, or express affection. They were looked down upon for being expressive when they were younger, and they learned to hold things in as adults. The aim of treatment is to get them to see that emotional expression is good and healthy. People with the emotional inhibition lifetrap are usually unaware of the lack of connection felt by their loved ones. For Bill to connect with his wife and son, he needs to work to express himself and share what he is experiencing with those closest to him. He should schedule family talks so he can practise doing this regularly in a safe environment. Adriane and their son can help by encouraging him and being patient as he works to find what he wants to share.

SCRIPTURES FOR MEDITATION

• John 13:34-35   • Romans 12:11   • I Thessalonians 5:19

Failure

The core message of the failure lifetrap is, *"I am fundamentally incompetent and have failed, am failing, and will fail again in the future. I am less talented and successful than other people."* The focus of this lifetrap is on achievement and **external** status symbols of success, rather than on the **internal** feeling of shame and inferiority that is present in the case of the defectiveness lifetrap.

Others may tell individuals who have the failure lifetrap that they have done a great job, but in their heart, they don't believe it. Instead, they always feel like a failure, in relation to their accomplishments, wealth, status, or academic pursuits. Whatever success they have managed to achieve, they attribute to luck, or they just believe that the people giving them encouragement are mistaken. People with this lifetrap believe they have failed and are destined to fail, and usually do not try very hard to succeed. They feel this way because they constantly make silent comparisons with others (peers, family members, friends or acquaintances). Others may have a healthier view of them than they do. Whatever talents they have, they believe that they are not that special, just ordinary. They do not feel they have what it takes to succeed. (The failure lifetrap is often linked with the defectiveness lifetrap.)

How the lifetrap of failure is manifested in the three coping styles, particularly in marriage…

Surrender – Surrendered people with this lifetrap believe their negative inner voice and accept they are failures when compared to others. They give in to their fear that they cannot be successful. As a result, their motivation to try to do their best gets diminished and they often end up failing at what they do, which in turn reinforces their lifetrap! When seeking a marriage partner, they may feel that their partner is a great success compared to them, or they may choose a less than satisfactory partner simply because they feel they are so unworthy. In times of conflict or trouble, they view themselves as doomed to failure and can be very passive and unable to work through problems (see Figure 16).

Avoidance – Avoiders with this lifetrap will sometimes make excuses for not pushing themselves. They may procrastinate when others want them to perform tasks. They flee from what feels like the reality of their belief that they cannot succeed, and often avoid work or challenge completely.

Figure 16: Failure Lifetrap

Overcompensation – Counterattackers who are haunted by the failure lifetrap respond by proving that they are not a failure. They fight the belief that they will inevitably fail by pushing themselves extraordinarily hard, constantly driving themselves to achieve more and more. They swing to the other extreme, and work very hard to prove to themselves and others that they are wrong, because any sense of failure is too uncomfortable for them. Many neglect meeting needs in order to gain successes in other areas of their life. They neglect their spouses or families so that they can push ahead in education or at work in order to not feel like a failure compared to peers or friends.

Possible Early Family Environment
- Your parents emphasised success in something that was not your strength. They may have focused on the sciences, but you may have been good at the arts.
- When you did not succeed, your parents were harsh with their criticism and called you a failure.
- Your parents focused attention on what you could not do, and not on the places where you achieved success.
- You did not receive much encouragement from your parents about your strengths, and were constantly trying to get their attention.
- Your parents compared you with your siblings or cousins or you may have heard how much they bragged about them but not about you, so you lost motivation to give your best.
- Friends, teachers or peers looked down on you early on in life, and you believed them.

THE FAILURE QUESTIONNAIRE

This questionnaire will measure the strength of your failure lifetrap. Please read each statement and decide how well it describes you and/or your beliefs. When you are not sure, base your answer on what you emotionally **feel**, not on what you **think** to be true. If you desire, reword the statement so that the statement would be even more accurate in describing you (but do not change the basic meaning of the question). Then choose the **highest rating from 1 to 6** that describes you (including your revisions), and write the number in the space before the statement.

RATING SCALE:
1 = Completely untrue of me
2 = Mostly untrue of me
3 = Slightly more true than untrue
4 = Moderately true of me
5 = Mostly true of me
6 = Describes me perfectly

Score	Description
	1. Almost nothing I do at work (or school) is as good as other people can do.
	2. I'm a failure.
	3. I'm not as talented as most people are at their work.
	4. I often compare my accomplishments with others and feel they are much more successful.
	Your Total Score (Add your scores together for questions 1-4. Maximum Score: 24)

Interpreting Your Failure Score

4-8:	Very low. This lifetrap does not apply to you.
9-11:	Fairly low. This lifetrap is very weak in your life.
12-15:	Moderate. This lifetrap is weak in your life.
16-19:	High. This lifetrap is fairly strong in your life.
20-24:	Very high. This lifetrap is very strong in your life.

This is a limited questionnaire taken from Young Schema Questionnaire, 3rd Edition (YSQ-L3). Used with permission.[101]

Case Study: Failure

Although Sharon had proven herself in the art world, and was making a reasonable living for herself (as opposed to being a starving artist), she still felt like a failure. After being married to Lionel for 13 years, Sharon came for therapy and explained the problems she was having in her marriage.

Sharon: *I feel so sad about my marriage. My husband always puts me down. At least once a month, he tells me that I should be a lot further along in my career. I do not feel that I am able to match up to his expectations. I feel so unloved. He doesn't even think that being an artist counts as having a career.*

Therapist: *Is it fair to say that you have done well in your business, been self-supporting, and even received some recognition for your artwork?*

Sharon: *Well, I think in my heart that people make this out to be a bigger*

---

[101] Copyright © 2005, Jeffrey Young, Ph.D. Unauthorised reproduction without written consent of the authors is prohibited. You may order/purchase the complete version of the questionnaire at www.schematherapy.com, or write to: Cognitive Therapy Center of New York, 130 West 42nd St., Suite 501, New York, NY 10036.

accomplishment than it actually is. And being an artist is not really very important at all, not a way to be a success in life.

Therapist: *So, I see that it is hard for you to take compliments and recognise what you have achieved.*

As our sessions continued, she made a connection with her upbringing.

Sharon: *Although when I was growing up I did relatively well at school, I remember feeling that if I could just excel in science, then I would really be smart. I didn't do badly, but my strengths were more in the arts, and I did not get as much encouragement from that as I would have if I had excelled in science and math.*

After further sessions, Sharon concluded that the negative messages had not necessarily come from her parents; rather she was hearing the voice of the society in which she grew up—one that looked down on her passion for the arts.

Sharon: *Since everyone around me seemed to value science and math, I felt a failure if I did not do well in them. So in one sense, deep down, I felt that I did not have what it takes to do well. I looked up to my husband, an accomplished professional, and felt that he was right to say that I was a failure, and I believed him. However, I eventually got tired of his put-downs and took a stand. My husband just doesn't understand how he has made me feel over the years. Being unloved is sad and I am not able to take it from him anymore.*

So, here is a person, who from all accounts is successful, but deep down in her heart, feels like a failure. While she identified with the defectiveness lifetrap, she could relate to the failure lifetrap more. Once Sharon came to this realisation, she was able to slowly begin to loosen up and think about pursuing her own dreams and passions rather than proving to others that she was successful.

Focus of Change
People with the lifetrap of failure make unfair comparisons with others about where they are in life. Sharon needed to realise that she was more successful than she believed. Some people will not be as successful as others financially,

and everyone has limitations in some areas. In fact, it is good for people to be sober about where they are—but people with this lifetrap need to not go to the other extreme. Therefore, part of the aim of therapy is to help people with this lifetrap make fair comparisons, and reduce the intensity with which they get triggered when meeting new people or hearing of someone else's success. Sharon was encouraged to excel in areas of strength, not conform to the expectations of others.

In marriage, some people with this lifetrap try to compensate for feelings of failure by choosing a partner with a high paying job or from a prominent family, who is supposedly a "good catch". Such is the case with Sharon, who is married to someone with such rigid standards that she has never been able to be a success in his eyes, therefore reinforcing her sense of failure. She struggles to value herself and her own accomplishments in the world rather than to measure herself against the accomplishments and talents of others. It is difficult for her to believe she can achieve success on her own, but she is working on it, and she hopes that her husband will get help for his issues.

SCRIPTURES FOR MEDITATION
• I Samuel 16:7   • Luke 16:14-15   • Romans 15:7

THE DOMAIN OF IMPAIRED AUTONOMY & PERFORMANCE
Vulnerability To Harm Or Illness

The core message of the vulnerability lifetrap is, *"Catastrophe is just around the corner. Bad things are about to happen and I am powerless to do anything about it."*

People with this lifetrap live in fear that danger is imminent. They are sure that they will contract a serious illness, lose money, or that an accident or attack or some other bad thing is going to happen to them. The fear is so exaggerated that it may manifest in the form of anxiety or panic attacks. They may go for medical check-ups over and over again. Any sign of illness is interpreted as something serious, like a heart attack. They are often able to function on a day-to-day basis but there is always a sense that danger is very close. People with this lifetrap tend to be very vigilant and go to great lengths to stop these things from taking place. Sometimes it may show up as excessive worry, such as trying to save large sums of money for the future since they believe that they might be left stranded. This worry may then induce some form of actual stress-related illnesses, which will then confirm their fears, resulting in more worry. They get stuck in a cycle, and resort to all kinds of medications and special diets in order to be prepared when danger strikes.

How the lifetrap of vulnerability is manifested in the three coping styles, particularly in marriage…

Surrender – Surrendered types with this lifetrap act from a place of fright that tragedy is about to take place and they must be constantly on their toes. They are super vigilant and pay excessive attention to catastrophes in the news. Sometimes they are unable to sleep because of this fear. As a result, their spouse may feel the need to constantly provide assurance and comfort, telling them that their fears are greatly exaggerated. This may lead to tension. They may also take precautionary measures, and this may frustrate their spouse, who may feel that they have gone too far. They may be anxious frequently and have a difficult time relaxing with their spouse. They worry about all sorts of matters, such as kids' homework, kids getting into trouble, personal illness, not having enough money in the future, not having enough insurance, etc. They will voice out their need for protection but nothing seems to assure them that their fears are invalid or excessive (see Figure 17).

Avoidance – Avoiders with this lifetrap will avoid any and all kinds of situations that may pose any form of danger, even if they are likely to be safe. They are fleeing their fear that something bad will inevitably happen to them or to their family. They often do not feel safe doing things like driving at night, going into a city alone, flying in a plane, taking the subway alone, or walking at night in a safe neighbourhood. In the end, their spouse gets affected as there will be a lot of activities that they will not be able to do, and needs will not get met. Their spouse will get very frustrated, because of the many restrictions.

Overcompensation – Counterattackers with this lifetrap may develop some kind of obsessive-compulsive disorder. Sometimes they will perform rituals to combat the dangers that are up against them. They may rely on superstitious beliefs to fight against these fears. Alternatively, they may participate in all kinds of risky behaviours as an overreaction to prove that nothing terrible will happen to them.

Possible Early Family Environment
- Your parents lived out this lifetrap and you imitated it. They talked incessantly about illness, (or about having no money, or getting attacked, etc.) and they told you stories of other people's tragedies.
- Your parents were excessively in control of your life, trying to make sure that you were not in danger.
- You faced a traumatic event as a child that rendered you fearful of all situations.
- You saw someone you love die from an accident, illness or tragedy and you internalised this and concluded that you should be on guard at all times.

Figure 17: Vulnerability Lifetrap

- Your childhood home or environment was not a safe place for you or was unstable and unpredictable.

THE VULNERABILITY TO HARM OR ILLNESS QUESTIONNAIRE

This questionnaire will measure the strength of your vulnerability lifetrap. Please read each statement and decide how well it describes you and/or your beliefs. When you are not sure, base your answer on what you emotionally **feel**, not on what you **think** to be true. If you desire, reword the statement so that the statement would be even more accurate in describing you (but do not change the basic meaning of the question). Then choose the **highest rating from 1 to 6** that describes you (including your revisions), and write the number in the space before the statement.

RATING SCALE:

1 = Completely untrue of me
2 = Mostly untrue of me
3 = Slightly more true than untrue
4 = Moderately true of me
5 = Mostly true of me
6 = Describes me perfectly

Score	Description
	1. I take great precautions to avoid getting sick or hurt.
	2. I am a fearful person.
	3. I worry a lot about the bad things happening in the world, such as crime, pollution, etc.
	4. I feel that the world is a dangerous place.
	Your Total Score (Add your scores together for questions 1-4. Maximum Score: 24)

Interpreting Your Vulnerability Score

4-8:	Very low. This lifetrap does not apply to you.
9-11:	Fairly low. This lifetrap is very weak in your life.
12-15:	Moderate. This lifetrap is weak in your life.
16-19:	High. This lifetrap is fairly strong in your life.
20-24:	Very high. This lifetrap is very strong in your life.

This is a limited questionnaire taken from Young Schema Questionnaire, 3rd Edition (YSQ-L3). Used with permission.[102]

---

[102] Copyright © 2005, Jeffrey Young, Ph.D. Unauthorised reproduction without written consent of the authors is prohibited. You may order/purchase the complete version of the questionnaire at www.schematherapy.com, or write to: Cognitive Therapy Center of New York, 130 West 42nd St., Suite 501, New York, NY 10036.

Case Study: Vulnerability

Stephan is deeply religious, has a great job, a radiant wife, healthy children, a nice bungalow, pretty much everything…except that he always feels that his health is in jeopardy.

Highly educated with several prestigious degrees and a large pay check, he has been married to Mary for almost two decades. However, for the past few years, he hasn't been able to enjoy his success because of excessive worry about his health issues. At home, after work, he has a hard time relaxing. At night, he wakes up frequently. Although he has been given a clean bill of health by the doctors, he still feels that something is amiss. All of this finally drove him to counselling.

Stephan: *It feels like I'm having a heart attack. My doctors gave me some medication, which helped, but I am so afraid that I will die, or lose my job or my family.*

Stephan's lifetrap of vulnerability was causing problems in his marriage.

Mary: *I don't know what is wrong with him. I am getting frustrated with him, and feel that that he is making all of this into a big deal. I told him over and over again to relax but we are not getting anywhere. And his constant thinking that something is wrong with his health is just too much.*

His fears about his health have increased over the years. As a middle-aged man, he doesn't view the general wear and tear that everyone experiences with age as normal, but feels it is all a part of a bigger problem. He worries excessively and has tremendous anxiety. Although intellectually he knows he is not in imminent danger, he still has to battle with his lifetrap. In therapy, Stephan revealed that his late mother had been obsessed about her health as well.

Stephan: *I remember my mother constantly being on guard about her health. She would talk about it all the time. She also talked about how dangerous the world was and how I better be careful of this and mindful of that. There was a period growing up when my mother worried that she might have diabetes, and she asked me to test her sugar content on a daily basis. She was obsessed by it. I even have memories of my mum performing bizarre rituals that she believed would keep our family safe—no wonder I am always worried!*

Focus of Change

People with the lifetrap of vulnerability usually developed this lifetrap from observing one or both parents being obsessed about health and safety issues. The aim for helping Stephan with this lifetrap is for him to gain confidence that his feeling of being in danger is greatly exaggerated.

Stephan's coping style is surrender—he has surrendered to this lifetrap, giving into the belief that his health has been constantly in jeopardy. During counselling, he decided to go for a very thorough check-up, and to place the results in a prominent place, so that he would be able to see it every day and remind himself that all is well. Even though there is always a possibility, the *probability* of a tragedy is very low. Stephan is working towards looking at life from a vantage point of *probabilities*, not possibilities.

⊰ SCRIPTURES FOR MEDITATION ⊱

- Psalm 23   • Job 1:10   • Matthew 24:6

Dependence / Incompetence

The core message of the dependence lifetrap is, *"I cannot take care of myself. I need to rely on those around me in order to survive. I cannot solve problems or make decisions on my own."*

People with the dependence lifetrap cannot handle life with all of its responsibilities and tasks. They are not at all confident of their own ability and have the need for someone else to constantly be around. Left alone, they feel completely useless, and feel that they will make wrong decisions. They feel that they do not have the skills to operate on their own, hence their dependence on others to do things for them or to help them. They may vacillate and be double-minded about what to do, and worry about whether a previous decision was right. People with this lifetrap may function well in some settings, but be very dependent on others.

How the lifetrap of dependence is manifested in the three coping styles, particularly in marriage…

Surrender – Surrenderers give in to the fright that they cannot rely on themselves to make decisions or handle finances. Lacking confidence, married people in this situation depend on their spouse for many things that others would be able to do themselves. This causes their spouse to babysit them, and this frustrates the spouse, who will feel like they have to look after another child. Spouses of people who have surrendered to their dependence will be severely restricted. This will probably produce resentment towards them for being so dependent. As in the case with vulnerability, options will be restricted and many activities that other couples enjoy doing could not be done. The surrendered person may even become entitled and make more and more demands on the spouse, which will eventually trigger the spouse (see Figure 18).

Avoidance – Avoiders with this lifetrap will try to get out of making decisions. They will flee from the stress they would feel in situations that force them to confront the fear that they cannot take care of themselves or be independent. They will avoid taking responsibility and avoid learning how to do tasks effectively. This will frustrate their spouse, as he/she will think that they are stuck having to do all the things that the dependent party could otherwise learn.

Overcompensation – Counterattackers may swing to the extreme and not be dependent on others at all, even when it would be advisable to do so. They fight against their belief that they need help from others or are not competent by acting in the opposite way. So a form of unhealthy independence may develop and their spouse may feel left out of many decisions. They will prove to themselves and others that they are able to take care of themselves. Even though they may be able to manage well, underneath there is still this lack of confidence and anxiety. They both may then lead separate lives, and not meet each other's needs.

Possible Early Family Environment
- Your parents were over-protective. They were so cautious that they did not allow you to develop a healthy autonomy. When other children were allowed to travel by themselves, you were not allowed to do so. When they were allowed to learn tasks, you were not given the opportunity.
- Your parents valued something (eg. grades, music or sports), and allowed you to focus only on that. As such, you never learned to do the tasks that your peers learned.
- You were given unusually strict boundaries. You may not have been allowed to go out of the house, or participate in extra activities, such as swimming or cycling, or playing team sports.

Figure 18: Dependence Lifetrap

- Your parents made all decisions about your life, or you were rescued by one parent in many situations.
- Your homework was done, or overly supervised, by one of your parents. When this was repeated many times, you thought you couldn't do it anyway, and you may have also developed a sense of laziness.
- You were criticised for making bad decisions so you lost your confidence. Your parents gladly stepped in when you hesitated, so you never quite developed the confidence to act on your own.

THE DEPENDENCE / INCOMPETENCE QUESTIONNAIRE

This questionnaire will measure the strength of your dependence lifetrap. Please read each statement and decide how well it describes you and/or your beliefs. When you are not sure, base your answer on what you emotionally **feel**, not on what you **think** to be true. If you desire, reword the statement so that the statement would be even more accurate in describing you (but do not change the basic meaning of the question). Then choose the **highest rating from 1 to 6** that describes you (including your revisions), and write the number in the space before the statement.

RATING SCALE:
1 = Completely untrue of me
2 = Mostly untrue of me
3 = Slightly more true than untrue
4 = Moderately true of me
5 = Mostly true of me
6 = Describes me perfectly

Score	Description
	1. When it comes to everyday functioning, I think of myself as a dependent person, .
	2. If I trust my judgment in everyday situations, I'll make the wrong decision.
	3. I don't feel confident about my ability to solve everyday problems that come up.
	4. I feel I always need someone I can rely on to give me advice about practical issues.
	Your Total Score (Add your scores together for questions 1-4. Maximum Score: 24)

Interpreting Your Dependence Score

4-8: Very low. This lifetrap does not apply to you.
9-11: Fairly low. This lifetrap is very weak in your life.
12-15: Moderate. This lifetrap is weak in your life.
16-19: High. This lifetrap is fairly strong in your life.
20-24: Very high. This lifetrap is very strong in your life.

This is a limited questionnaire taken from Young Schema Questionnaire, 3rd Edition (YSQ-L3). Used with permission.[103]

Case Study: Dependence

Geoffrey and Cynthia have been married for 15 years and have two young children. They own a small restaurant. When they came to therapy, she was

---

[103] Copyright © 2005, Jeffrey Young, Ph.D. Unauthorised reproduction without written consent of the authors is prohibited. You may order/purchase the complete version of the questionnaire at www.schematherapy.com, or write to: Cognitive Therapy Center of New York, 130 West 42nd St., Suite 501, New York, NY 10036.

at wits' end. At the same time, Geoffrey felt cornered by his wife, who was constantly taking out her frustration on him.

Cynthia: *I feel that I have to babysit my husband. I have to do everything for him. Things that he should be able to do, I end up doing. I am so tired. I have my own responsibilities and now I have to look over his. I am sick of this life.*

Cynthia cried throughout the session. Her husband looked dumbfounded.

Geoffrey: *I feel constantly criticised by her and I hate this feeling. It reminds me of the same criticism I got from my mother when I was a child.*

In subsequent sessions, Geoffrey shared about his mother:

Geoffrey: *My mother was so protective of me. She is a professor in a famous university, and she constantly found fault with me and my sister. She belittled us about everything. I was not allowed to go anywhere unless she was with me. Until I was a teenager, I never once was allowed to leave the house alone. I did not know how to take a bus and do stuff that other kids could do. She was so down on me, she even controlled my homework. I guess you could say I got used to letting my mother do everything for me. Not my father, though...he was never around.*

Geoffrey brought this dependence into his marriage. His wife ended up doing most of his work and got tired of it. Initially, he thought she was the problem, and could not understand why she was always in a bad mood. When Cynthia would become angry with him for repeatedly forgetting important details pertaining to their restaurant business, he felt that she should have been more understanding. Geoffrey was so dependent that he felt it was his right to rely on the women in his life in an unhealthy manner.

Through counselling, Cynthia decided it was best for them not to work in the same business, so she got her own job. She had thought of leaving him as well, but decided against. With counselling, Geoffrey also saw the entitlement that accompanied his dependence lifetrap and decided to make an effort to grow and do things by himself and become less dependent on others.

Focus of Change
People with the lifetrap of dependence do not know how frustrated others feel about their unhealthy reliance on them for daily tasks. They lack the confidence

to be able to make decisions and take care of things by themselves. Geoffrey thought he was just expecting normal support from his spouse and friends, and didn't realise that he was dependant on others for almost everything in his life. Therapy centred on increasing Geoffrey's ability to make decisions and to accomplish everyday tasks, and decreasing his dependence on others. Geoffrey and Cynthia were advised to start with simple responsibilities and then gradually make their way towards more difficult ones.

Rather than get frustrated, spouses of those with the dependence lifetrap should empathise with the problems created by their partner's upbringing. When they empathise with them instead of criticising them, it will help the dependant party to feel confident and accepted, rather than attacked.

⟪ SCRIPTURES FOR MEDITATION ⟫

• I Corinthians 13:11   • Galatians 6:5   • James 1:2-4

Enmeshment / Undeveloped Self

The core message of the enmeshment lifetrap is, *"I cannot survive on my own without constant contact and closeness with my parent or partner. I need to know what they think in order to be sure of what I think."* This is about an underdeveloped sense of self as a separate person.

Sometimes it is not that people are dependent on others to accomplish tasks, but they are intertwined emotionally. For persons with the enmeshment lifetrap, it is hard to tell where one ends and the other begins. They are so closely interrelated to the other person, they are unable to tell themselves apart from that person. They feel empty and are often afraid of existing on their own. People can be enmeshed with their parents, their spouse, their children, a sibling, or their best friend. This is very difficult in marriage, because if a person is enmeshed with their spouse, the spouse feels smothered, and if a person is enmeshed with a parent, the spouse feels left out.

Adults enmeshed with a parent (usually the mother) communicate more with that parent than with their spouse. Their mother is the first to know about what names they are thinking to pick for their child, or what kind of house they would like to buy, or which job they will possibly take. This kind of interaction has usually existed all through their life and neither they nor their parent ever quite made a break. This carries into adulthood, and even into the marriage. Enmeshed individuals feel the need to constantly talk with their parent and tell them everything. There is a sense that the two of them are, in a strange way, one person.

When people are enmeshed with their spouse, the problem becomes one of too much closeness, with a lack of separation between the two partners. This can be suffocating and inhibit the leading of separate healthy lives. It is also difficult for children, as the parents are overly focused on each other at the expense of the family.

How the lifetrap of enmeshment is manifested in the three coping styles, particularly in marriage…

Figure 19: Enmeshment Lifetrap

Surrender – Surrendered people with this lifetrap feel they are afraid to be separate and on their own. They must remain in constant contact with their parent. They have a tremendous need to confide in their parent(s) all the time. They do not believe they should be different or independent. They are more attached to their parent (it could also be a big brother or sister) than to their spouse. Their parent knows about their feelings before their spouse. Their parent's opinion matters to them more than their spouse's opinion, or at least that is how it comes across (see Figure 19). As a result, resentment towards the in-laws will develop. Tension between the dependant person's spouse and the in-laws will be high, but the people who have surrendered to their enmeshment will think that their spouse is making a big deal out of it—after all it is right to be close to your parents. Their spouse will feel sidelined and unimportant. In turn, he/she may respond to this in a negative way.

Avoidance – Avoiders with this lifetrap are unable to maintain a healthy independence. They need to keep themselves separate and aloof, over-stressing independence, in order to have a sense of themselves separate from their parents and possibly their spouse and others as well. They tell themselves they must keep away from close relationships in order to keep their sense of self and be independent. They fear that if they are close to others, they will not know what they think on their own.

Overcompensation – Individuals who counterattack the enmeshment lifetrap will tell themselves, "I must fight my inclination to be like my parents or spouse and behave in exactly the opposite way. Whatever they do, I will do the opposite." They will seek to be separate in obvious ways. If their parents prefer big houses, they will choose a small house. This may seem like separation, but it is not. Their decisions are less about what they really want than wanting to not "be" their parents. They are still not in touch with who they really are. This is hard in marriage as they may be very antagonistic and rigid with their choices.

CHOOSE AWARENESS

Possible Early Family Environment

- There was a very close bond between you and one of your parents. You were so close that you were able to easily read one another's non-verbal communication and know what the other person was thinking. This kind of excessive attachment began very early on and continued into adulthood.
- Your parents were very controlling and did not allow you to make decisions on your own.
- Your parents were rigid in their thinking and opinions and did not allow for diversity.
- Your parents were over-protective (see "Possible Early Family Environment" under "Dependence Lifetrap").
- You were taught to not set boundaries with the parents, and when it was done, it produced unhealthy guilt.

THE ENMESHMENT / UNDEVELOPED SELF QUESTIONNAIRE

This questionnaire will measure the strength of your enmeshment lifetrap. Please read each statement and decide how well it describes you and/or your beliefs. When you are not sure, base your answer on what you emotionally **feel**, not on what you **think** to be true. If you desire, reword the statement so that the statement would be even more accurate in describing you (but do not change the basic meaning of the question). Then choose the **highest rating from 1 to 6** that describes you (including your revisions), and write the number in the space before the statement.

RATING SCALE:

1 = Completely untrue of me
2 = Mostly untrue of me
3 = Slightly more true than untrue
4 = Moderately true of me
5 = Mostly true of me
6 = Describes me perfectly

Score	Description
	1. I have not been able to separate myself from my parent(s), the way other people my age seem to do.
	2. It is very difficult for my parent(s) and me to keep intimate details from each other, without feeling betrayed or guilty.
	3. My parent(s) and I have to speak to each other almost every day or else one of us feels guilty, hurt, disappointed, or alone.
	4. I often feel that I do not have a separate identity from parent(s) or partner.
	5. I often feel as if my parent(s) are living through me—I don't have a life of my own.

Score	Description
	6. It is very difficult for me to maintain any distance from the people I am intimate with; I have trouble keeping any separate sense of myself.
	Your Total Score (Add your scores together for questions 1-6. Maximum Score: 36)

Interpreting Your Enmeshment Score

6-11:	Very low. This lifetrap does not apply to you.
12-17:	Fairly low. This lifetrap is very weak in your life.
18-23:	Moderate. This lifetrap is weak in your life.
24-29:	High. This lifetrap is a fairly strong in your life.
30-36:	Very high. This lifetrap is very strong in your life.

This is a limited questionnaire taken from Young Schema Questionnaire, 3rd Edition (YSQ-L3). Used with permission.[104]

Case Study: Enmeshment

Helen is threatening to leave Joseph, her husband of six years, because she feels that he values his mother more than her. By the time she came for counselling, she was incredibly frustrated with her marriage.

Helen: *For years, I have tolerated this. My husband is more loyal to his mother than he is to me. He values her more than he does me. For example, when we bought the present apartment that we live in, he sought her advice before he sought mine. I came in second after his mother. When it comes to other matters, it's the same thing. He goes to her for parenting advice, for suggestions on where to eat... He even calls her more than he calls me. Who is he really married to?*

Therapist: *Have you brought this up to him before?*

Helen: *I have done so, again and again, but to no avail. He says he has to honour his mum. Frankly, he is a mummy's boy. When we were dating, I thought he just respected his parents, which was endearing. But this is too much! My in-laws are a real issue with me. I can't take this anymore.*

---

[104] Copyright © 2005, Jeffrey Young, Ph.D. Unauthorised reproduction without written consent of the authors is prohibited. You may order/purchase the complete version of the questionnaire at www.schematherapy.com, or write to: Cognitive Therapy Center of New York, 130 West 42nd St., Suite 501, New York, NY 10036.

He does not even want to come for therapy with me. He thinks that the problem is with me.

Joseph is enmeshed with his mother. Helen is resentful about how she is ranked with respect to her in-laws. This is common in cases where one spouse is enmeshed with a parent, usually a mother. Tension develops and the enmeshed spouse usually is in the dark about how he treats his spouse. Enmeshed people get so emotionally close to their parents, it is as though they both are one entity. Marriage is supposed to be the only relationship where the two become one, so obviously being enmeshed with a parent would threaten the closeness of married life. (And even in the closeness of marriage, it is still important that each person has a healthy individual identity.)

Focus of Change
People with the enmeshment lifetrap have a hard time making decisions without first considering their parent's opinions. Helen needed Joseph to learn to live without constantly seeking out his mother's approval. The aim here is for the enmeshed individual to express his/her true self without interference from the parents. As Joseph makes progress, he will learn to make Helen feel special and not be so glued to his mother. This is all a part of learning to set healthy boundaries, which enmeshed individuals do not learn in childhood.

---------- ❖ **SCRIPTURES FOR MEDITATION** ❖ ----------

• Genesis 2:24   • Proverbs 22:6   • I Corinthians 13:4-7

Abandonment / Instability

The core message of the abandonment lifetrap is, *"I cannot count on anyone for consistent support, caring, and connection. I will be rejected; people I love and need will die; and people I love and need cannot be relied upon to be there when I need them."*

People who have the abandonment lifetrap fear that everyone they love will leave them. They believe that ultimately they will be alone, and that they cannot really count on people to be there for them. They have a constant need to hear that their spouse loves them, misses them and will not leave them. When their spouse does not communicate that, they get resentful.

Underneath their anger and hurt, they do not feel secure and literally believe that they are destined for loneliness.

How the lifetrap of abandonment is manifested in the three coping styles, particularly in marriage…

Surrender – Individuals with this coping style surrender to the belief that they cannot count on their partner. They gravitate to people who are unstable and who, ironically, will *not* be there for them. They may also give in to their thinking that they will always be alone. They put up with instability but ultimately they will get depressed because they feel they have been alone for a long time. Operating from a place of fear, they accuse their partners of cheating or being about to leave them because they **expect** to be abandoned (see Figure 20). They run the risk of driving their partners away and making their worst fears become true. They are unwilling to express this to their spouse, either because they believe they are fated to be lonely or because they are afraid that it will make the other party leave.

Avoidance – Individuals with this coping style tend to avoid the relating part of relationships as much as possible. They are in flight from their fear that their partner will not be there to care about them. People with this lifetrap are particularly vulnerable to substance abuse. What is difficult in marriage is that it is the relationship itself they avoid. This avoidance results in the other partner feeling abandoned, and sets up a cycle, which reinforces the belief that spouses are not there for each other. As avoiders sense their spouses getting distant, they may pull away even further. They avoid getting close for fear that they themselves will be abandoned.

Overcompensation – Individuals who counterattack operate from the fight position of "I will leave you first because I know you are going to leave me." Or they will fight by clinging to their partner, questioning them constantly about what they do when they are away, or even attacking during brief periods of separation. They will get angry, misinterpreting the behaviours of their spouse to mean that the spouse is abandoning them, one way or another. Overcompensators will react with almost no provocation, and be filled with resentment. They are in danger of pushing their partner away and all too often, because of their off-putting behaviour, the abandonment becomes a reality.

CHOOSE AWARENESS

Figure 20: Abandonment Lifetrap

Possible Early Family Environment
- One of your parents left home, or died, or lived somewhere else.
- You were given up for adoption.
- You were forced to live with someone other than your parents for a period of time during childhood, perhaps because of difficult circumstances (e.g., divorce, illness, financial problems, war).
- One of your parents was too ill to look after you.
- There was intense marital conflict between your parents.
- Someone else in the family took the attention away from you, for example a very ill sibling, or one with special needs, or one who was favoured over you.

Drs Jeffrey Young & Janet Klosko[105] say that abandonment starts very early in life, before a child has words to describe what is happening, and so a person may not have any memory of being abandoned *per se*. Others may remember when one of their parents left them during childhood, particularly in the case of death of a parent, or divorce, or being given up for adoption. In our opinion, it should not come as a surprise that children who are adopted, even by the most nurturing of parents, will feel some form of abandonment at some point in their lives.

THE ABANDONMENT / INSTABILITY QUESTIONNAIRE

This questionnaire will measure the strength of your abandonment lifetrap. Please read each statement and decide how well it describes you and/or your beliefs. When you are not sure, base your answer on what you emotionally **feel**, not on what you **think** to be true. If you desire, reword the statement so that the statement would be even more accurate in describing you (but do not change the basic meaning of the question). Then choose the **highest rating from 1 to 6** that describes you (including your revisions), and write the number in the space before the statement.

RATING SCALE:

1 = Completely untrue of me
2 = Mostly untrue of me
3 = Slightly more true than untrue
4 = Moderately true of me
5 = Mostly true of me
6 = Describes me perfectly

Score	Description
	1. I worry that the people I feel close to will leave me or abandon me.
	2. I don't feel that important relationships will last; I expect them to end.
	3. I become upset when someone leaves me alone, even for a short period of time.
	4. I can't count on people who support me to be there on a regular basis.
	5. I can't let myself get really close to other people, because I can't be sure they'll always be there.
	6. I can't be myself or express what I really feel, or people will leave me.
	Your Total Score (Add your scores together for questions 1-6. Maximum Score: 36)

---

[105] Young, J. E., & Klosko, J. S. (1994). *Reinventing your life*. New York: Plume. 62-65.

	Interpreting Your Abandonment Score
6-11:	Very low. This lifetrap does not apply to you.
12-17:	Fairly low. This lifetrap is very weak in your life.
18-23:	Moderate. This lifetrap is weak in your life.
24-29:	High. This lifetrap is a fairly strong in your life.
30-36:	Very high. This lifetrap is very strong in your life.

This is a limited questionnaire taken from Young Schema Questionnaire, 3rd Edition (YSQ-L3). Used with permission.[106]

Case Study: Abandonment

Sally and Stewart have been married for 12 years. Sally is a very intelligent woman. A mother of young children, she holds a professional job and is highly successful. Unfortunately, she worries that Stewart will abandon her whenever they have a disagreement.

Sally: *Whenever my husband gets angry with me, my immediate reaction is that he would take off and abandon me. So, to prevent that, I counterattack, thinking that I can stop what I fear from happening. Deep down in my heart, I know that I am not so upset about whatever small thing we are arguing about as much as I am giving into my fear about him leaving. This lifetrap is very strong—I did not know how much it was and is affecting me.*

She relates it to her childhood.

Sally: *Growing up was very difficult for me. My father was violent towards my mother and he left us when I was eight years old. I remember begging my father not to leave the family and cried many tears but he left anyway. I would constantly wait at home for him to come back. Because I did well in junior high school, I was sent away to a prestigious boarding school for high school. I was lonely and felt abandoned. I would pray for my mum to come see me. Thankfully she visited me frequently, but the separation was intense. I can still remember the pain, although I am over forty years old.*

---

[106] Copyright © 2005, Jeffrey Young, Ph.D. Unauthorised reproduction without written consent of the authors is prohibited. You may order/purchase the complete version of the questionnaire at www.schematherapy.com, or write to: Cognitive Therapy Center of New York, 130 West 42nd St., Suite 501, New York, NY 10036.

Focus of Change

People with the lifetrap of abandonment will have exaggerated feelings of instability in their closest relationships. The aim of treatment in regards to marriage is for them to become confident with their spouse, and to not be afraid that their relationship will end because of the normal ebb and flow of life. Sally is learning to look at conflict independently of her fear of being abandoned. When Sally counterattacks, her avoiding husband retreats, thus reinforcing her abandonment lifetrap. Both Sally and Stewart are working on not letting their coping styles trigger each other's lifetraps.

☙ SCRIPTURES FOR MEDITATION ❧

• Isaiah 43:1-5   • Romans 8:37-39   • Hebrews 13:5

Subjugation

The core message of the subjugation lifetrap is, *"I must submit to the needs and desires of others before my own or I will be rejected by the anger or abandonment of people who are important to me."* The internal slogan is *"I'm number two."* Subjugation is about **needs**—not showing preferences, desires, decisions and opinions, or **emotions**—not showing feelings, particularly anger.

People who have the subjugation lifetrap will feel that their desires, needs and opinions are neither significant nor important. They tend to repress expressing themselves, which leads to passive aggressive thoughts and behaviour, withdrawing, and ultimately, intense anger. They believe they *have to* always put others' needs and opinions above their own. They will often neglect themselves and give in to others because they are extremely afraid of conflict, which they fear will lead to some kind of punishment or loss of love and affection. They rarely express their own opinions, and even if they do, they won't treat their own opinion as being as important as their spouse's opinion because of their fear of conflict or rejection. They take care of their spouse more than themselves because they constantly worry about their partner's reactions and opinions about them.

In the end, after being subjugated for a while, feelings of anger and resentment will start to surface because they have not paid any attention to their own needs, and they haven't asked their spouse to meet their needs. They may feel very little excitement in life, because they have been too busy meeting others' needs.

People around them will share that this is their strength, but it is actually their weakness. People with this lifetrap will not experience the kind of intimacy they want because all of their attention is focused on meeting their partner's needs and wants, with nothing left over for themselves. When a subjugated person does start feeling the need for self-care, he/she will feel afraid that he/she will be rejected in anger or abandonment. Eventually, people with this lifetrap will hit a wall. They will blow up and then become aggressive. Often this takes their partners by surprise and they think that their subjugated spouse is having a problem, when it is really about them coming out of subjugation, though not in a healthy way. This may lead to the subjugated person overreacting, swinging to the other extreme, becoming defiant of authority, and refusing to follow any form of rules, and may be mistaken for entitlement.

How the lifetrap of subjugation is manifested in the three coping styles, particularly in marriage...

Surrender – Subjugated partners with the surrender coping style are extremely compliant, giving in to the wants and wishes of their spouse. They seldom express their own needs, because they feel that the needs of their spouse are more important. The bottom line is that they give in because they are afraid of either conflict or rejection (see Figure 21).

Avoidance – Subjugated people with this coping style will be conflict avoiders *par excellence*. They want to keep the peace. They avoid getting into a discussion with their partners if they feel there will be a difference of opinion that might cause conflict. They may try different avenues to get their way, but not at the risk of causing conflict. Conflict itself brings about a lot of stress. If they happen to be married to counterattackers, they will make themselves busy with other activities, and may even pick up an addiction.

Overcompensation – Individuals who counterattack act as if their needs should come first, but are coming from a confusing place. This coping mode is used when they just can't give in to the lifetrap anymore. Since they are fighting the belief that they should not express their needs or feelings, when they do try to put themselves first, it comes across as very rigid and demanding. They do not really believe that they can express themselves and not be rejected, so there is sometimes an intense pressure that their need should be met, since they so rarely put themselves first.

Possible Early Family Environment
- Your parents were abusive when you did not yield to their wishes.
- Your parents were over-controlling to the point that there was little autonomy on your part to make your own decisions.
- You saw one of your parents give in to the other and learned it was the best way to keep the peace.
- You were made to feel guilty if your needs were given attention before others.

Figure 21: Subjugation Lifetrap

THE SUBJUGATION QUESTIONNAIRE

This questionnaire will measure the strength of your subjugation lifetrap. Please read each statement and decide how well it describes you and/or your beliefs. When you are not sure, base your answer on what you emotionally **feel**, not on what you **think** to be true. If you desire, reword the statement so that the statement would be even more accurate in describing you (but do not change the basic meaning of the question). Then choose the **highest rating from 1 to 6** that describes you (including your revisions), and write the number in the space before the statement.

RATING SCALE:
1 = Completely untrue of me
2 = Mostly untrue of me
3 = Slightly more true than untrue
4 = Moderately true of me
5 = Mostly true of me
6 = Describes me perfectly

Score	Description
	1. I let other people have their way, because I fear the consequences.
	2. I believe that if I do what I want, I'm only asking for trouble.
	3. In relationships, I let the other person have the upper hand.
	4. I've always let others make choices for me, so I really don't know what I want for myself.
	5. I get back at people in little ways instead of showing my anger.
	Your Total Score (Add your scores together for questions 1-5. Maximum Score: 30)

Interpreting Your Subjugation Score	
5-9:	Very low. This lifetrap does not apply to you.
10-14:	Fairly low. This lifetrap is very weak in your life.
15-19:	Moderate. This lifetrap is weak in your life.
20-24:	High. This lifetrap is fairly strong in your life.
25-30:	Very high. This lifetrap is very strong in your life.

This is a limited questionnaire taken from Young Schema Questionnaire, 3rd Edition (YSQ-L3). Used with permission.[107]

Case Study: Subjugation

Harry and his wife, Elaine, came for therapy as their marital relationship took a turn for the worse. Harry feels stifled by his strong-willed wife. Elaine is perplexed at her husband's new-found anger.

---

[107] Copyright © 2005, Jeffrey Young, Ph.D. Unauthorised reproduction without written consent of the authors is prohibited. You may order/purchase the complete version of the questionnaire at www.schematherapy.com, or write to: Cognitive Therapy Center of New York, 130 West 42nd St., Suite 501, New York, NY 10036.

Harry: *We have been married for a while now, and all along, I have allowed her to take the lead and make most of the major decisions. There were times when I disagreed, but I gave in because I knew that we would have a conflict. Even when I had a good point, she would keep coming back until she got her way. On top of that, Elaine constantly criticises me. I own a business, and I am able to make decisions there, but she acts like everything I do is wrong. I took the heat, but now I feel that I can't take it anymore. I'm almost forty years old—life is too short to put my needs by the wayside. I am finally speaking out, and she hates it. I find myself getting really angry now.*

After a few sessions, Harry linked this feeling of subjugation to his early years.

Harry: *All my life, I had to give in to people. First there was my father. He wanted me to accomplish **his** dreams, not mine. I gave in because I was afraid of the consequences. I had no choice. When I was a teenager, he decided which school I should attend, and which course I should take. My mother was also like that. She was controlling and decided which sports I should participate in. Everyone else decided what I should do. When I moved overseas to study, I lived on campus and ended up being subjugated with my roommate. We shared a room and when he wanted it for his own private use, I was told to leave. I could not even enter my own room. I had so many feelings in my heart. Later, when I got a job, and started attending church, I also did what others expected of me. When others wanted me to be a lay leader at church, I followed. I am so used to doing things for people, I am not even confident in making my own decisions and expressing my needs properly.*

In subsequent sessions, Harry admitted that now, he was coming out of subjugation, and becoming very fed up with everyone.

Harry: *Sometimes I get angry and blow up at my wife, and I then I just walk off. Sometimes, I take it out on my employees, and show my anger. I now know that it is "me" coming out of subjugation, but in an unhealthy way.*

Focus of Change
People who are subjugated do not prioritise their needs for fear of conflict if they do not do what others want of them. Doing this over and over again eventually will catch up with them, and at some point they will explode.

They do that because of years of unmet needs for fear of conflict, rejection or abandonment.

The aim here is to help them see that they have the right to have their needs met. However, they should do so in an appropriate manner, not wait and then blow up in a rage and hurt the people closest to them. They should also learn to draw boundaries with unhealthy people and not interact with them.

Harry needs to begin sharing decision-making with Elaine and allowing his opinions to be part of the process. By starting with small decisions such as where to go for dinner, they can increase intimacy and closeness in their marriage. While dominant partners like Elaine *seem* satisfied because they always get their way, they can also feel lonely as the other person withdraws by just saying yes.

Harry needs to learn to express his needs appropriately to his wife, instead of alternating between being passive and aggressive. Rather, he should aim to be assertive and learn to share himself with Elaine.

SCRIPTURES FOR MEDITATION

- Matthew 10:28-31 • Ephesians 4:25-26 • I John 4:16b-18

Negativity / Pessimism

The core message of the negativity lifetrap is, *"I am destined to make a serious mistake that will result in big problems. Things will inevitably go wrong. Bad things will happen to me."* The negative aspects of life are emphasised at the expense of those things which are positive and potentially joy-bringing.

People with this lifetrap feel down. Everything is seen and experienced with a negative spin on it. The cup is never half-full; it is always half-empty. They hate making mistakes and the supposed consequences that may arise. They worry about the loss and humiliation that may come from taking risks. They would rather be safe than sorry, and take the path that would least expose them to such risks. Usually their negativity is not accurate but blown out of proportion.

How the lifetrap of negativity is manifested in the three coping styles, particularly in marriage…

Surrender – People who tend to be surrendered with this lifetrap give in to their negativity at once, and take the negative side of scenarios. They give in to their fright that things are bad and will stay bad, and ignore positive evidence that contradicts their pessimistic outlook. Their spouses may get fed up trying to talk with them, so they may then take matters into their own hands and make decisions accordingly. Talking with a spouse who is negative can be very draining. All options, when explored (going on a holiday, making an investment, taking a class, etc) will be met with negative remarks and there will be an insistence that other factors have not been taken into account (see Figure 22). Surrendered types view making mistakes as being catastrophic. Conversations will usually not go well, and will cease at some point. Partners may gravitate towards people who are more optimistic.

Avoidance – Avoiders with this lifetrap do not find fulfilment being in this state of negativity, so they resort to drinking, substance abuse, or other escapist activities to suppress these feelings. They seek to distract themselves to flee from the discomfort they would feel if they were conscious of their pessimistic views. Sometimes rather than expressing their negative feelings, they keep a low profile and have very low expectations of the outcome. They avoid talking about issues where they need to process both pros and cons.

Overcompensation – Counterattackers may pretend to be positive, and come across as a bit fake. They work hard to fight their belief that bad things will happen. They do not take into account real and reasonable issues. In their hearts they are still negative, but for the sake of going with the flow they act positive. Eventually their partners will see this duplicity.

Possible Early Family Environment
- Your parents talked about things from a negative point of view. One of them may have painted such a negative picture of life that you assumed that outlook as well.
- Your parents went through very hard times, and so a strong signal was sent to avoid this fate at all costs, and to avoid making mistakes.
- You actually experienced many negative events in your childhood, which reinforced what your negative parents told you about the world.
- You have a more negative temperament, and your parents didn't train you to be more positive.

CHOOSE AWARENESS

Figure 22: Negativity Lifetrap

THE NEGATIVITY / PESSIMISM QUESTIONNAIRE

This questionnaire will measure the strength of your negativity lifetrap. Please read each statement and decide how well it describes you and/or your beliefs. When you are not sure, base your answer on what you emotionally **feel**, not on what you **think** to be true. If you desire, reword the statement so that the statement would be even more accurate in describing you (but do not change the basic meaning of the question). Then choose the **highest rating from 1 to 6** that describes you (including your revisions), and write the number in the space before the statement.

RATING SCALE:

1 = Completely untrue of me   4 = Moderately true of me
2 = Mostly untrue of me   5 = Mostly true of me
3 = Slightly more true than untrue   6 = Describes me perfectly

Score	Description
	1. Even when things seem to be going well, I feel that it is only temporary.
	2. If something good happens, I worry that something bad is likely to follow.
	3. I worry that a wrong decision could lead to disaster.
	4. I often obsess over minor decisions, because the consequences of making a mistake seem so serious.
	5. I feel better assuming that things will not work out for me, so that I don't feel disappointed if things go wrong.
	6. I focus more on the negative aspects of life and of events than on the positive.
	Your Total Score (Add your scores together for questions 1-6. Maximum Score: 36)

Interpreting Your Negativity Score

6-11:	Very low. This lifetrap does not apply to you.
12-17:	Fairly low. This lifetrap is very weak in your life.
18-23:	Moderate. This lifetrap is weak in your life.
24-29:	High. This lifetrap is a fairly strong in your life.
30-36:	Very high. This lifetrap is very strong in your life.

This is a limited questionnaire taken from Young Schema Questionnaire, 3rd Edition (YSQ-L3). Used with permission.[108]

Case Study: Negativity

Sylvia's husband, Gerald, initiated therapy. He feels that his marriage is on the rocks. According to him, she is not much fun to be with, and Sylvia's negativity is making Gerald feel discouraged. He claims that she says no to all his suggestions.

Gerald: *It is difficult to make plans with her. When I want to take the family out, she says no and comes up with some kind of excuse. When I want to inject some fun into the family, like taking the kids swimming, she does not get excited about it. When I propose to go on a holiday, it takes a lot to convince her. I am tired, and I sometimes become enraged at her negativity.*

---

[108] Copyright © 2005, Jeffrey Young, Ph.D. Unauthorised reproduction without written consent of the authors is prohibited. You may order/purchase the complete version of the questionnaire at www.schematherapy.com, or write to: Cognitive Therapy Center of New York, 130 West 42nd St., Suite 501, New York, NY 10036.

Sylvia: *Well, it is not that I don't want to go, but I feel that we need to get prepared. What if it rains? What if something happens and we are not prepared? I am just trying to be thorough. I would rather him plan everything out before we try something new.*

Therapist: *How much planning do you think is needed for a nice day in the park with the children?*

Sylvia: *Well, it gets very hot, so we need to have drinks ready, hand wipes, a blanket, an umbrella.*

Sylvia is "Madam No". All plans have to be vetted carefully. During further counselling, she realised that she is afraid to take chances because she is afraid of making mistakes. She traced this lifetrap back to her mum.

Sylvia: *My mother was negative all the time. I still hear her voice in my head. "No" to this, "no" to that. She painted a negative picture of why things would go wrong. I guess, over time, I imitated her. I also got criticised a lot. There was a lot of emphasis on success and doing well and so mistakes were highlighted a lot.*

Focus of Change

People with the lifetrap of negativity are generally very afraid to make mistakes. Perhaps they were made to feel ashamed when they were growing up. They want to avoid the shame that accompanies risk-taking, so they put up a wall and would rather take no risk so they don't have to make mistakes. Sylvia's negativity was extremely off-putting to Gerald, who would then avoid getting into conversations with Sylvia, which meant that neither of them were getting their needs met.

The aim here is for Sylvia to feel that it is fine to make mistakes, that making mistakes is part of being human, and that part of learning comes from making mistakes. She also needs to understand that an overly negative outlook on life is causing harm to her relationships with her spouse and kids, who she deeply loves.

SCRIPTURES FOR MEDITATION

- 2 Corinthians 10:5
- Philippians 4:8-9
- Colossians 3:2

THE DOMAIN OF IMPAIRED LIMITS

Entitlement / Grandiosity

The core message of the entitlement lifetrap is, *"I am special and better than other people. Rules should not apply to me. I should always come first."* This lifetrap is rooted in a desire for power and control.

It is important to understand there are two types of entitlement. One is "pure entitlement", which results when people are spoiled as children and do not learn to take other people into consideration. These people are pure narcissists, unable to be thoughtful of others. If your spouse is like this, what is most important is to be able to set limits and not allow yourself to be pushed around.

The second type of entitlement is a bit more complicated. This is called "fragile entitlement". This form of the lifetrap comes not from being spoiled, but is a **reaction** to unmet core needs, and rooted in either the defectiveness lifetrap or the emotional deprivation lifetrap. When needs for caring and recognition are not met, a response of "I have to take it for myself" and "No one else is looking out for me" develops. The lifestyle and behaviour looks the same as "pure entitlement", but it is important to understand that the behaviour of these narcissists is covering up a lot of pain and unmet needs.

People with the entitlement lifetrap believe that what they want or need should always be a priority. It is okay for them to cheat on their spouse, and they minimise it. They do not need to fasten the seat belt when the plane is taking off, they can park illegally, and they generally get angry when they do not get their way. Entitled individuals do not care if getting their way disadvantages others. They will change the rules when playing a game. As long as they win, that is what matters. They feel good when they win and get their way, but they do not have any awareness of the pain others feel. They have a warped sense of fairness, and accuse their spouse of being selfish instead. They rarely, if ever, put themselves in other people's shoes. They are usually not in tune with their spouse's feelings, but are totally in tune with their own. When challenged about their behaviour, they often think that people should accept them the way they are.

Entitled people will sometimes rise up in their organisations; they will boast about being no-nonsense leaders who are go-getters, and who don't take no for an answer. (Highly entitled individuals do not like to hear the word no.) They may receive compliments for these traits, and for being so determined in life. They do not like to work under others, since they do not like rules, but they do not mind enforcing rules with others. They generally hate sharing about their weaknesses, but love boasting about their strengths.

Very few people with this lifetrap volunteer to seek help or see their need to change. Why? Because life is good, since they get their way most of the time. Because of their bullying, they have power, and they achieve results by infringing on other people's rights. So why ask for help? What's to change?

How the lifetrap of entitlement is manifested in the three coping styles, particularly in marriage…

Surrender – Individuals who surrender to the entitlement lifetrap act as if their needs should always be first, that what they want matters more than anything else. Underneath this entitlement is the fright that if they do not make themselves number one, no one else will take care of them or see them as special. Individuals with entitlement surrender to the inner voice that tells them they are special. They brag about themselves, making sure that everyone is aware of their accomplishments.

They do not give consideration to their partner's needs, only to their own. They have outbursts of anger, and pout when they do not get their way, though sometimes only inwardly. They are not able to take feedback well and they hate their flaws being exposed. They do not follow the same rules that they expect their spouse to follow, and they do not think it is a big deal (see Figure 23).

Avoidance – Avoiders who have the entitlement lifetrap avoid situations where they are not able to excel, because they hate losing and feeling that someone is one up on them. They flee from situations that would challenge their belief that they are special and superior to others. They will pull away and avoid conflict and closeness, a kind of pouting behaviour to make sure that their needs are met. When they fail at something, they give excuses and move on to something else. They do this so they can soothe themselves and make themselves feel good about their new success, which might mean a new marriage.

Figure 23: Entitlement Lifetrap

Overcompensation – Counterattackers with the entitlement lifetrap overcompensate for their inner selfishness by paying excessive attention to what other people want and need. They fight against their core belief that what they need is most important. While their behaviour may appear selfless, they may easily become upset when they are not recognised and rewarded for their actions. This may look like "Why are you not praising me and rewarding me for being so good to you?" Even when taking care of others, the underlying belief is "I am a great and special person—look at all that I am giving."

Possible Early Family Environment
- You were shamed a lot growing up. To avoid feeling shame, you overcompensated and shamed others.
- There were no proper boundaries in your life early on. You set your own limits. Even if there were limits, they were few, and revolved around you achieving excellence in one or more areas.
- You were allowed to throw tantrums and often got your way. Your parents gave in because of your strong will. Your anger was a manipulative tool to get what you wanted.
- You were spoilt growing up. You got what you wanted and had an intimidating pout when you did not.
- You were taught, either explicitly or implicitly by your parents, to not follow rules.
- You were not taught to care about others. Your parents valued achievement and status and you did not want to go through the shame of not achieving these things. You went to the ends of the earth to make things happen in your life, with little regard for others.
- Insufficient attention was given to recognising your accomplishments and you were unduly criticised as a child. Attention was not paid to what you needed on a consistent basis. Your response was to become excessively demanding.

THE ENTITLEMENT / GRANDIOSITY QUESTIONNAIRE

This questionnaire will measure the strength of your entitlement lifetrap. Please read each statement and decide how well it describes you and/or your beliefs. When you are not sure, base your answer on what you emotionally **feel**, not on what you **think** to be true. If you desire, reword the statement so that the statement would be even more accurate in describing you (but do not change the basic meaning of the question). Then choose the **highest rating from 1 to 6** that describes you (including your revisions), and write the number in the space before the statement.

RATING SCALE:
1 = Completely untrue of me
2 = Mostly untrue of me
3 = Slightly more true than untrue
4 = Moderately true of me
5 = Mostly true of me
6 = Describes me perfectly

Score	Description
	1. I feel that what I have to offer is of greater value than the contributions of others.
	2. I usually put my needs ahead of the needs of others.
	3. I often find that I am so involved in my own priorities that I don't have time to give to friends or family.
	4. People often tell me I am very controlling about the ways things are done.
	5. I get very irritated when people won't do what I ask of them.
	6. I can't tolerate other people telling me what to do.
	Your Total Score (Add your scores together for questions 1-6. Maximum Score: 36)

Interpreting Your Entitlement Score

6-11: Very low. This lifetrap does not apply to you.
12-17: Fairly low. This lifetrap is very weak in your life.
18-23: Moderate. This lifetrap is weak in your life.
24-29: High. This lifetrap is a fairly strong in your life.
30-36: Very high. This lifetrap is very strong in your life.

This is a limited questionnaire taken from Young Schema Questionnaire, 3rd Edition (YSQ-L3). Used with permission.[109]

Case Study: Entitlement

When Chris and Suzanne came for counselling, there was so much anger, they came in separate cars. She felt like getting a divorce, and he felt that *she* needed therapy. During that session, she was angry and terribly unhappy and cried several times. He was also angry and felt that she needed help. He saw himself as a generous husband who had been taken advantage of. As always, each had a story to tell.

Suzanne (in tears): *He has no respect for me. He had an affair and I found out about it from his cell phone. Of course I got angry.*

---

[109] Copyright © 2005, Jeffrey Young, Ph.D. Unauthorised reproduction without written consent of the authors is prohibited. You may order/purchase the complete version of the questionnaire at www.schematherapy.com, or write to: Cognitive Therapy Center of New York, 130 West 42nd St., Suite 501, New York, NY 10036.

Chris: *Well, yes, I went out with someone and had an affair, but I am not in touch with her anymore. (To Suzanne) You have such a good life—I give you money, a car, household help, and a driver. What else do you want? You use my credit card and spend money without any consideration! (To therapist) This is why she needs to see a therapist—she needs help. She's sick.*

As the sessions went on, Suzanne disclosed that Chris had been with other women as well, and had flirted with still others. In a session with him alone, he was confronted.

Therapist: *Did you have any other relationships with women?*

Chris: *Well, yes, here and there, but what can I do? They jump me, like the other night. Then Suzanne saw a packet of condoms in the house. I was stupid to have left those there.*

Several observations could be made about Chris. He came late for therapy and on several occasions, he completely forgot and didn't show up at all. When reminded, he said that he would prefer to have the sessions closer to his home, for the sake of convenience. And when asked to read a book which could help him improve his marriage, he could not be bothered.

Suzanne has her issues as well, but Chris' entitlement lifetrap is strong. He has completely surrendered to his entitlement and feels that rules don't apply to him, such as:
- Crossing the boundaries of marriage and being unfaithful to his wife
- Not reciprocating in a relationship
- Punctuality to appointments
- Ignoring homework given to help his marriage.

Further, Chris has little empathy for Suzanne. He does not see her suffering, nor is he at all remorseful about what he has done by having a string of affairs. It is not a big deal to him. Successful in his chosen field, he feels that rules should apply to others, but not to him. Like a spoilt child, he feels that people owe him favours and requests. He is finely attuned to his own needs, but not the needs of others. He demands that his needs be met by others, but is not able to feel for others when they want him to meet their needs.

One of the issues with the entitlement lifetrap is that success in their endeavours makes entitled individuals feel superior. They may be determined and work hard at their job, but they also work hard at being demanding in their relationships. They don't take no for an answer at work, so they are often successful. They bring this mindset into their relationships with others and demand that their needs be met. They bend rules at work to be successful, and also bend rules in their relationships with people. They have double standards at work and double standards at home. Entitled individuals who are successful in their careers should not automatically think that what works at work should apply at home. After all, the people at work are getting paid to be there—the ones at home are not. As bosses, they are not empathetic to those under them—they push their employees hard and get somewhere because of that drive—but are void of empathy at home with their spouses. As a result, success has a way of blinding them to the fact that they are causing harm to their closest relationships. Dr Young says that while many entitled people are successful, there are also many entitled people who are in jail! Perhaps the clever ones know how to not get caught.

Focus of Change
People who have the entitlement lifetrap don't usually come for therapy, or if they do, they come to get their spouse fixed. Therefore, the aim is for them to learn that they do, in fact, need to work on their lifetrap, and that other people have rights and needs just like they do. In the same way they want their needs to be met, they should seek to meet their spouse's needs, not set a double standard and make their relationships "one-way". In this relationship, Chris has been encouraged to practise being empathic toward his wife, and to try to meet her needs as often as he expects her to meet his. At the time of this writing, Suzanne is deciding whether or not she should stay with someone who is a serial womaniser.

As stated earlier, the entitlement lifetrap is often a reaction to the emotional deprivation lifetrap or the defectiveness lifetrap. Overcompensators with the former begin to demand that others give them what they want or need because they do not believe they will be taken care of, and with the latter feel put down and try to one-up their spouse. Chris needs to see that relationships are a two-way street, and that by becoming open and vulnerable, rather than being demanding, self-serving, or bullying, he is more likely to get what he really needs—a satisfying and caring relationship.

SCRIPTURES FOR MEDITATION

• Philippians 2:3-5 • 2 Timothy 3:1-5 • Hebrews 12:7-11

Insufficient Self-Control / Self-Discipline

The core message of the insufficient self-control lifetrap is, *"I should not be uncomfortable."* This lifetrap leads people to express their emotion negatively, avoid difficult tasks, and give in to temptation. This lifetrap interferes with healthy adult behaviour of reciprocity in relationships, and setting and achieving goals.

People with this lifetrap have difficulty controlling their impulses, such as uncontrolled anger, sexual promiscuity, or over-eating. These may evolve into addictions. They also may have trouble sitting down and doing work for what others would consider a reasonable length of time. Such tasks are not completed because they are seen as being too boring. People with this lifetrap may set out to do a task, but then get easily distracted. If a task seems too difficult, they will give up after starting it. If they are in a position of authority, they will delegate more than others would delegate in their position. They often have a hard time finishing anything that they have started. Discipline is a challenge for them. They often do not have a long-term view of things. Much of what they do is based on their desires, and they are rash in their decision-making. Only when this lifetrap brings them to a low point in life as a result of not being self-controlled will they start to realise that they have to deal with this problem. (People with this lifetrap are sometimes quite likeable because their spontaneous side is very attractive. This charm may carry them far, in spite of their lack of discipline.)

How the lifetrap of insufficient self-control is manifested in the three coping styles, particularly in marriage…

Surrender – Surrendered types with this lifetrap do not take the completion of tasks seriously, as they appear too hard and too boring. As a result, their spouse has to step in and complete tasks for them, which may cause resentment. In order for the surrendered person to complete a difficult task, he/she would need many reminders. They may start something only to give it up, which will cause their spouse to lose respect for them. In the event that the surrendered person does attempt the task, he/she may take short cuts or get others to do the job.

People with this lifetrap make decisions about what is good for them based on what feels good in the short term, not on what is actually good for them in the long term. Surrendered types are likely to be addicted to substances, shopping, Internet pornography, gambling, or sexual promiscuity. They may find it difficult to control their anger, for example, and experience bursts of rage. Their spouse may find it unpleasant to live with them as a result and will avoid being with them. They will then not have their needs met by their spouse but through addictions, which, of course, are not actually fulfilling (see Figure 24).

Avoidance – Avoiders will flee from the discomfort of situations that involve commitment or responsibility they do not wish to handle. This can be alternately fun and frustrating in marriage. Both avoiders and surrenderers will focus on fun at the expense of tasks that need to be accomplished to take care of home and family. The avoider's spouse may get tired of always taking up slack for the person with no self-control and then blow up in anger, from time to time, as a result of being frustrated. The avoider will feel that his/her spouse looks down on him/her and may seek acceptance elsewhere. Addiction is also a possibility here to numb the emotional pain and aid in escape.

Overcompensation – Counterattackers fight their discomfort with self-control by acting in the opposite way. They exercise excessive control, often allowing themselves little pleasure, as they are afraid if they let go they will be out of control. Even when they are very disciplined, they operate from a fear that they have insufficient control over themselves. They can be quite rigid and difficult to live with.

Possible Early Family Environment
- Your parents were not very involved with you while you were growing up. Your parents left you to set your own limits at too young of an age, such as when to sleep, how long to play, what to eat, how much TV to watch. Early on, you were allowed to act on your desires.

- No consequences were set when you got out of line. Because your parents were not involved, they did not know what you were up to. Your parents were too busy with their own work and schedules.
- Since your parents were too busy, you were brought up by grandparents or by nannies, who spoilt you and gave you whatever you wanted.
- You are naturally talented. You didn't have to try that hard to succeed early on in life, and your parents didn't sense the need to teach you perseverance. As life became more challenging, you avoided pursuits that would require much perseverance.
- You watched your parents procrastinate, give into their emotions, or live with addictions.

Figure 24: Insufficient Self-Control Lifetrap

THE INSUFFICIENT SELF-CONTROL / SELF-DISCIPLINE QUESTIONNAIRE

This questionnaire will measure the strength of your insufficient self-control lifetrap. Please read each statement and decide how well it describes you and/or your beliefs. When you are not sure, base your answer on what you emotionally **feel**, not on what you **think** to be true. If you desire, reword the statement so that the statement would be even more accurate in describing you (but do not change the basic meaning of the question). Then choose the **highest rating from 1 to 6** that describes you (including your revisions), and write the number in the space before the statement.

RATING SCALE:
1 = Completely untrue of me   4 = Moderately true of me
2 = Mostly untrue of me   5 = Mostly true of me
3 = Slightly more true than untrue   6 = Describes me perfectly

Score	Description
	1. It often happens that, once I start to get angry, I just can't control it.
	2. I tend to overdo things, even though I know they are bad for me.
	3. I get bored easily.
	4. When tasks become difficult, I usually cannot persevere and complete them.
	5. I can't concentrate on anything for too long.
	6. I can't force myself to do things I don't enjoy, even when I know it's for my own good.
	Your Total Score (Add your scores together for questions 1-6. Maximum Score: 36)

Interpreting Your Insufficient Self-Control Score

6-11:   Very low. This lifetrap does not apply to you.
12-17: Fairly low. This lifetrap is very weak in your life.
18-23: Moderate. This lifetrap is weak in your life.
24-29: High. This lifetrap is a fairly strong in your life.
30-36: Very high. This lifetrap is very strong in your life.

This is a limited questionnaire taken from Young Schema Questionnaire, 3rd Edition (YSQ-L3). Used with permission.[110]

---

[110] Copyright © 2005, Jeffrey Young, Ph.D. Unauthorised reproduction without written consent of the authors is prohibited. You may order/purchase the complete version of the questionnaire at www.schematherapy.com, or write to: Cognitive Therapy Center of New York, 130 West 42nd St., Suite 501, New York, NY 10036.

Case Study: Insufficient Self-Control

Donald and Maria have been married for a decade. Maria has a hard time exercising self-control. From the beginning of therapy, Donald spoke of his wife's lack of discipline, and how it affected her work, her family life, and their marriage.

Donald: *We own our own business and I am the head of operations. It is crucial that Maria keeps to her deadlines, but many times, I don't know what she is up to. At night, when I am working hard, she watches television and talks on the phone. When I question her, she denies it.*

Maria: *I have told him many times that I need my relaxation time. He just doesn't trust me. Yes, I read books and watch TV, but it isn't so terrible. He is so critical of me!*

Later, Maria admitted to being very undisciplined and talked about her childhood.

Maria: *Everything came easy for me at school. I was naturally good at sports, music, and academics, and I rarely had to work hard. I suppose I never had to learn discipline or perseverance, so now I find it really hard to do things I don't feel like doing.*

In subsequent sessions, Maria confided that she actually did want to work on having more self-control.

Therapist: *How would having more self-control make things different?*

Maria: *Well, I think that if I stop procrastinating on major tasks, and start following through on each project, as long as Donald is not berating me, I should be fine. I don't even mind his reminders, as long as they are said with kindness; after all, he is not just my boss, but also my husband! One more thing—I need to stop smoking. It sounds like a tall order, but I am worried about my health—I don't think I can afford to put off these changes.*

Focus of Change

People with the lifetrap of insufficient self-control have a hard time denying themselves, making themselves uncomfortable, or delaying gratification. The aim here is to help them understand the value of persevering and getting tasks accomplished, and that in the long run, they would be much better off not giving into short-term pleasure.

Maria decided to first work on the issues that affected their business, and when she had seen some victories in that area, she would then try to quit smoking.

◁ SCRIPTURES FOR MEDITATION ▷

• Proverbs 6:6-11 • Galatians 5:19-23 • 2 Peter 1:5-9

Approval-Seeking / Recognition-Seeking

The core message of the approval-seeking lifetrap is, *"I must seek the approval of others above all else. If other people do not approve of me, something is very wrong."* This pattern of thinking is about defining who we are through the eyes of others rather than paying attention to our own needs and desires.

People with this lifetrap struggle to form an opinion about themselves outside of what others think and feel about them. When push comes to shove, what people think of them determines how they feel about themselves. The opinion of others is the primary factor in forming a good opinion about themselves. It is not about achieving a high standard that they made up for themselves, as in the case of unrelenting standards, or entitlement, where people want to feel one up on others. It is also not about compensating for their defectiveness by pushing themselves. It is about craving other people's approval. If people's opinion of them is poor, they feel lousy about themselves. Their world collapses when they sense that others do not have a high opinion of them. If people think highly of them, they feel elevated and happy about themselves. Much of their effort is geared towards drawing attention towards their good deeds. Given how much they are controlled by what others think, they do not really develop an authentic sense of self with their own values and preferences. As a result, they are not truly fulfilled.

How the lifetrap of approval-seeking is manifested in the three coping styles, particularly in marriage...

Surrender – Surrendered types with this lifetrap may give in to their spouse's desires for them in order to be pleasing to the spouse. They function in the world from a place of fright that others must approve of them or they will have to confront their belief that they are not okay. They work hard to impress other people. They may also annoy their spouse by caring too much about what others think, which can cause tension in the marriage. Sometimes, it may be the spouse's opinion of him/her that matters the most, so any form of feedback will completely crush their world. The other spouse then feels that they have to tip toe around their partner when they express an opinion that is different (see Figure 25).

Figure 25: Approval-Seeking Lifetrap

Avoidance – Avoiders with this lifetrap tend to keep away from people whose admiration they may never receive. They flee the place of discomfort they would feel if they allowed themselves to be aware how much they need their approval. They deliberately do not want to spend time with them, even if it might mean steering clear of in-laws, parents, or siblings. This may be misconstrued as selfishness, but it is more related to the frustration they feel from a lack of approval.

Overcompensation – Counterattackers with this lifetrap might eventually become defiant and not care about the approval of others. They fight their belief that others must approve of them. They may even go out of their way to misbehave. They will not try to get others' approval, although in their hearts, they still are haunted by what people think of them. In this case, the behaviour provokes the opposite response to what the person is actually seeking.

Possible Early Family Environment
- Your parents emphasised the need for status, looking good, or recognition in such a way that it was part of their normal family conversation.
- Your parents boasted about themselves. If and when they were praised by others (eg. success at work, appearing in the media), they made it into a big deal.
- Your parents bragged about their achievements and who they knew.
- Your parents focused more on how things looked at home, rather than what was inside the hearts and minds of their children.
- Self-esteem had nothing to do with you liking yourself, and everything to do with others approving of you.

THE APPROVAL-SEEKING / RECOGNITION-SEEKING QUESTIONNAIRE

This questionnaire will measure the strength of your approval-seeking lifetrap. Please read each statement and decide how well it describes you and/or your beliefs. When you are not sure, base your answer on what you emotionally **feel**, not on what you **think** to be true. If you desire, reword the statement so that the statement would be even more accurate in describing you (but do not change the basic meaning of the question). Then choose the **highest rating from 1 to 6** that describes you (including your revisions), and write the number in the space before the statement.

RATING SCALE:
1 = Completely untrue of me
2 = Mostly untrue of me
3 = Slightly more true than untrue
4 = Moderately true of me
5 = Mostly true of me
6 = Describes me perfectly

Score	Description
	1. It is important to me to be liked by almost everyone I know.
	2. I change myself depending on the people I'm with, so they'll like me more.
	3. My self-esteem is based mostly on how other people view me.
	4. Having money and knowing important people make me feel worthwhile.
	5. When I look at my life decisions, I see that I made most of them with other people's approval in mind.
	6. Lots of praise and compliments make me feel like a worthwhile person.
	Your Total Score (Add your scores together for questions 1-6. Maximum Score: 36)

Interpreting Your Approval-Seeking Score

6-11: Very low. This lifetrap does not apply to you.
12-17: Fairly low. This lifetrap is very weak in your life.
18-23: Moderate. This lifetrap is weak in your life.
24-29: High. This lifetrap is a fairly strong in your life.
30-36: Very high. This lifetrap is very strong in your life.

This is a limited questionnaire taken from Young Schema Questionnaire, 3rd Edition (YSQ-L3). Used with permission.[111]

Case Study: Approval-Seeking

Olivia has been married to her husband, Henry, for about five years. She seeks her husband's approval for all of her decisions. On the positive side, that means that they rarely argue. However, they work in the same business together and she is always thinking about how to make decisions in order to gain his approval. This has become annoying to her husband, so Olivia came for therapy.

---

[111] Copyright © 2005, Jeffrey Young, Ph.D. Unauthorised reproduction without written consent of the authors is prohibited. You may order/purchase the complete version of the questionnaire at www.schematherapy.com, or write to: Cognitive Therapy Center of New York, 130 West 42nd St., Suite 501, New York, NY 10036.

Olivia: *I don't feel confident about making decisions because I keep wondering if my husband would be happy with me. Consequently, I talk to him about everything, which makes him feel frustrated. I act the same way with my leaders at church, I am constantly in touch with them to ensure that I am doing what they like because I am afraid of displeasing them.*

Therapist: *How do you feel that this developed?*

Olivia: *Growing up, I lost my father when I was six years old. My mother was lonely, and remarried quickly. My stepfather was mean to me. He abused me and put me down because of my low marks at school. He beat me a lot. In everything I did, I tried to make him happy with me. I had a stepsister, whom my stepfather favoured. So I went the extra mile to make sure that my stepfather was pleased with me. Trying to please him consumed me.*

Focus of Change

People with this lifetrap are constantly consumed with what others think of them. Even if they are doing a great job, it is the approval of others that will decide how they feel about themselves. The response of others is more important than their own opinion. They lack their own convictions.

The aim here is for them to own their own values, beliefs and convictions, not borrow from others. They should not suppress their own preferences at the expense of being liked by others.

Olivia was advised to start writing in a journal so that she could get in touch with her own feelings and desires, and to practise expressing herself in a healthy way. She was encouraged to write in her journal about the things that she does well whenever she feels tempted to seek approval from her husband.

⊰ SCRIPTURES FOR MEDITATION ⊱

- Mark 12:30 • John 12:42-43 • 2 Corinthians 5:9

THE DOMAIN OF EXAGGERATED EXPECTATIONS
Unrelenting Standards / Hypercriticalness

The core message of the unrelenting standards lifetrap is, *"I must work very, very hard to meet very high standards or I will be criticised. I do not have time to relax or have too much fun. I must always be efficient."* The driving words for this lifetrap are **"I should ..."**

Do you know someone who is not able to accept being anywhere other than at the top? People with the unrelenting standards lifetrap feel the need to constantly push themselves, and they work harder and harder to get somewhere because their present place in life is not good enough. They are always one position away from being content. It's no surprise that this lifetrap is related to the defectiveness lifetrap.

Early on in life, people with this lifetrap begin developing standards that *must* be in place, and they are critical of people who do not meet up with these standards. They might be hard on small mistakes made by their spouse. Perhaps the house is not clean enough or their spouse's clothing style is not to their satisfaction. The self-made rules are with them everywhere they go. They even impose them on their children. Little grace is shown to others when mistakes are made and they frequently look down on others who do not live up to their exceedingly high expectations. They pick on small issues like their teeth not being straight, though no one else would really notice. They are hypercritical of others for the pettiest of reasons. They push themselves so hard that taking time off makes them feel guilty. They find it difficult to relax, and all of this takes its toll on their health. They may be successful but it is usually at the expense of their marriage and other relationships. They are difficult to live with because they expect others to comply with their rules.

How the lifetrap of unrelenting standards is manifested in the three coping styles, particularly in marriage...

Surrender – Surrendered types with this lifetrap believe the truth of the excessive standards set by their inner voice and they do everything they can to get there. Their fright mode tells them that they must achieve and do everything perfectly. They are not satisfied with where they are in life and strive to do more and more, obsessed with status and position. They never take time off, always pushing themselves to the limit. They are not able to meet needs because they are busy trying to meet whatever standards they have set for themselves to achieve. There is little time set aside to relax with their spouse because they are always busy. They are very critical of themselves and those around them. This chips away at the marriage relationship because the spouse always feels that they are not good enough or have not performed well enough (see Figure 26).

Avoidance – Avoiders with this lifetrap will often procrastinate. They flee from the reality that they can never meet the unrealistic standards they set for themselves. They do not want to get started on something because the resources are not perfect, and everything is not in order. So, tasks are often

Figure 26: Unrelenting Standards Lifetrap

not done because they can't settle for something less than ideal. They may avoid doing something together with their spouse, such as taking up a hobby, or working together on something, because they feel that they may not do well in this area.

Overcompensation – Counterattackers fight against the high standards this lifetrap demands of them. Since the standards are set so high they can never be met, to fight them means not to try at all. Work is done quickly and often in a sloppy manner. They swing the pendulum and then give up all the standards, and underachieve. They overreact negatively to their spouse who expects reasonable standards but which are not good enough.

Possible Early Family Environment
- A parent (or both parents) set a standard of high expectations. One of them was a role model for you, and you ended up imitating this trait.
- The love of one or both of your parents was performance based. You did not experience unconditional love from them. Their approval and acceptance was based on some kind of achievement.
- Your parents' conversation was frequently about what you should achieve and be, not about good relationships. Character was more defined in terms of achievement, not about inner qualities.
- When you did not achieve, you were criticised and shamed. Nothing was ever good enough for your parents (or teacher or coach). You hardly received any encouragement.
- You developed these standards to soothe the inner pain in your life from a lack of deep relationships with others, in order to feel good.

THE UNRELENTING STANDARDS / HYPERCRITICALNESS QUESTIONNAIRE
This questionnaire will measure the strength of your unrelenting standards lifetrap. Please read each statement and decide how well it describes you and/or your beliefs. When you are not sure, base your answer on what you emotionally **feel**, not on what you **think** to be true. If you desire, reword the statement so that the statement would be even more accurate in describing you (but do not change the basic meaning of the question). Then choose the **highest rating from 1 to 6** that describes you (including your revisions), and write the number in the space before the statement.

RATING SCALE:
1 = Completely untrue of me
2 = Mostly untrue of me
3 = Slightly more true than untrue
4 = Moderately true of me
5 = Mostly true of me
6 = Describes me perfectly

Score	Description
	1. Almost nothing I do is quite good enough; I can always do better.
	2. I must meet all my responsibilities.
	3. I feel there is constant pressure for me to achieve and get things done.
	4. I often sacrifice pleasure and happiness to meet my own standards.
	5. I can't let myself off the hook easily or make excuses for my mistakes.
	Your Total Score (Add your scores together for questions 1-5. Maximum Score: 30)

Interpreting Your Unrelenting Standards Score

5-9:	Very low. This lifetrap does not apply to you.
10-14:	Fairly low. This lifetrap is very weak in your life.
15-19:	Moderate. This lifetrap is weak in your life.
20-24:	High. This lifetrap is a fairly strong in your life.
25-30:	Very high. This lifetrap is very strong in your life.

This is a limited questionnaire taken from Young Schema Questionnaire, 3rd Edition (YSQ-L3). Used with permission.[112]

Case Study: Unrelenting Standards

Simon and his wife, Carol, came together for therapy. She feels that he looks down on her and she is not able to meet up to his expectations. His unrelenting standards were obvious from the start.

Carol: *He makes me feel like an idiot. He thinks I can't do anything right.*

(The therapist discusses with Carol all of the things she does at work and at home and with their two daughters who are in primary school.)

Therapist: *Simon, do you hear Carol saying that she feels that you think she cannot do anything right? Do you know why she might feel that way?*

---

[112] Copyright © 2005, Jeffrey Young, Ph.D. Unauthorised reproduction without written consent of the authors is prohibited. You may order/purchase the complete version of the questionnaire at www.schematherapy.com, or write to: Cognitive Therapy Center of New York, 130 West 42nd St., Suite 501, New York, NY 10036.

Simon: *I get so frustrated with her when she does not listen to me. She has a hard time following directions.*

Therapist: *Just now you heard us discussing what a great job she has done at work and at home, bringing up the children. To me, she seems like an intelligent woman.*

Simon: *You think she's smart? I don't. I don't think she is intelligent at all.*

Therapist: *Well, I know she attended a university that is ranked among the top 30 in the whole world, so I don't think she is not intelligent.*

Simon: *Here's the proof—the kids do not do well enough in their exams—she's just not pulling through. I want my kids to do excellently. I believe they can, but my wife is not rising to the occasion. Also, the house is not clean enough. She's just a housewife. Come on, I work hard all day—the least she can do is keep the house clean! Also, I expect her to take better care of her looks.*

Carol: *I am trying. I feel looked down upon, and do not feel good enough for him. As a result, I get withdrawn and then I don't feel like being giving to him emotionally. We really have a problem. I have thought of leaving him. I can't take this anymore.*

Simon's unrelenting standards have eroded his wife's self-esteem and triggered her defectiveness. He counterattacks her when tasks are not done to a certain standard because *he* is driven to meet that standard. At work, with his uncompromising standards, he excels. He is extremely driven to succeed. He gets his job done well, and for that he receives praise and promotion. However, at home, his high standards are at the expense of a harmonious relationship with his wife, and for that matter, with his two daughters. Even over relatively small issues, he insists that his standards be kept. At any given moment, he is seldom happy in life, but he blames it on others' inability to please him, and doesn't see his need to lower his standards.

Focus of Change
People with the lifetrap of unrelenting standards think that their standards are normal and that others are stupid, shoddy, careless, lazy, unkempt, inept, or slow. Simon's reactions to situations, his opinion of others, and condemnation of others, are usually out of proportion with the reality of the situation.

The aim here is to get people with this lifetrap to see the damage that results from their unrelenting standards. Simon needs to see that his self-imposed standards are ruining his relationships with the people he cares about the most and are not worth the pursuit. He also needs to see that not meeting these standards is not the end of the world.

◆ SCRIPTURES FOR MEDITATION ◆

• Luke 18:9-14 • Philippians 4:4-7 • I Peter 3:8

Punitiveness

The core message of the punitiveness lifetrap is, *"Mistakes have consequences—I should be punished for making mistakes and so should everyone else. It is not okay to make a mistake. We should constantly strive for and demand perfection."*

People with the punitive lifetrap do not give grace or mercy, either to themselves or to people who make mistakes. They are people who usually do not forgive easily. Rather, they see all mistakes as crimes that should be punished. They have a very strong sense of justice, of right and wrong, seeing things in black and white. They come across as blaming when they see a mistake. They view people who show mercy as weak and feeble. Mistakes are mistakes, whether committed unintentionally or deliberately.

Sometimes (not always) they are punitive towards themselves and do not forgive themselves for their past mistakes. They keep letting their past mistakes haunt them. They talk about their mistakes repeatedly. Some people with this lifetrap are only hard on others, but soft on themselves. They mask their punitiveness as seeking justice and being fair.

How the lifetrap of punitiveness is manifested in the three coping styles, particularly in marriage…

Surrender – The surrendered types give in to their thoughts about punishment, but it may be that the person they want to punish is themselves. They will be quick to admit a wrong, but they will beat themselves up over it for a long time. In giving in to their belief, they become very harsh critics of themselves and others around them. Even small mistakes will result in harsh consequences. Spouses will feel frustrated because they are not given grace (see Figure 27).

Avoidance – Avoiders tend to withdraw from relationships with others, as they flee their belief that they will be punished. They avoid feedback and situations where they would be evaluated for fear that they would be punished. They are afraid to admit making mistakes for fear that they themselves would be punished. If they are struggling to forgive themselves, they may fall into addictions or escapist activities.

Figure 27: Punitiveness Lifetrap

Overcompensation – Counterattackers who are punitive will be very angry people. Their marriages are full of blaming and they will not forgive their spouses easily. They often feel that their partners get away with mistakes. Their spouses will feel reluctant to be transparent with them or confess their shortcomings for fear that these things will be held against them for a long time. Overcompensators with this lifetrap keep bringing up the same issues over and over again in future arguments although they may not be related. This is a sign that these matters have not been settled in their hearts. Spouses feel little empathy from their punitive husbands or wives, but will feel that they are blamed for almost everything that goes wrong in the marriage. Since punitive people feel that forgiveness and mercy are for weaklings, they will usually assume that their partners should learn the lesson through experiencing major consequences. Often the consequences are far worse than the crime committed. Spouses will gravitate to others who are more accepting of them.

Possible Early Family Environment
- Your parents blamed you for things, and used a condemning tone when they were berating you and your siblings; your parent's voice remains in your head even in adulthood.
- You attended a school where others were punished frequently for their mistakes. Little grace was shown. Forgiveness was hardly mentioned.
- Your parents did not talk much about grace or forgiveness. They had a negative view of people who held such views.
- Your parents were either always right and blamed others, or held grudges.
- Your parents got hurt growing up and ruminated on memories of this hurt. They took this out on others in different situations later on in life, and you bore the brunt.
- You were brought up in a very negative religious atmosphere where hellfire and brimstone and the wrath of God were used as deterrents for undesirable behaviour.

THE PUNITIVENESS QUESTIONNAIRE

This questionnaire will measure the strength of your punitiveness lifetrap. Please read each statement and decide how well it describes you and/or your beliefs. When you are not sure, base your answer on what you emotionally **feel**, not on what you **think** to be true. If you desire, reword the statement so that the statement would be even more accurate in describing you (but do not change the basic meaning of the question). Then choose the **highest rating from 1 to 6** that describes you (including your revisions), and write the number in the space before the statement.

RATING SCALE:
1 = Completely untrue of me
2 = Mostly untrue of me
3 = Slightly more true than untrue
4 = Moderately true of me
5 = Mostly true of me
6 = Describes me perfectly

Score	Description
	1. If I make a mistake, I deserve to be punished.
	2. Most of the time, I don't accept the excuses other people make. They're just not willing to accept responsibility and pay the consequences.
	3. I often think about mistakes I've made and feel angry with myself.
	4. When people do something bad, I have trouble applying the phrase, "forgive and forget".
	5. I get upset when I think someone has been "let off the hook" too easily.
Your Total Score (Add your scores together for questions 1-5. Maximum Score: 30)	

Interpreting Your Punitiveness Score

5-9:	Very low. This lifetrap does not apply to you.
10-14:	Fairly low. This lifetrap is very weak in your life.
15-19:	Moderate. This lifetrap is weak in your life.
20-24:	High. This lifetrap is a fairly strong in your life.
25-30:	Very high. This lifetrap is very strong in your life.

This is a limited questionnaire taken from Young Schema Questionnaire, 3rd Edition (YSQ-L3). Used with permission.[113]

---

[113] Copyright © 2005, Jeffrey Young, Ph.D. Unauthorised reproduction without written consent of the authors is prohibited. You may order/purchase the complete version of the questionnaire at www.schematherapy.com, or write to: Cognitive Therapy Center of New York, 130 West 42nd St., Suite 501, New York, NY 10036.

Case Study: Punitiveness

Justin and Nathalie have been married for five years, and came for counselling after yet another intense and bitter argument. Justin has a hard time forgiving people. He is a meticulous person who prides himself on not suffering fools gladly. He has had run-ins with many people in his life, at times coming to blows. He notices people's mistakes, and feels that they need to be punished. This attitude has taken a toll on his marriage, and his work.

Nathalie says that no matter how many times she apologises, Justin keeps bringing up things he is hurt about. She says that he ruminates on the episodes over and over again, and she feels that there isn't a closing chapter to the mistakes she or others have made. This has affected their marriage, since he gets triggered by her at the slightest mistake and feels that she should pay.

Therapist: *What kind of things does Nathalie do that make you upset?*

Justin: *She doesn't take care of the kids properly—I saw one of our children fall down on the way to kindergarten and my wife didn't do anything to prevent it.*

Therapist: *Well, every child falls down. What about another example. Has your wife apologised for something she did that hurt you?*

Justin: *Yes, but she was not sincere. Her "sorry" was not from the heart. I put up with a lot, and all she can do is say "sorry".*

To a punitive person, an apology has to match the amount of hurt that he/she endured. A punitive person feels that he/she has had to pay a big price for his/her mistakes. Grace and forgiveness are not easy for him/her to extend. People who are punitive are also in a state of rage and anger much of the time. They lash out at others. People usually do not like to hang out with punitive individuals—they're not much fun.

Focus of Change

People with the lifetrap of punitiveness believe that one should pay for one's mistakes. The aim here is for people with this lifetrap to understand grace, and gain a good understanding of forgiveness. They need to appreciate the benefits of forgiving, which will improve their health and relationships as well. They need to realise that the best way to change people is not necessarily punishment, but through extending grace and forgiveness. Justin was advised to look at his own weaknesses, and be grateful for grace, and to extend the same grace to his loved ones.

> **SCRIPTURES FOR MEDITATION**
>
> • Psalm 103:8-18 • Romans 12:17-21 • Ephesians 4:32

Self-Sacrifice

The core message of the self-sacrifice lifetrap is, *"I must meet the needs of others before my own. I do not want to feel selfish or cause any pain to others."* This pattern of thinking and behaving appears very kind but creates problems in the long run as it results in imbalanced relationships, and problems with unmet needs.

People who have this lifetrap are usually very endearing, unless they flaunt their sacrifice in martyrdom. They genuinely care for people and are in tune with others' pain and feelings. They empathise by taking on responsibilities in order to relieve others of discomfort. They prefer to suffer, rather than allow others to be inconvenienced. They strive to make other people feel better. The decision to do so does not come from wanting to please them, or to avoid conflict or a threat, but it is a decision to relieve others because they empathise with them and feel that it is their responsibility. If they do not sacrifice for others, they feel guilty. This becomes a danger and a lifetrap when these self-sacrificing people do not get their own needs met and eventually experience burnout. This may cause physical health problems or even mental health problems, such as depression or breakdown.

Note: Some people with the entitlement lifetrap soothe their consciences by giving to others. However, they find it such a burden that they end up thinking that they have the self-sacrificing lifetrap.

How the lifetrap of self-sacrifice is manifested in the three coping styles, particularly in marriage...

Surrender – Surrendered types with this lifetrap yield to the desire to help others and be responsible for everything and everyone, and they put others' needs as a priority. They give in to their belief that their own needs should not be a priority. They attend to their spouse's needs, often going the extra mile to help them with their chores and responsibilities (see Figure 28). Even with shared responsibilities, they end up doing most of the work. In the end, after long periods of serving and giving, anger will result and the partner with this lifetrap will feel that the relationship is very much one way. They will feel that they do all the giving, but little receiving. Partners married to them may also take them for granted and get used to their serving nature, neither showing appreciation nor sharing the responsibilities.

Avoidance – Since people with the self-sacrificing lifetrap feel guilty receiving and are more comfortable giving, they tend to feel guilty asking and will avoid situations where they are at the receiving end for a change. They flee from the discomfort they feel when their needs or desires are made a priority. They feel guilty taking time off for themselves, receiving pleasure in sexual intercourse, or rewarding themselves with gifts. They may eschew birthday parties and tell everyone to not give them gifts. It comes across as not being appreciative and partners may read this wrongly, and assume that it is selfishness.

Figure 28: Self-Sacrifice Lifetrap

Overcompensation – Counterattackers fight their core belief that their focus should be on others by giving as little as possible. Perhaps after doing a lot of one-way giving, and feeling that they have not received in return, they become completely inward focused and do not want to give, even in reasonable situations. The pain of not receiving in the past has been too great. They are not able to go on, and they get resentful towards those who did not respond to their giving. They feel that everyone is the same and that no one appreciates them. This happens when they experience burnout. They change so much that they are now a different person. In marriage, we find giving partners finally blowing their top and drawing thick boundaries. They feel that they have learned the lesson and will not allow others to take advantage of them again. They are now bent on not being in that situation, and assert themselves in every possible situation.

Possible Early Family Environment
- Your parents were unable, for whatever reason, to take care of you or your younger siblings, so you stepped in and assumed this responsibility.
- Your parents modelled sacrifice for you. Perhaps they were in one of the helping professions, such as nursing, counselling, or church leadership, or perhaps they were very involved with volunteer work.
- You had to work or help out in your parents' business very early on in life because of your parents' financial problems or poor health.
- You assumed the role of the parent (parenting the parent) at too early an age, even though it should have been the other way round. For example, one of your parents may have been an alcoholic, or may have been abused severely by the other parent or other relatives.

THE SELF-SACRIFICE QUESTIONNAIRE

This questionnaire will measure the strength of your self-sacrifice lifetrap. Please read each statement and decide how well it describes you and/or your beliefs. When you are not sure, base your answer on what you emotionally **feel**, not on what you **think** to be true. If you desire, reword the statement so that the statement would be even more accurate in describing you (but do not change the basic meaning of the question). Then choose the **highest rating from 1 to 6** that describes you (including your revisions), and write the number in the space before the statement.

RATING SCALE:
1 = Completely untrue of me
2 = Mostly untrue of me
3 = Slightly more true than untrue
4 = Moderately true of me
5 = Mostly true of me
6 = Describes me perfectly

Score	Description
	1. I feel guilty when I let other people down or disappoint them.
	2. I'm the one who usually ends up taking care of the people I'm close to.
	3. I can get by on very little, because my needs are minimal.
	4. No matter how much I give, it is never enough.
	5. If I do what I want, I feel very uncomfortable.
	6. It's very difficult for me to ask others to take care of my needs.
	Your Total Score (Add your scores together for questions 1-6. Maximum Score: 36)

Interpreting Your Self-Sacrifice Score

6-11:   Very low. This lifetrap does not apply to you.
12-17: Fairly low. This lifetrap is very weak in your life.
18-23: Moderate. This lifetrap is weak in your life.
24-29: High. This lifetrap is a fairly strong in your life.
30-36: Very high. This lifetrap is very strong in your life.

This is a limited questionnaire taken from Young Schema Questionnaire, 3rd Edition (YSQ-L3). Used with permission.[114]

Case Study: Self-Sacrifice

Jane and Roland have been married for seven years. Jane's self-sacrifice has hurt her marriage because Roland gets annoyed at how much she feels for and gives to others.

Roland: *I get so ticked off with her. She feels for people all the time, and then expects me to do the same. Sometimes she helps homeless people, sometimes she works with addicts. I appreciate her heart, on the one hand, but on the other hand, I hate it when these very needy people end up getting so attached to my wife. There were times when my wife even had some of them come and live with us, and she sometimes has arranged for it without my knowledge. On several occasions, we have had big arguments as a result.*

---

[114] Copyright © 2005, Jeffrey Young, Ph.D. Unauthorised reproduction without written consent of the authors is prohibited. You may order/purchase the complete version of the questionnaire at www.schematherapy.com, or write to: Cognitive Therapy Center of New York, 130 West 42nd St., Suite 501, New York, NY 10036.

Jane: *Well, I feel for these people. Some of them have been abused by their parents or husbands. Some of them are now estranged from their families as a result of their addictions. My life is so nice—I feel guilty if I don't help these people. And my parents taught me to always help others. "Do unto others" was their motto. My dad didn't think much of people who were lazy, and he was generous to a fault, so I guess it is just in my blood.*

Therapist: *What part of her helping people do you not like?*

Roland: *I don't mind her helping. I feel for those people as well. I gave some of them money, I found a job for one of those cases, and was happy for my wife to help one of them find a place to live. It is just that I get irritated when Jane places their needs before her health, her work, or before meeting my needs. I have tried to express this, but then I see my wife ignoring me and not ignoring them. When she goes overboard and helps these people to the point that they become dependent on her, I think it is unhealthy. I believe that my wife's motives are great, but this has gone too far.*

Jane is an example of a self-sacrificing person who went too far. She has a tremendous ability to feel for people, which can be a great strength, but it will also breed resentments in her family members, and eventually, even in her, unless she deals with her issues.

Focus of Change
When people with the self-sacrifice lifetrap give and give, they eventually experience burn out. They are often compassionate people who feel guilty if they meet their own needs instead of meeting others' needs, so this moves them to put others' needs before theirs.

The aim here, as with subjugation, is for them to recognise their own needs and not feel guilty meeting them. Often they neglect themselves for the sake of caring for others. They should not quench their ability to empathise with others, which is a strength, but they should strike a balance. When this balance is achieved, they will end up being healthy givers for long periods of time without getting burnt out. Jane learned that sometimes her serving was actually enabling others' weaknesses. This encouraged her to learn to say no, to not neglect her family, and to make time for herself.

SCRIPTURES FOR MEDITATION

• Exodus 20:8-11   • Ecclesiastes 3:1-8   • Mark 12:31

Vortex of Conflict Escalation

In light of what we have learned so far with regards to lifetraps and coping styles, we would like to point out that conflict often escalates when our lifetraps and coping styles work together and trigger each other. Allow us to use our own marriage to illustrate this principle. Lifetraps in **green**, Coping Styles in **blue**.

Stage One: Karen says something that triggers John's defectiveness lifetrap. (It might not have actually been a put-down, but at least he *perceived* it as one.)

Stage Two: As a result of feeling put down, he counterattacks, turning the criticism he believes he heard from Karen back into criticism of her.

Stage Three: This unhealthy coping style of overcompensating triggers Karen's lifetrap of subjugation. She believes she has to give in to John, and doesn't want to argue…

Stage Four: She retreats in accordance with her coping style of avoidance, which triggers John again because…

Stage Five: He misinterprets her avoidance to mean that she doesn't care about the situation or about him. In turn, John's mistrust lifetrap gets triggered.

Stage Six: He counterattacks again, asserting passionately about how she doesn't care, which changes the subject of the argument. (Sound familiar?)

Stage Seven: His coping style of overcompensating triggers her insufficient self-control.

Stage Eight: And, in accordance with her avoidance coping style, she resorts to reading novels, watching TV, emotional eating, or surfing the internet, in order to avoid her feelings around conflict. But in John's mind, Karen avoids in order to get out of resolving the tension, or to avoid him, or as proof that she is undisciplined!

Stage Nine: His mistrust lifestrap is triggered again, and he then lashes out at her lack of discipline, and a full-blown cold war has erupted from an accidental remark.

What happened? This is what we call the "Vortex of Conflict Escalation" (see Figure 29). As our lifetraps get triggered, our coping styles trigger the other person's lifetraps. When this happens, eventually the conflict will escalate. The emotional part of our brain (with the memory) works faster than the rational part of the brain—that's why the vortex can escalate so quickly!

Some couples are afraid of any conflict. They don't argue at all but they are also usually not on the same page on many issues. They have both chosen to avoid talking. They have decided to put their differences aside and function as two people living under the same roof, with nothing more than some Mutual Affection for each other. But is this a healthy partnership? Would this bring about the closeness that the couple desires? In Love Connection, couples should bring things out in the open in such a way as to cause growth.

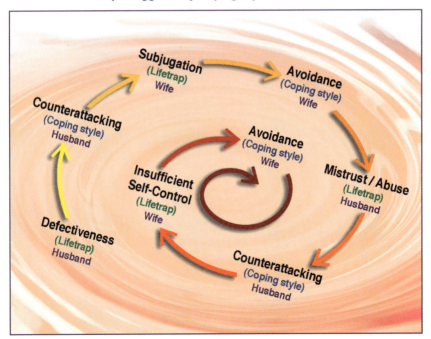

Figure 29: Vortex of Conflict Escalation

On the other hand, constant bickering brings another set of pain and hurts. So, given that differences are bound to happen, couples need to learn to develop skills and insights on how to not allow conflicts to escalate. What causes hurt and pain is when the conflict escalates to an unhealthy level. When we say an unhealthy level, we mean pouting, sulking, retreating, uncontrollable anger, accusations, finger pointing, shouting, put-downs or other similar behaviours and, in extreme cases, violence.

John Gottman, after over two decades of research, found that the four most corrosive behaviours in marriage are criticism, defensiveness, contempt and stonewalling.[115] All of these have elements of both the overcompensating and avoidance coping styles. He goes on to say this about conflict escalation:

> I can tell 96 percent of the time whether a marital discussion will resolve a conflict, after the first three minutes of that discussion.[116]

In other words, when our lifetraps are triggered, we should try to be aware of, and not resort to, one of the three coping styles. They do no good in marriage other then trigger the spouse's lifetrap and a vortex will begin that will take us to an unhealthy place. This can lead to resentment and bitterness, which shifts both partners into a hostile situation, making it more difficult to resolve the initial conflict.

What about your marriage? Do the exercise below and see the pattern of your own vortex.

---

[115] Gottman, J. M. (1999). *The marriage clinic: A scientifically-based marital therapy.* New York: W. W. Norton & Company, Inc. 41-47.

[116] Gottman, J. M., & Silver, N. (1999). *The seven principles for making marriage work.* New York: Three Rivers Press. 40.

CHOOSE **AWARENESS** 175

Vortex of Conflict Escalation Exercise
Answer each of the following questions.

Questions
1. Think about your last conflict. Write down which lifetrap in you or your spouse was triggered first. Triggered lifetrap was Who was triggered?
2. What coping style followed as a result? Coping style was Whose?
3. What lifetrap in you or your spouse got triggered as a result of the coping style in no. 2 above?
4. What coping style followed as a result of the lifetrap being triggered in no. 3 above?
5. What lifetrap got triggered in you or your spouse as a result of the coping style of your spouse in no. 4?
6. What coping style followed as a result of the lifetrap being triggered in no. 5 above?

Do you see how each other's coping style triggers off the spouse's lifetrap, and how the vortex begins to escalate the conflict? Conflict escalation can erode our marriages quickly. Our coping styles and lifetraps work against us to escalate the conflict.

So, what do we do if our lifetraps are triggered? How do we avoid getting into the "Vortex of Conflict Escalation"? The answer lies in being vulnerable.

No wonder we get stuck from time to time—our lifetraps have been getting triggered and our coping styles sucked us into a vortex! So how do we get out? Better yet, how do we get healed?

CHAPTER 4

CHOOSE TO BE VULNERABLE

We began this book by talking about the importance of marriage, and how we need to leave behind the Infatuation phase and choose Love Connection. We saw how Love Connection comes when we build our marriage on a foundation of love and respect, and then we focused on growing in awareness of our lifetraps and coping styles, the true obstacles to Love Connection.

Understanding our lifetraps, how and why they get triggered, and identifying our particular coping style all help us understand conflict in our marriage. Which lifetraps do *you* have? What is causing harm in *your* marriage? How do lifetraps and coping styles factor in to the conflicts between you and your spouse?

Typically, when we fight with our spouse, we have some form of the same fight over and over again. What's worse, it is often not even our spouse that we are really fighting; i.e., when one or more of our lifetraps get triggered, we are re-experiencing the trauma of our needs that were not met when we were children. We are in a place of very old and very great pain. This place is the root of the conflicts we have with our spouse, and the place where we need to work to create lasting change.

At this point, we would like to introduce a crucial term to help us overcome the power of our lifetraps: being vulnerable. (Not to be confused with the lifetrap of vulnerability to harm or illness.) One of the most consistent predictors of divorce is not angry fighting *per se*, but rather arguments and interactions that are full of contempt and defensiveness.[117] When we are vulnerable, we

---

[117] Gottman, J. M. (1994). *Why marriages succeed or fail.* New York: Simon & Schuster. 68-102.

avoid these toxic qualities. Being vulnerable encourages humility, respect, tenderness and courage. It strengthens our Love Connection. Our spouse now becomes a source of healing. He/she is a friendly partner, not a sparring partner. The same issues that trigger our lifetraps and make us flare up in anger or withdrawal are the issues with which we need the most help from our partner in order to heal. Being vulnerable is about moving away from patterns of defensiveness, fear, avoidance, and angry counterattacking to a place where we allow our partners (and ourselves) to see us as we really are. We shall now explain this term, and how being vulnerable with our spouse brings Love Connection.

Being Vulnerable—A Pathway to Healing

When we are vulnerable with our spouse, we allow ourselves to be known in a much more intimate way. We will move toward healing as we vulnerably discuss our lifetraps, our coping styles, and their origins. We are assuming that most of you do feel safe enough with your spouse to do this. If you do not, then find others with whom you feel safe and share vulnerably, but work towards being safe with your spouse. God gave us our spouse to help us meet the core needs that weren't met during childhood. Helping each other to meet needs that weren't met during childhood is a sacred privilege.

One of the findings in the field of counselling and therapy is that treatment success is the greatest in an atmosphere where the patient or client feels safe and respected.[118] In fact, this is rated to be a more successful predictor than the skill of the therapist or the type of therapy employed. So a safe environment with our spouse, or even with a group of supportive church friends, to which we will refer in this book as a "small group", will make all the difference in how well we will heal. Sometimes when we share, we will experience an "aha" moment. When this happens, we are getting into what experts call the "child side". We believe that Jesus was talking about this concept in the following passage:

> *¹At that time the disciples came to Jesus and asked, "Who is the greatest in the kingdom of heaven?" ²He called a little child and had him stand*

---

[118] Clients, not practitioners, make therapy work - British Association for Counselling & Psychotherapy. (2008, October 17). *Medical News Today*. Retrieved May 28, 2010, from http://www.medicalnewstoday.com

among them. ³And he said: "I tell you the truth, unless you change and become like little children, you will never enter the kingdom of heaven. ⁴Therefore, whoever humbles himself like this child is the greatest in the kingdom of heaven." (Matthew 18:1-4)

What exactly did Jesus mean when He taught that we should be like little children? Certainly being childish, immature and undisciplined were not the traits He had in mind. Rather, Jesus meant for us to imitate the godly qualities of a child—the side where we do not put up a front but are transparent about how we really feel and what we really need. This is what we see in children. Children are genuine in their demeanour. If they are angry, it shows. If they are happy, it shows! Jesus admired these qualities in children and taught us to bring back those innocent, genuine feelings that have been tucked away, hidden within us all.

Different experts have seen the value of getting in touch with the child side. Drs Alice Miller, Donald Winnicott, and Emmet Fox all taught that we should experience the child side of ourselves, or our true self.[119] Dr Charles Whitfield defines the child side as "who we are when we feel most authentic, genuine or spirited."[120]

Our child side experiences the feelings of joy and pain, and wants and needs to express these feelings without fear or judgment. This is seen clearly in young children. It is one of the reasons why they are so endearing. We don't completely lose our child side, even as adults; we only become good at hiding it. This child side is who we truly are. It is the side that expresses what we need, when we are weak, when we are happy and contented, when we are sad, and when we are afraid. When children start experiencing unhealthy guilt or shame or fear at a young age, they are usually at a loss, not knowing how to cope with these emotions. Often, the people who induce such feelings of unhealthy shame, guilt and fear are our parents, and some of them are grossly ignorant about healthy parenting skills and principles. In fact, Dr Virginia Satir and Dr Felitti, pioneers in family therapy, found that between

---

[119] Whitfield, C. L. (2006). *Healing the child within*. Deerfield Beach, FL: Health Communications, Inc. 1.
[120] Whitfield, C. L. (2006). *Healing the child within*. Deerfield Beach, FL: Health Communications, Inc. 9.

only 5-20% of the population receive a healthy amount of guidance, love and nurturing. The remaining 80-95% people do not.[121] As a result, most people grow up with feelings of unhealthy guilt, shame or fear from a young age.

When needs are not met, a child develops a false sense of who he/she is. Children rely on their parents to meet their core needs. When a child does not feel loved and accepted by his/her parents, or when the messages he/she receives are negative, the child is powerless to know that these messages are false. Since these negative messages get repeated over and over, the child comes to believe them, and accepts them as the truth about himself/herself. Lifetraps develop. The more powerful the negative messages and life experiences are, the more powerfully the lifetrap will develop. For example, if a child is constantly criticised and made to feel incompetent, or asked to do things beyond his/her ability, the defectiveness lifetrap will develop. (Some readers will remember Dorothy Law Nolte's poem, "If children live with criticism, they learn to condemn..."[122]).

As adults, we carry these lifetraps forward into our definition of ourselves. They become the inner truth of who we are. Rather than seeing ourselves as truly lovable, having intrinsic value and being acceptable as we are (created by God), we struggle with false understandings of ourselves. In order to manage the pain and fear these lifetraps cause us, we develop a false front in the form of unhealthy coping styles that hide our needs and desires. As adults, we are so in the habit of using our coping style(s) to respond to our fears, we no longer know we are shutting ourselves off from our innermost thoughts and feelings.

Eventually, with repetition, our child side gets completely hidden and comes out only here and there; our false side has now become a very natural part of our makeup and personality. It is deeply embedded in us, and the more we rely on this side of ourselves, the less we are in touch with our child side.

Moreover, as adults, our vocabulary is more extensive than when we were children, and we know what to say to confuse people and deter them from getting to our child side. As a result, little healing takes place. When we

---

[121] Whitfield, C. L. (2006). *Healing the child within*. Deerfield Beach, FL: Health Communications, Inc. 2.

[122] Nolte, D. L. (1972). *Children learn what they live*. Retrieved January 15, 2010, from http://www.empowermentresources.com

CHOOSE TO BE **VULNERABLE**

don't nurture our child side, the false unhealthy coping style takes over. This coping style is not our true inner self. When Jesus tells us to be like a little child, we believe that He is calling on us to bring out our child side, which is genuine, sincere and teachable. This side comes out when we are vulnerable. Believing the false truth of our lifetraps and using our coping styles will only prolong the pain and keep us from healing.

For example, when we quarrel with our spouse, rather than being vulnerable, we might act tough, and pretend that we don't need anyone and that we are fine, which is an avoidant coping style. In our avoidant style, by being busy, we keep ourselves detached from our true child side. Our coping style of avoidance may put us on the path of getting involved in an addiction or being a workaholic. Whatever it is, it will prevent us from being in touch with our real self, our child side.

When feelings of guilt or shame arise, some of us counterattack in order to protect ourselves. Since we are not being vulnerable, the child side is hidden, but a false angry side comes out instead by way of the counterattacking coping style.

Then there are those of us who are surrendered because we hear a critical parent voice and give in, thinking that everything is our fault. While this may not lead us to start a volatile quarrel the way a counterattacking coping style would, we are still not vulnerable, and so the child side of us stays tucked away. We think this is humility, but if we were truly being humble, *we* would not be the focus of attention. Whatever our coping style, we have learned to respond to pain by hiding our inner self, the child side, and have become accustomed to a façade.

When we start being vulnerable, we will suddenly feel confusion, fear, excitement, sadness and even anger. When this happens, it is actually good news. We are finally getting in touch with our child side! However, many people will give up at this point because they feel awkward and hurt. It is easier to stay in touch with their old, false self and the coping style to which they have been accustomed for so long. They would rather stay with the *familiar* than move towards something *healthier*.[123]

---

[123] Young, J. E., & Klosko, J. S. (1994). *Reinventing your life.* New York: Plume. 24.

As we practise being vulnerable, we should not let the awkward feelings dissuade us from pressing on. We should not give into our fear, rather, we should allow ourselves to feel our old fears, and look to our spouse to help us feel safe and comfortable. This can be a place of real healing rather than the false place of relating through our lifetraps and coping styles. If we feel more comfortable writing instead of talking and sharing, it is fine to do so, as long as we are being vulnerable. When we get there, we will feel Love Connection with our spouse like never before. It is such a wonderful place to be, but it takes humility and courage. We can take responsibility for our own healing. It may take a while. We may need to have a "do over" now and again, but with each attempt, we will get closer and closer to being healed. When we say being healed, we mean getting healed emotionally and mentally, and spiritually, and as a result, attaining a sense of peace.

All of us, from every corner of the globe, yearn for this kind of peace—the rich, the poor, the young and the old. The alternative is holding in our feelings until they become unbearable. How is that a better option? Our feelings have a way of coming out, whether we want them to or not. Somehow they will come out, through our present unhealthy coping style, which may lead to all sorts of self-destructive behaviour, including dependence on alcohol, smoking, or sexual promiscuity, or through counterattacking others. While this is happening, we may feel numb as we go about our routine. We will not feel quite as alive with our partner. Our child side is the energetic side that is waiting to come out. It has to be drawn out carefully, through being vulnerable.

Men are notorious for frowning at the thought of being vulnerable with their spouse, with a small group or a support group. Usually they view this as girl talk. They laugh, and look down on such things, but truthfully, it is their avoidant side that is reacting. Little do they realise that suppressed feelings lead to stress, distress and illness,[124] simply because this part of them is not liberated. They end up experiencing less personal growth, and miss out on how wonderful it is to get in touch with their child side.

As comfortable as we may be with our false self (coping style), it is not able to help us get healed, by virtue of it being *false*. Only the child side, the true self, can take us to a healthier place. Staying with the false messages of our

---

[124] Whitfield, C. L. (2006). *Healing the child within*. Deerfield Beach, FL: Health Communications, Inc. 58.

lifetraps through our coping styles will only prolong the pain and hold back the healing. They function to hide our child side. So, let's get our child side out and be vulnerable! Whitfield says that most of us expose our child side for only about 15 minutes a day! The other times are filled with the false self, and our unhealthy coping styles.[125]

Whether with our spouse or with other safe friends, it is time to get started. We should be patient with each other and help each other go through this process. This is what love for each other is all about; making the effort to help our selves and others change, as Dr M. Scott Peck defines love in his book "The Road Less Travelled":

> (Love is) the will to extend one's self for the purpose of nurturing one's own or another's spiritual growth.[126]

In marriage, love is not only acting on a feeling. It is a decision we make based on what is best for our spouse and ourselves. When we commit ourselves to loving our spouse in this manner, there will be growth on both sides. Love, looked at in this way, means creating the kind of environment that is able to nurture growth in ourselves and our partner. It may be uncomfortable at the beginning to be vulnerable, but the feelings will change.

Having explained how vulnerability is related to meeting the needs of our child side, let's get specific and talk about how to be vulnerable.

How To Be Vulnerable

When it comes to communicating in a vulnerable way with our spouse, we like to think of vulnerability as having three or four components: sharing our weakness (such as our lifetraps, coping styles), our feelings (such as fears, sadness, anger), our need (Love and Respect), and apologising where necessary.

i) Sharing our weakness means sharing gut-wrenching soul baring information without fear of how we are perceived. This is the hardest part! Instead of reacting when we get triggered, we need to take stock of what lifetrap is getting triggered and then admit our weaknesses, such as our harmful coping styles

---

[125] Whitfield, C. L. (2006). *Healing the child within*. Deerfield Beach, FL: Health Communications, Inc. 11.
[126] Scott Peck, M. (1978). *The road less travelled*. New York: Touchstone. 81.

While this is being done, our spouse will hopefully be listening and trying to understand our feelings, and not jump in and start lecturing or giving solutions. This is embarrassing, humbling and difficult, and may in turn trigger more defectiveness, but with God's grace we should press on and share vulnerably. Healing will take place when we admit our weaknesses, not when we hide behind the mask of our typical coping style. "Honey, I felt angry just now when you made that comment. In hindsight, I can see that it was because I felt guilty for not being home more with the kids, and I became insecure that you thought I wasn't a good parent. My defectiveness got triggered."

ii) Sharing our feelings respectfully means that instead of being rude and angry, stuffing, or sulking, we honestly share our pain and hurt, as lovingly as possible. "To be honest, my ego got a bit bruised when I thought you meant that I wasn't a good parent. However, I am sorry for my rudeness."

iii) Expressing our need means that we ask for our spouse to meet our need for Love and Respect (Chapter 2), rather than being demanding. This works best in a gentle tone of voice. We can express what the partner could have done that would have been more helpful. "Maybe it would help me if I could hear you being a bit more appreciative of the times I am with the kids, so that I don't feel that you 'never notice' the good things I do. However, that is no excuse for my outburst!"

iv) Apologising when necessary is just that—if there is something for which we need to apologise, we should do it here. See the examples in the two paragraphs above. The last sentence in both examples is an apology. Humility is always endearing.

Bear in mind the following:
- We need to see our spouse as a person who needs us and whose needs we are able to meet.
- Our spouse is human and has weaknesses, just like we have. Our spouse has his/her own hurts. Let us have feelings of compassion for our spouse.
- We should accept our spouse for who he/she is, knowing that over time, we will both grow into more loving and helpful partners, able to better meet each other's needs.
- "…Change and become like little children…" Being vulnerable can bring tears of refreshing…Experience a renewed sense of unity and closeness: Love Connection.

Now that we have learned how to communicate in a vulnerable way, we shall move to the section on how to use our vulnerability with each other to overcome the power of the negative and false message of our lifetraps.

Helping Each Other Heal: A Ten Point Plan for Weakening Lifetraps and Coping Styles

1) Identify your Lifetraps and Coping Styles
Fill out the lifetrap questionnaires from Chapter 3, and if desired, you may fill out an additional form from the Schema Therapy website. The YSQ-S3 version is available from schematherapy.com or you may write to:

Schema Therapy Institute,
120 West 42nd Street, Suite 501,
New York, NY 10036

It is important that you do not make this an academic exercise; rather see this as a crucial moment to gain insight into yourself and your spouse. We have found that people who realise their lifetraps and coping styles, who have eureka moments, are the ones who change the most. Conversely, those who gloss over their lifetraps and coping styles will change little. If you acknowledge that a lifetrap or coping style is the roadblock in your marriage, then this insight should help. Another important bit of advice: Work on the most dysfunctional lifetrap first—the one that is causing you the most harm in your marriage. It usually comes out in other close relationships as well. Do not work on five lifetraps at once. It would overwhelm you. Work on one or two at a time. As you defeat and weaken the lifetrap you are focusing on, you will feel liberated from self-defeating patterns.

2) Get to The Root
As we help each other heal, we will do well to get to the root, rather than focus only on the symptoms. Delving into our past may be painful, but we will be rewarded as we see our marriages improve and even make progress in other areas of our lives. For illustration purposes, we will look at four common issues—conflict avoiding, outbursts of anger, selfishness, and depression—to see how getting to the root improves the healing process.

Issue: Conflict Avoiding
There are many reasons why people avoid conflict. *Why* are they unassertive? What is underneath what we see? Perhaps one woman has a surrendered

coping style and a subjugation lifetrap. She is very afraid of conflict with others and feels that if she asserts herself, conflict will arise. The second woman is also unassertive but is so because of her mistrust lifetrap and her avoidance coping style. In particular, she is unassertive with her spouse, and avoids facing it by getting involved with other tasks, like being obsessed about her work. A third woman has a surrendered coping style and her predominant lifetrap is the defectiveness lifetrap. She also needs help in being assertive because she has bought into the belief that when there is conflict, it is entirely her fault. Giving these women training on assertiveness *per se* will not get to the root. On the other hand, if you get to the origin of their lifetraps and coping styles, you will see them make progress in other areas of their lives when the same lifetrap interferes. It pays to get to the bottom of a person's lifetrap.

Issue: Outbursts of Anger

Let's look at another example—outbursts of anger, which is a common problem in many marriages and relationships. Let's say that one man has the defectiveness lifetrap and is an overcompensator. He would be triggered at the slightest perceived put-down from his wife, and then react, in anger, to put down his wife. A second man has an abandonment lifetrap and perceives that his wife will leave him for someone else, and counterattacks in anger when he feels triggered by his wife. Yet another man has the surrendered coping style and the subjugation lifetrap, but he has had enough of giving in to other people. Now he is ready to blow his top and rebel in anger at his wife's slightest attempt to make him comply. A fourth man is angry because he is a counterattacker with the mistrust lifetrap. Outbursts of anger are evident in all of these men, but the root of their anger is different. Telling them to stop being angry will only go so far. It pays to get to the root of things. By dealing with the right lifetrap and coping style, you will then deal not only with the issue at hand, but also help the person have victories in other areas of his/her life where the lifetrap also interferes.

Issue: Self-centredness

A woman has the emotional deprivation lifetrap and counterattacks. She makes unrealistic demands from her spouse to meet her needs, and comes across as being selfish or self-centred. A second woman has the entitlement lifetrap and acts as if rules do not apply to her. She seems to only care about her needs getting met. She would also be labelled self-centred. A third woman has been self-sacrificing for years and has now had enough. She no longer shows appreciation to her spouse and refuses to do anything for him. Again, this appears as self-centred behaviour. So all the above examples exhibit self-centred behaviour but they are rooted in different lifetraps. Getting the lifetraps and coping styles correct will do more to solve the problem than simply telling them to stop being self-centred or selfish.

Issue: Depression

Let's look at a final example, a person who is depressed. One person with the self-sacrificing lifetrap and the surrendered coping style becomes depressed because he got burnt out from being giving to others all his life, and is feeling down because for so long his own needs were not met. A second person gets depressed because she has unrelenting standards and has never been able to achieve the standards that she has imposed onto herself at work, in marriage and in any other relationship. Again, both these lifetraps and coping styles can lead to depression but the root is different. It pays to be correct in our assessment of the lifetrap and coping style leading to the depression. There are numerous other combinations of lifetraps and coping styles that exhibit the same symptoms but have different underlying lifetraps triggering them. When it comes to symptoms, Young and Klosko say that almost all lifetraps can result in depression, anxiety, substance abuse, psychosomatic symptoms or sexual dysfunction.[127]

People benefit when they gain awareness of what exactly is bothering them. It is hard work to get to the bottom of things, but the dividends are huge if we do. Understanding the origin of our lifetraps and coping styles makes change a lot easier. This is not about just feeling good temporarily. It is about changing for the better. When we become aware of our destructive lifetraps and coping styles, and see the damage they have done to our marriage and relationships in general, we finally get sick of them. We need to really dislike our lifetraps and coping styles. Once we are really sick of them, we will use this awareness and make the appropriate changes. Anthony de Mello says, "Only when you are finally sick of your sickness, will you decide to get rid of

---

[127] Young, J. E., Klosko, J. S., & Weishaar, M. E. (2003). *Schema therapy: A practitioner's guide.* New York: The Guilford Press. 65.

it."[128] When both husband and wife make an effort to understand and change together, it will lead both of them to a better place in their marriage. So many times, we think that our marriage will only change if our partner changes. We shift the blame to others; it is more our wife's fault or our husband's fault than it is ours. By taking stock of our lifetraps and coping styles, we are taking personal responsibility for our own issues. We may not be able to change our spouse, but we can change ourselves! If both partners have this attitude, and get to the root of their issues, the marriage will quickly accelerate into the Love Connection phase as healing takes place.

3) Keep a Journal of Your Lifetraps and Coping Styles
One very helpful exercise that facilitates getting to the root of our issues is to monitor our lifetraps and coping styles in a journal. Remember, with some lifetraps our coping styles may be different; for example, we may have the defectiveness lifetrap and be a counterattacker at home, but with our boss at work, we may surrender with the subjugated lifetrap, afraid to speak up for fear of conflict. A person with the vulnerability lifetrap may also be very surrendered in his coping style since he/she feels that danger is around the corner, but he may cope with the mistrust lifetrap by counterattacking people who trigger him/her. While we probably have one *predominant* style, coping styles can vary from lifetrap to lifetrap and monitoring them as we go about the week will open our eyes to how we come across to others, especially our spouse.

An example of such a journal is found in the Appendix. (Please refer to Appendix 6, *A Journal for Your Lifetraps & Coping Styles*). There are several columns to be filled in. In the trigger column, write down who triggered you and what they said or did that triggered you. The next column is for which coping style was used. Write down how you coped when the lifetrap was triggered, including what you said and did. In the last column, write down how you felt after the interaction. If you are vigilant about keeping this journal, you will see patterns emerging. By sharing this with your spouse and maybe some trusted friends, you will then see which lifetraps are causing the most harm in your life and which ones need the most attention.

---

[128] Anthony de Mello, S. J. (1990). *Awareness.* New York: Doubleday. 12.

Some people do not like this exercise because of the trouble it takes to write down their thoughts and actions. However, the benefits are immense. When our blind spots get the better of us, we may not see the thread of one lifetrap going through many of our relationships and causing harm along the way. When we are able to see how damaging our lifetraps and coping styles are, and then focus on them, we will make progress in our marriage and in other aspects of our lives.

4) Share Vulnerably Before Conflict Escalates
Now let's talk about how to use our vulnerability with each other to prevent an escalation of conflict with our spouse. When you are analysing a particular conflict, help each other see the evidence for and against the lifetrap. (Because lifetraps are distorted, we will usually be able to find evidence to prove that our lifetraps are wrong.)

For example, speaking from John's point of view: When my wife disagrees with me in front of others, my defectiveness lifetrap gets triggered. Being an overcompensator, I feel "put down" by my wife, and as a result, when we are alone, I sometimes take the opportunity to put her down! (This has happened more times than I would like to admit!) Now that I am trying to be vulnerable, rather than allowing my counterattacking coping style to take over, I am trying to pause and take a reality check. I analyse the situation and ask myself if Karen was indeed putting me down in front of others. Often our lifetraps are wrong, or they exaggerate the situation. If we press our "pause" button and talk with our spouse in a vulnerable way, we won't get sucked into the Vortex of Conflict Escalation that we discussed at the end of the previous chapter. We have a choice when we get triggered. Choose vulnerability. When our child side comes out, it rarely triggers our spouse's lifetraps.

On the other hand, if we let our lifetraps and coping styles take over, they will very likely trigger our spouse. Being vulnerable has a way of endearing us to our spouse, and he/she will respond in such a way so as to meet our emotional core needs. As we communicate in this manner, we will realise how distorted and wrong our lifetraps are. We will then feel better because we did not listen to our lifetraps. So, right after our lifetraps are triggered, we should create an opportunity to talk vulnerably with our spouse, thus saving ourselves from heartache, hurt and pain. When we feel our lifetraps getting triggered, it sometimes helps to take a short break and talk sense to ourselves or others first so that when we go back to our spouse, we will have decent dialogue instead of escalating into a vortex!

The path of listening to our lifetraps and going back to our usual coping styles will not weaken our lifetraps, unless there is reconciliation at some point in the future. So when lifetraps are triggered, take the opportunity to share vulnerably with each other. Again, don't let the vortex suck you in!

And while we are being vulnerable, it helps if we engage in some form of loving touch, such as holding hands or a neck rub. Why on earth would we do that, you ask? Consider this finding from the University of Zurich. Couples who used a nasal spray containing oxytocin (one of the brain chemicals found in infatuation which fosters feelings of trust and attachment) before discussing an ongoing marital conflict were more likely to engage in friendly positive communication than those who didn't take a whiff. Oxytocin is stimulated naturally with touch![129] (Maybe it's time to sign up for that couples massage class you've been putting off.)

To summarise, being vulnerable helps us by:
- Weakening our lifetraps
- Bringing out our child side
- Helping our spouse to meet our needs as he/she hears the child side
- Not triggering our spouse's lifetraps and coping style
- Strengthening our Love Connection.

Since being vulnerable is so crucial to the healing process of having our core needs met and weakening our lifetraps, we would like to give you some examples on how to be vulnerable when your lifetraps are triggered.

---

[129] Fisher, H. (2009, December 17). Real aphrodisiacs to boost desire. *O, The Oprah Magazine*. Retrieved January 18, 2010 from http://www.oprah.com/relationships/Real-Aphrodisiacs-to-Boost-Desire

CHOOSE TO BE VULNERABLE

> Being VULNERABLE means:
> - Expressing your Feelings respectfully in a gentle tone
>   (such as fears, sadness, anger, abandonment)
> - Expressing your Weaknesses
>   (such as lifetraps and coping styles)
> - Expressing your Needs
>   (such as needs for Love and Respect)
> - Apologising when Necessary.

The following are examples of wives making vulnerable statements to their husbands. (Remember statements such as these "go down better" when delivered with a gentle tone of voice.)

Scenario: The wife feels that her husband has begun to prioritise work over their relationship. She brings it up in a negative and angry way and they argue. Later she speaks vulnerably.

- Feelings: *"Honey, sometimes I'm afraid that I'm an unlovable wife, that you're not happy with me and I feel rejected and disconnected from you."*
- Weakness: *"When you work late almost every night and are not home with me, it makes me feel unloved and uncared for, and reinforces those negative thoughts I have about myself. I get depressed and then critical of you. This is my weakness, and I don't want to do that."*
- Need: *"I know that you have a desire to do well in your work, but I do feel the need for your love and affection, because it gives me security. I need you and I want to be with you."*
- Apology: *"I am sorry I criticised and 'went after you' for this. Please accept my apology."*

Scenario: The wife fears that her husband might be paying attention to another woman.

- Feelings: *"Honey, sometimes I feel that I'm an unlovable wife, and I'm afraid that you're not happy with me and I feel rejected and disconnected from you. I know that you get tempted, and I totally understand that. Would you mind if we talked about it honestly?"*

- Weakness: *"Dear, sometimes I feel that you think about how other women are more beautiful than I am, and I feel unattractive. I do feel insecure and get down on myself. I know I have my weakness and I may not be meeting your needs well. I want to get your honest thoughts about this."*
- Need: *"I need your assurance that your eyes are only for me, because sometimes I get the feeling that you are paying attention to this particular (or another) woman, and it feels like a stab in my heart. I need to feel connected to and loved by you."*
- Apology: *"Perhaps I am making something out of nothing, and if so, I am sorry."*

Scenario: The wife feels that her husband is critical of her parenting skills.
- Feelings: *"Honey, sometimes when you criticize me I feel worthless. Sometimes I worry that I'm not a good mother, or that I am not doing my best when it comes to the kids."*
- Weakness: *"When I feel worthless, I get tempted to not give me best, because I think, 'What's the point?' and lose motivation. This is my weakness when I get down."*
- Need: *"I need you to encourage me when I do right as well and not come across like you are picking on me. I need you to talk to me like we're on the same team. I want us to be on the same team."*
- Apology: *"I am sure I can do some things better and I open to getting feedback from you. I am sorry if I have disappointed you in some way."*

Scenario: The wife feels that her husband interrupts while she is talking and gives her a solution right away.
- Feelings: *"When you interrupt like this it really makes me feel that I am not valued as a wife. I know that you are good at giving solutions, and I am not saying you don't care; I am just saying that it feels uncaring when you don't let me finish saying my bit."*
- Weakness: *"When I get interrupted like this, it sort of makes me feel that you are not interested in what I have to say, and it feels like you don't care about what I have to say. Then I get tempted to feel insecure about myself and my abilities and then I think that what I am saying is not worth listening to. Then I get down on myself or even irritated at you and this is my weakness and I need to be aware of that."*

CHOOSE TO BE **VULNERABLE**

- Need: *"I really need to feel that you care, and you can do that by letting me finish instead of interrupting, which would help me feel accepted by you and believe that you think my opinion matters."*
- Apology: *"I may be triggering you, in which case, please let me know. I am willing to apologise and listen."*

Scenario: The wife feels that her husband is not helping the children to be self-disciplined with their homework.

- Feelings: *"Sweetie, sometimes I am overwhelmed with life. I love our children, but sometimes sorting everything out is more than I can take."*
- Weakness: *"When you see that I am feeling frustrated with the kids, and you don't step in and help out, it feels like you don't want to be involved. I know that is probably not how you feel, but it comes across as unconcerned. I don't want to get negative towards you and I know this is my weakness and I need to take responsibility for this."*
- Need: *"I really need your help and authority as a father. I know that you are tired after work, but it would help me, and also help the children, if we could work as a team."*
- Apology: *"Please let me know if there is something I can do better to help you want to be on that team."*

The following are examples of husbands making vulnerable statements to their wives. (Remember statements such as these "go down better" when delivered with a gentle tone of voice.)

Scenario: The husband feels that his wife does not respect his goals and aspirations at work, especially when she brings up mistakes from the past.

- Feelings: *"Honey, you may not believe this, but I sometimes doubt myself and worry that I will not be a good provider, and I hear negative 'voices in my head' telling me I am useless. When you make belittling remarks about my job and aspirations, it feels disrespectful. I am sure this is not what you mean but it can come across like this."*
- Weakness: *"When I don't feel appreciated by you I do not look forward to coming home. I avoid you by going out with colleagues for no reason; this is my weakness and I do not want to do that."*
- Need: *"I really need you to show appreciation to me for working hard, and express appreciation for the way I provide for the family. I know that I do make mistakes sometimes, but I need you to be supportive."*

- Apology: *"Please let me know if there is something I have done that contributed to you being critical of me. If I have done something, let me know so I can take responsibility for it."*

Scenario: The husband feels that his wife does not include him when making decisions about the kids.
- Feelings: *"Dear, sometimes I'm afraid I might not be a good father. At the same time, I want to be, but then when you make decisions about the kids without letting me know and I only find out later, I feel terrible – it makes me feel like you don't think I am important."*
- Weakness: *"I need the kids to know that their dad takes an interest in them; that you and I are a team."*
- Need: *"I really need to be included and I want both of us together to look out for what is best for the children."*
- Apology: *"What can I do to make sure we communicate better about the kids? I am willing to change and I am sorry if I have not been there for you."*

Scenario: The husband feels that his wife is not interested in "participating in the bedroom".
- Feelings: *"Sweetheart, the world is full of temptations and I see beautiful women who are half dressed every time I go to work. Even the trains are full of ads about sex in some way or another. I want you to know that I am attracted to you and I want to express my physical love with you and you only. However, it seems to me that for the last few months, when I want to be with you in that way, you are always 'too tired'. After I while, it makes me feel hurt and unloved, because it makes me feel that you don't care about my needs, or that you think I am 'oversexed'".*
- Weakness: *"I get tempted and I do not want to be drawn to any other woman but you. This is my weakness and I would love for you to help me with this."*
- Need: *"I need intimacy with you frequently. I feel close to you when we improve this aspect of our marriage. God has given us each other – you are the only one who can satisfy me in this area."*
- Apology: *"Is there something I can do to help you not feel so tired? I want and need for us to be close in every way."* (Note: Best said after the husband has washed the dishes!)

Scenario: The husband feels that his wife often jumps to conclusions about his inability to handle the household finances.
- Feelings: *"Darling, I know I am not the best when it comes to working out our finances and I really want to get better. I need you to encourage me rather than tell me how irresponsible I am. When you say things like that, I feel put down. I am trying hard to provide for the family and I know that I am not perfect, but it was a real stab in my heart when you said those words."*
- Weakness: *"I can do better in my discipline and I know that this has always been my weakness. I hope we can talk about this and perhaps discuss how you can help me with it."*
- Need: *"I need your encouragement as that really makes a difference because I care about what you think more than anyone else."*
- Apology: *"I am sorry that I haven't asked you for help in this area before. It hurts my ego to lean on you for support and that is my fault."*

When you communicate vulnerably, rather than with negative coping styles, you will be able to use what you are learning about lifetraps to help yourself, your spouse, and your relationship.

5) Do an Imagery Exercise with Your Spouse
What if the unhealthy pattern gets repeated so often that the vulnerable talks are not making much headway? We would like to introduce a simple imagery exercise, where you both will be engaging in an experiential process. This is not something that you need to do every time you have a conflict, but if you have never done this before with your spouse and did not take time in the past to get to know his/her child side, then this would be a helpful exercise. (Some of us are able to handle this intense self-reflection and self-disclosure, but others will need help from friends and counsellors, perhaps even professionals, since the issues can be quite intense.)

Allow us to comment on why an experiential process is powerful before we introduce it to you.

An experiential process that is done well will do a lot more healing than just casually talking about the past. Experiential sharing gets deeper into our emotions. It helps us get in touch with our lifetraps emotionally rather than just intellectually. Lifetraps are strong and stubborn, and they bring out emotions like loneliness, anger, sadness and anxiety when they are triggered. When we see how false our lifetraps are at an emotional level, the healing power to weaken the lifetrap is greater.[130]

During an experiential exercise, you will learn more about each other's past. The more you understand, the more you will appreciate your spouse. For some of you, unlocking past secrets will bond you both together like nothing else. Your connection will get deeper and you will know how to better meet each other's needs. The more you know about yourself, the healthier you will become. As a result, you will be a better spouse and parent, and you will feel lighter and more at peace. Isn't this a great gift to give yourself and to your loved ones? Though it may be painful at first, don't avoid the process. The sooner we know ourselves, the sooner we will be a better husband or wife and parent. Many of you know about your spouse's past in an abstract way. You have heard some stories, but you have never spent time really knowing your partner's past in a way that will take your Love Connection deeper. It is a new level of *knowing*. When you are at this level, it is amazing how much more accepting of and compassionate towards each other you will be. (Please refer to Appendix 7, *Healing Imagery Exercise*.)

6) Strengthen Your Healthy Spiritual Side

We all have two sides. There is the side of us that wants to do what's right but we end up not doing it. Then there is the side where we know the wrong, but we still end up doing it. The passage from Romans 7 that we quoted in Chapter 3 bears repeating:

> [14]*We know that the law is spiritual; but I am unspiritual, sold as a slave to sin.* [15]*I do not understand what I do. For what I want to do I do not do, but what I hate I do.* [16]*And if I do what I do not want to do, I agree that the law is good.* [17]*As it is, it is no longer I myself who do it, but it is sin living in me.* [18]*I know that nothing good lives in me, that is, in my sinful nature. For I have the desire to do what is good, but I cannot carry it out.* [19]*For what I do is not the good I want to do; no, the evil I do not want to do—this I keep on doing.* [20]*Now if I do what I do not want to*

---

[130] Young, J. E., Klosko, J. S., & Weishaar, M. E. (2003). *Schema therapy: A practitioner's guide.* New York: The Guilford Press. 110-145.

do, it is no longer I who do it, but it is sin living in me that does it. ²¹So I find this law at work: When I want to do good, evil is right there with me. ²²For in my inner being I delight in God's law; ²³but I see another law at work in the members of my body, waging war against the law of my mind and making me a prisoner of the law of sin at work within my members. ²⁴What a wretched man I am! Who will rescue me from this body of death? ²⁵Thanks be to God—through Jesus Christ our Lord! So then, I myself in my mind am a slave to God's law, but in the sinful nature a slave to the law of sin.

Our lifetraps and coping styles block us from a healthy relationship with God and with our spouse and others. (Thank God for His grace!) When we strengthen our healthy spiritual side, we weaken our lifetraps. This is why we should never abandon or compromise our Bible study and prayer times. They should not be viewed as "routines", rather, habitual prayer and Bible study help weaken our lifetraps and give our healthy spiritual side the power and strength to defeat those negative distorted lifetraps. A good Quiet Time connects us to God and helps us. How we react to our spouse either positively or negatively will reflect to a large degree how strong or weak we are spiritually. Praying together, sharing biblical insights and having family devotionals will strengthen our healthy spiritual side and dramatically weaken our lifetraps.

Whether we like it or not, our lifetraps are a part of us. The triggering of our lifetraps is not in our direct control. Lifetraps are a part of our brain make-up, the way we have stored information about what has happened to us and the meaning we have given to these experiences. We do, however, have control over our coping response. The stronger our spiritual healthy side is, and the more we can rely on our relationship with God to help us, the better we are able to respond in a loving, spiritual way when our lifetraps are triggered.

We have all seen the unfortunate scenario of old, mature disciples losing their love for God and then over time becoming less and less spiritual, and as a result, more and more ungodly. Often it comes down to them not digging deep in their relationship with God through vigilant prayer and Bible study. Lifetraps are part of our sinful nature; they want to be in control. They lurk under the surface, seeking means and ways to out-talk our spiritual side.

Lifetraps are relentless; they push us into responding through coping styles that are sinful and destructive, such as sexual addiction and substance abuse. Our best defence against our lifetraps is to strengthen our spiritual side!

7) Strengthen Your Close Relationships with Trustworthy People

We firmly believe that married couples should spend time regularly with other married couples. This enables us to influence one another for the better. Many of us are blessed to have awesome, loving married couples in our lives who help us when we go through difficult times. This is such a crucial form of support. The scripture in Ephesians 4:15-16 comes to mind:

> [15]*Instead, speaking the truth in love, we will in all things grow up into him who is the Head, that is, Christ.* [16]*From him the whole body, joined and held together by every supporting ligament, grows and builds itself up in love, as each part does its work.*

In order to achieve growth, it is helpful for married couples to get connected with one another. When we have trusting and meaningful friendships with other couples, it will help us strengthen our healthy side. When we are struggling, their voices will help strengthen our healthy spiritual side to battle against our lifetraps. God uses "one another" in the church to keep us strong and spiritual. In fact, our marriages may not survive unless we invite people into our lives to help talk sense to us when we are listening to our lifetraps (and to Satan). Don't fight your marriage battles alone; it's too hard. Build genuine relationships with other people. We feel blessed to be a part of a church that really feels like a family, where we can talk about our marriage in a safe atmosphere. If you are a part of a healthy church, we strongly encourage you to do the same. (Or find a like-minded support group). Solid, genuine and meaningful relationships with other people can make a huge difference in our lives and in our marriages. Conversely, being isolated and alone will take us into a downward spiral, and facilitate Mutual Affection or the Disintegration phase.

Studies show that the more isolated we are, the less healthy mentally we are. A book entitled *Loneliness*,[131] by JT Cacioppo and Patrick William, spells out how people who are isolated and lonely experience more wear and tear

---

[131] Cacioppo, J. T., & William, P. (2008). *Loneliness.* New York: W. W. Norton & Company, Inc.

mentally and physically later on in life than the non-lonely people who have meaningful relationships. Here are some of the findings:
- People with high levels of loneliness reported to have lower levels of social support, higher levels of shyness, poorer social skills, higher anger, higher anxiety, lower self esteem, lower positive mood and higher negative mood.[132]
- Lonely and isolated people have less of an ability to empathise with others.[133]
- An article in Science Magazine reported that in terms of physical illness, lonely people are on par with those with have high-blood pressure, who are obese, who do not exercise, who smoke and who suffer an early death.[134]

We don't know exactly how it all works, but having quality meaningful relationships will strengthen us mentally and physically; inevitably this will have an effect on our lifetraps. On the other hand, being isolated, without quality meaningful relationships, will only strengthen our negative thinking and lifetraps. Our lifetraps are not the truth, but they are real to us, often painfully so. The more isolated you become, the stronger the false truth of your lifetrap becomes. The closer you are to healthy, supportive people who care about you and share God's love for you, the more opportunities are created for you to see how false the messages of your lifetraps actually are. The stronger your healthy spiritual side, the less you need to use your negative coping styles!

8) Continue to Practise Being Vulnerable with Each Other
Although we have been focusing on being vulnerable before a conflict escalates, it is also helpful to be vulnerable with each other when there is no conflict. As mentioned earlier in Chapter 2, we recommend for couples to spend at least eight hours per week together. Watching TV together doesn't count! Do not let these opportunities slip by. Talk to each other and vulnerably share your ups and downs. Get into each other's child side. The more you practise being vulnerable during everyday conversations, the easier it is to do when a conflict is about to rise. It is tough, especially for men, but it is a powerful skill that is worth practising.

---

[132] Cacioppo, J. T., & William, P. (2008). *Loneliness*. New York: W. W. Norton & Company, Inc. 88.

[133] Cacioppo, J. T., & William, P. (2008). *Loneliness*. New York: W. W. Norton & Company, Inc. 166.

[134] House, J. A., Landis, K. R., & Umbertson, D. (1988). Social relationships and health. *Science, 241*, 540-545.

9) Be Giving To Others
Something about being outwardly focused and volunteering to help others (taking on a service role at church, befriending elderly shut-ins, tutoring special needs children, studying the Bible with others consistently, helping those who are struggling, coaching a Little League team, etc.) without expecting anything in return, has a way of giving us a positive mental boost. Social scientists do not quite know how it all works, but giving to others instead of "Help me first!" has a way of helping us to not get so caught up in our own world of negativity. Reaching out to someone in pain helps to ease our own. Some of the most healthy and joyful people we know are the ones who set aside time to help others. Psychologists call that kind of joyful feeling the "helpers high".[135]

Again, we would like to qualify that this does not mean that we should throw ourselves completely into helping others and become self-sacrificing in an unhealthy way, and not take care of our own needs. It is about getting the right balance of helping others as we also seek ways to help ourselves.

10) Work Towards Forgiving Your Spouse and Parents
We shall deal with the subject of forgiveness and reconciliation in the last chapter. Suffice it to say that when people hurt us, we hear their voices in our heads again and again. Sometimes our recollection changes because of bitterness. As the story evolves, we end up with a distorted memory, but after genuinely forgiving, these voices will not have such a negative impact. (See Chapter 6, *Choose Reconciliation.*)

---

[135] Cacioppo, J. T., & William, P. (2008). *Loneliness.* New York: W. W. Norton & Company, Inc. 228.

Speaking of being honest with each other about our most vulnerable issues, I have been very tempted at work. One of my colleagues is giving me the kind of attention that would make my spouse uncomfortable, and should make me uncomfortable. Do you have any information that could help me?

CHAPTER 5

CHOOSE FIDELITY

Marriage vows should be honoured "until death do us part". We are called to be faithful to our spouse. Our spouse is given to us by God to meet some of our most important core needs. It is a lifelong commitment. If we are unfaithful, we will face the judgment of God Himself.

> *Marriage should be honoured by all, and the marriage bed kept pure, for God will judge the adulterer and all the sexually immoral. Keep your lives free from the love of money and be content with what you have, because God has said, "Never will I leave you; never will I forsake you."* (Hebrews 13:4-5)

If we are trying to build Love Connection in our marriage, having an affair should be the farthest thing from our mind. Infidelity breaks our spouse's heart. Unfortunately, this view is seen as more and more old fashioned, if not in belief, than at least in practice. Dr Neuman, to whom we referred in Chapter 2, concludes that one in every three couples will be affected by an affair,[136] and Ruth Houston believes that almost three out of every four men are guilty of cheating on their wives.[137] Dr Annette Lawson surprisingly found that affairs occur sooner rather than later. According to her:

> The various researchers arrived at a general consensus… suggesting that above one-quarter to about one-half of married women have at least one lover after they are married in any given marriage. Married men

---

[136] Neuman, G. (2008). *The truth about cheating: Why men stray and what you can do to prevent it.* Hoboken, NJ: John Wiley & Sons, Inc. 4.
[137] Houston, R. (2002). *Is he cheating on you? 829 telltale signs.* New York: Lifestyle Publications. 24.

probably still stray more often than married women—perhaps from 50 percent to 65 percent by the age of forty.[138]

Whatever the exact statistics are, infidelity is a lot more common than we think. Many of the victims interviewed by these experts were caught off guard and totally shocked to learn about their spouse's betrayal. They never dreamt it would happen to them, simply because they did not think that their marriages were on the rocks. And even those who were suspicious didn't get very far. Says Dr Neuman:

> Without being questioned, a mere 7 percent admitted to their wives that they had cheated. And unfortunately, few men admit to it even after multiple questioning. Shockingly, 68 percent never admit to cheating or only do so after their wives have concrete evidence of the affairs.[139]

Definition of An Affair

As marriage counsellors, we define an affair as an attraction-based relationship developed with someone other than your spouse, featuring emotional attachment, longing, and flirtation of some kind. There may or may not be frequent lustful fantasies or a physical relationship. Nevertheless, such a relationship is a breach of trust of your marriage vows. *This includes relationships developed through cyberspace, phone sex or getting involved with chat lines.*

Some people claim that it is not really cheating if no sex is involved, if they just have an emotional attachment to the other person. However, we agree with Dr Neuman, who calls this kind of relationship an "emotional affair".[140]

Marriage is about developing an intimate relationship and oneness in spirit and destiny with someone of the opposite gender. No one else should come close to taking this place. If there is someone outside with whom you are developing such a relationship, then it is an affair. If you have any hope of developing Love Connection with your spouse, the affair needs to be stopped immediately! (More on that later.)

---

[138] Lawson, A. (1988). *Adultery: An analysis of love and betrayal.* New York: Basic Books. 75.
[139] Neuman, G. (2008). *The truth about cheating: Why men stray and what you can do to prevent it.* Hoboken, NJ: John Wiley & Sons, Inc. 4.
[140] Neuman, G. (2001). *Emotional infidelity.* New York: Random House Inc. 26.

Why Does Anyone Cheat?

According to Neuman's research into what sort of marital dissatisfaction contributed to husbands committing adultery, 59% said their dissatisfaction in the marriage was emotional, 29% said it was sexual, and 12% attributed the dissatisfaction to other causes.[141]

Neuman's conclusion, also mentioned in Chapter 2 of this book, is that men do not cheat because of the sex *per se*, but because of a lack of emotional connection with their spouse. (We are addressing all affairs, including women cheating on their husbands. However, since Neuman's book is about why *men* cheat, some of our statistics only apply to husbands' affairs.) For years, men have been labelled as being unemotional creatures. On the contrary, we agree with Neuman's analysis that men can be *very* emotional; they just have a difficult time *expressing* their emotions.

If men do not feel Love Connection with their wives (and vice versa), it does not take much for infatuation and chemistry to develop. When this happens, there is an unfair competition going on between the two—the new interest who would be conjuring all of the brain chemistry present in the Infatuation phase, and the spouse, stuck in the Mutual Affection or Disintegration phase with its lack of positive feelings.

And since a lack of emotional connection is behind most affairs, is it any surprise that so many affairs take place? No, because so many marriages are hurting and many of the needs of love and respect are not being met by husbands and wives, but by someone else. Again, we are back to what we stated in Chapters 1 & 2—we need to constantly make an effort to have Love Connection, which starts with love and respect. When husbands are considerate listeners, responsible leaders and romantic lovers, and when wives make their husbands feel appreciated, enter into their world and participate in the bedroom, spouses will feel emotionally connected with each other. Not only will Love Connection be strong, but couples will also have the added motivation and strength to not even come close to crossing the line of infidelity.

---

[141] Neuman, G. (2008). *The truth about cheating: Why men stray and what you can do to prevent it.* Hoboken, NJ: John Wiley & Sons, Inc. 17.

Affairs Do Not Happen Overnight

Rarely does an affair develop over night. *The Chicago Tribune* reported that 73% of straying men and 42% of women who cheat meet their extramarital partner at their workplace.[142] Guess what? In America, as of 2009, more women are now working than men.[143] In Singapore, the number of women in the workforce has doubled since 1970.[144] What does that tell us? We must be on our guard—opportunities for temptation are higher now than ever before.

It starts with another person giving you attention, or with you doing something innocent. You wouldn't do anything wrong, *per se*, just have lunch together, or grab a quick cup of coffee, or go window-shopping. Perhaps for the sake of work, you travel together, and over time, chemistry develops. This chemistry absolutely will chip away at the bond you have with your spouse. If you find yourself in this situation, make a decision right now to re-channel your energy into your own marriage! Build Love Connection with your spouse, not with another person.

How does it feel to be caught up in an "emotional affair"? You think about the other person frequently. You long to be with them. You manoeuvre ways to see them or to be with them. You fantasise about them. You are extra polite with them, and eventually, you start sending them affectionate text messages and e-mails. While all this is happening, you become more critical of your spouse, spend less time at home, engage in sex less often with your spouse, and begin shirking responsibilities at home. All this usually happens over some time; it does not happen overnight.[145]

Here are some guidelines to avoid developing any form of emotional attachment at the workplace:
a. Avoid travelling alone with any colleague for whom you could have the slightest attraction. Tell your boss that you and your spouse would not

---

[142] Barnes, S. (1999). Immunized against infidelity: Want to avoid divorce? Then learn how to be faithful. *Chicago Tribune*. Retrieved Dec 16, 2009, from http://www.preventingaffairs.com
[143] Rampell, C. (2009, May 5). As layoffs surge, women may pass men in job force. *The New York Times*. Retrieved January 28, 2010, from http://www.nytimes.com
[144] Singapore Department of Statistics. (2009, August 13). *Statistics Singapore - Time series on labour force participation rate*. Retrieved January 14, 2010, from http://www.singstat.gov.sg/stats/themes/economy/hist/labour.html
[145] Houston, R. (2002). *Is he cheating on you? 829 telltale signs*. New York: Lifestyle Publications. 26.

feel comfortable about it. Do not underestimate what could come out of such trips. With all good intentions, you may end up having lunch, laughing and having a good time together. If repeated a few more times, you may develop an infatuation with him/her. If you are not able to avoid such travel arrangements, look into going together as a group, or consider bringing your spouse if possible.

b. Avoid having meals alone with your colleague. During lunch breaks, this can be a temptation. When you are with others, it is much more difficult for personal chemistry to develop.

c. Avoid working late nights at the office. When your lifetrap is telling you to work late nights at the expense of time with family or spouse, you are paving the way to develop a harmful relationship with someone else.

d. Avoid time alone with someone who might tempt you during work. Keep your conversation strictly business and if you need to be in an informal setting, do so in groups.

e. Avoid keeping your family life a secret. Tell others plainly that you are married. Have a picture on your desk, on your computer and in your wallet. Let them know how much you value your marriage. If possible, invite colleagues to come to church, and to join you in attending marriage and family workshops, or organise monthly lunch time speakers on family friendly topics. Others will come to respect you if you practise what you preach in this area.

f. Avoid intimate communication via all media such as text messaging, emailing, instant messaging, social networking, etc. Do not make your devices private; do not bar your spouse from looking at them. Computers, social networking sites and cell phones should be joint property in a marriage. If you are resistant in this area, ask yourself, "Why?" Your spouse has every right to know who is getting in touch with you and who is coming in and out of your life. In fact, rather than your spouse having to find things out, volunteer this information when you spend time together. Honesty will go a long way in building your Love Connection (see Chapter 2).

Along with all the above, we want to qualify that we feel that it is healthy to have deep friendships with other people, but it is not wise to spend time alone with those for whom you might have an attraction. One of the most helpful ways to improve your marriage is to let other married couples into your lives. Develop deep relationships with them. Learn from them. Be inspired by how they interact with each other. Allow them to give you advice and guide you. It makes a difference when you have other couples in your lives that are able to be there when you and your spouse are not getting along. Their input and love can help to pull you out of the Mutual Affection times, or even the Disintegration phase; just don't build dangerous friendships.

Since infidelity is so common, it may be necessary for you to do some homework yourself. Ruth Houston's research is based on interviews with people who figured out in hindsight the signals that they had not picked up on earlier. She feels that if people can be educated on the subject, they might be able to prevent a marriage disaster. Her message is: Don't pretend that it will turn out fine. You may be the last person to find out. Don't turn a blind eye. Your marriage and family are at stake. Act on your hunches, but with respect and honesty.[146] For more information, visit her website at infidelityadvice.com.

Having said all of this, please bear in mind that if your primary lifetrap is one or a combination of the following: mistrust, abandonment, emotional deprivation or defectiveness, you may be suspicious for no reason. There is a difference between a correct "gut feeling" and getting triggered by your lifetraps. You need to get advice, and walk through this with someone with whom you feel safe before acting on your hunches. Better still, if you are cheating on your spouse, just come out into the open now and be honest. You can't build Love Connection on a foundation of dishonesty. Don't delay any further. Confess your sins to each other:

> *Therefore confess your sins to each other and pray for each other so that you may be healed.* (James 5:16a)

If you have been flirting, come clean. Let your child side speak, not the false self that wants to look good. Talk to your spouse and to a few people whom you trust. Get guidance. Follow the instructions in this book. Make the effort to reignite the fire in your marriage. It is *your* marriage and only *you* can make a difference.

---

[146] Houston, R. (2002). *Is he cheating on you? 829 telltale signs.* New York: Lifestyle Publications. 46.

What If I'm No Longer Attracted to My Spouse?

One excuse that some people make for having an affair is that they have lost all attraction towards their spouse. Granted, there are cases where a husband or wife may have completely let themselves go, and that should be addressed since it probably is a sign of deeper issues. Usually, however, the person who is unhappy is making unfair comparisons that are highly inaccurate.

You may meet many people who are physically more attractive than your spouse, but bear in mind that there are many more important qualities that make a person attractive. (Not to mention that there are probably plenty of people more attractive than you!) The media puts way too much stock on physical beauty. Much more important are warmth, affection, compassion, patience, humility, generosity, and integrity; being responsible, encouraging, gracious, serving, forgiving, joyful, calm, selfless, and a great parent; as well as possessing intellect, wit, spirituality, and love for people. Your spouse has strong points and weak points just like you do, but take him/her as a whole and you will find that you probably married an incredible person! No one is so awesome that they are the best in every area. Such a person resides only in your imagination! Even if they did exist, ask yourself this question, "How would such an amazing person feel about being with you?"

The more important issue is, to what qualities are you attracted? On which areas do you place your focus primarily? Focusing on charm, beauty and wealth is shallow. Hollywood is full of such examples. Typically, how long do their marriages last? We should be grateful for something deeper and longer lasting than beauty and charm. At the end of the day, we want to be married to someone with whom we are able to connect, be intimate, and share heart and soul. The ability to achieve this with someone bears little or no correlation whatsoever with his/her outward appearance. There are absolutely no statistics to show that pretty, handsome and wealthy people have better marriages. It is a fantasy.

If Infidelity Has Occurred, What Next?

If this proves to be true then you will feel ashamed, betrayed, guilty, angry, and anxious, perhaps all of them in a given day. We have seen wives and husbands go through all of these emotions. For some marriages, the affair was the end. For others, it became a turning point. Lessons were learned, forgiveness was granted and changes were made.

No matter what the other spouse did wrong, there is no excuse for an affair. It does not matter. Cheating is always wrong. Period. Here are some guidelines for dealing with an unfaithful spouse as soon as the cheating surfaces:

1. **Confront Your Spouse** – This will be the most difficult conversation that you will have with him/her. There needs to be honesty. If either party is prone to fits of rage, then do it in the presence of someone with whom you can feel safe. Do not assume that the affair will just go away by itself. Nip it in the bud. An early confrontation may save the marriage.

2. **Look for Repentance** – The person who cheated should be very repentant and should extend heartfelt apologies. Sometimes couples learn more from a tragedy than they do at other times. So, this is a time to take stock of the relationship and move forward stronger than before. However, it is dangerous to move forward with someone who does not show remorse, or refuses to admit the truth. Usually it is a sign that he/she does not want to give up the affair, and that he/she has only apologised because he/she feels guilty for hurting his/her spouse, not because he/she is ready to stop cheating. The passage in Psalm 36:1-2 is appropriate to describe such a callous attitude:

    ^{1}An oracle is within my heart
    concerning the sinfulness of the wicked:
    There is no fear of God before his eyes.
    ^{2}For in his own eyes he flatters himself
    too much to detect or hate his sin.

    The guilty partner should not qualify his/her apology with, "I did this because you were…" Nothing will aggravate a betrayed spouse more than the guilty party not taking personal responsibility. At another time, the one who cheated may talk about what he/she would like their partner to change, but this is a separate issue altogether. That talk needs to happen eventually in order to deal with areas that are problematic, but it should not be part of the apology.

The guilty party should also allow his/her partner to express his/her hurt as a result of this affair. This may take time, but it needs to be done. Too often the guilty party wants the confession to be over and done with. There is pain watching someone express the hurt of betrayal, but this process will actually strengthen the healthy side of the betrayer and it will help the victim to forgive.

3. **Find Out Sufficient Details** – Too many details will not be helpful, such as in what ways the other person was more attractive. However, the unfaithful spouse should disclose information such as how they met and how it developed, how many times they interacted and the finances that were involved. This will also help to chart a new course of action to prevent a relapse.

4. **Make Immediate Changes** – If the person involved with your spouse is a colleague from work, then one of them needs to quit their job or change departments. It is radical, but it is probably what is needed to save the marriage. It does not take much for the chemistry to get re-ignited even if the affair is out in the open. If it is someone in the neighbourhood, move. Erase all details about the other person, such as phone numbers, addresses, emails, etc. The affair needs to stop immediately. It will not be convenient. Coming out of an affair will always be difficult. Thereafter, no more contact should be made. Touch no more, speak no more, hear no more, see no more.

5. **Do Not Fight Alone** – It is essential that another couple is there for you both. Couples with good, supportive friends have a better chance to make it through the painful rebuilding time. The other couple will have an objective view of your relationship and can help you both make the changes that need to be made for healing to take place. This may involve getting professional help. If couples are serious about changing, healing will take place soon, but remorse and cooperation are crucial. Things rarely change if only one side is making the effort. (If this is the case, and you still want to give things a try, then we recommend watching the movie, *Fireproof*, and getting the corresponding book, *The Love Dare*.[147])

---

[147] Kendrick, S., & Kendrick, A. (2008). *The love dare.* Nashville, TN: B & H Publishing Group.

6. **Grant Forgiveness** – The guilty party must be at a point where they can sincerely ask for forgiveness. The hurt party needs to process the entire episode and must forgive his/her partner. Forgiveness is not just about letting go, or forgetting about the incident. It is about going through your anger in a healthy way, combined with sincere forgiveness, rather than suppressing it under the guise of moving forward. (See Chapter 6, *Choose Reconciliation.*)

7. **Take Time to Decide** – Do not be rash. Give your spouse time to reflect. Sometimes it will take a crisis to get your partner to take the marriage seriously. For very self-centred men and women, crisis is the only way. So, allow the crisis to have an effect on him/her. Remember a lot is at stake when you go through a divorce, so do not make a rash decision. As stated earlier, we usually look for remorse. If there is no remorse and a lot of blame-shifting, then it may be time to move towards a separation.

8. **Secure Your Finances** – If you feel that separation is inevitable, engage a lawyer and secure your position. Finances and child custody rarely have straight forward outcomes. The stress that ensues from ugly battles over these two issues is what gives divorce top ranking in mental health stress measurement charts, so please count the cost.

The steps we have outlined above may not happen in exactly the order we have laid out, and the discussions you have will certainly not be smooth sailing. It would be wise to get professional help. You will definitely want to talk in the presence of trusted and safe advisors. And by all means, keep reading—the next chapter is about forgiveness!

Wow, that was heavy, but necessary! The truth is, whether or not we have to talk about any fidelity issues, we definitely need to discuss some things that will need forgiveness on both sides. We've tried saying, "I'm sorry" before but it doesn't always feel resolved. Any suggestions?

CHAPTER 6

CHOOSE RECONCILIATION

When we first got married in 1987, we thought then that the sign of a healthy marriage was very few fights. However, over the years, we have had enough altercations and disputes (not to mention quarrels, spats, and tiffs, but no fisticuffs) to abandon that yardstick. Now we reassure couples that everyone has conflicts, but the important thing is how well we heal from our hurts and wounds, and how well we can learn to meet each other's needs instead of triggering each other.

This does not mean that just because you end with resolution, all kinds of conflict are fine—high-level conflict is harmful to both spouses and to the children.[148] Therefore knowing how to prevent conflict from escalating is essential, but along with that, being able to forgive and repair a relationship is also essential. In fact, being able to truly reconcile after disagreements is proof that we are in, or close to being in, the Love Connection phase.

Since we are all sinners, understanding forgiveness and knowing how to extend it to each other is a very crucial component of a healthy marriage. This is especially true for Christian marriages, seeing as how forgiveness is not exactly optional for followers of Jesus. Yet we have noticed how little emphasis forgiveness is given in major approaches to marriage therapy. Experts and writers come up with all kinds of attending, assessment and intervention skills, but only in rare cases is forgiveness given the attention it deserves.

---

[148] Amato, P. R., & Booth, A. (2001). Parental predivorce relations and offspring postdivorce well-being. *Journal of Marriage and the Family, 63*(1), 197-212.

Sadly, even many Christians do not know the correct biblical definition of forgiveness. We strongly believe that unless it is properly understood and rendered, the possibility of relapse will be high and couples will not grow and change as part of their marital journey together as husband and wife. It is no doubt difficult, but it is essential. When we forgive, the bitterness, resentment, and anger are swept away. The negative emotional energy is gone and is replaced by feelings of light-heartedness, freedom, and peace. Indeed, forgiveness *is* the corner stone for healing in our marriage relationship.

Defining Forgiveness

The scriptures take an unambiguous stand on forgiveness. God allows us to choose to forgive, just like He gives us the choice to accept His grace and come to Him in repentance. In the parable of the lost son, also known as the prodigal son (Luke 15), the father allowed the son to come to his senses of his own accord. The father waited patiently at home, looking at the horizon every day, longing to see his son make his way back in humility. When the son made the first move, the father ran and embraced him! (Luke 15:20) Even with all this compassion waiting to burst from the father's heart, he still gave his son the choice to return. God is the same way. Forgiveness is our choice, but the consequences are grave with regards to our salvation if we choose *not* to forgive:

> [21] Then Peter came to Jesus and asked, "Lord, how many times shall I forgive my brother when he sins against me? Up to seven times?" [22] Jesus answered, "I tell you, not seven times, but seventy-seven times. [23] Therefore, the kingdom of heaven is like a king who wanted to settle accounts with his servants. [24] As he began the settlement, a man who owed him ten thousand talents was brought to him. [25] Since he was not able to pay, the master ordered that he and his wife and his children and all that he had be sold to repay the debt.
>
> [26] "The servant fell on his knees before him. 'Be patient with me,' he begged, 'and I will pay back everything.' [27] The servant's master took pity on him, cancelled the debt and let him go. [28] But when that servant went out, he found one of his fellow servants who owed him a hundred denarii. He grabbed him and began to choke him. 'Pay back what you owe me!' he demanded. [29] His fellow servant fell to his knees and begged

> him, 'Be patient with me, and I will pay you back.' ³⁰But he refused. Instead, he went off and had the man thrown into prison until he could pay the debt. ³¹When the other servants saw what had happened, they were greatly distressed and went and told their master everything that had happened. ³²Then the master called the servant in. 'You wicked servant,' he said, 'I cancelled all that debt of yours because you begged me to. ³³Shouldn't you have had mercy on your fellow servant just as I had on you?' ³⁴In anger his master turned him over to the jailers to be tortured, until he should pay back all he owed. ³⁵This is how my heavenly Father will treat each of you unless you forgive your brother from your heart." (Matthew 18:21-35)

The last verse in the section above (verse 35) lets us know that God is not just *making a suggestion* when He tells us to forgive. For Christians, it seems that our salvation is linked to whether or not we have forgiven others.

Here are two more passages that are crucial to our understanding of forgiveness:

> ²¹You have heard that it was said to the people long ago, "Do not murder, and anyone who murders will be subject to judgment." ²²But I tell you that anyone who is angry with his brother will be subject to judgment. Again, anyone who says to his brother, "Raca," is answerable to the Sanhedrin. But anyone who says, "You fool!" will be in danger of the fire of hell. ²³Therefore, if you are offering your gift at the altar and there remember that your brother has something against you, ²⁴leave your gift there in front of the altar. First go and be reconciled to your brother; then come and offer your gift. (Matthew 5:21-24)

> ³⁷Do not judge, and you will not be judged. Do not condemn, and you will not be condemned. Forgive, and you will be forgiven. (Luke 6:37)
> ¹⁴Make every effort to live in peace with all men and to be holy; without holiness no one will see the Lord. ¹⁵See to it that no one misses the grace of God and that no bitter root grows up to cause trouble and defile many. (Hebrews 12:14-15)

When defining forgiveness, researchers make a distinction between the genuine and the superficial. Dr Robert Enright and Dr Everett Worthington are among the foremost experts on forgiveness in North America.

Dr Worthington writes:

> In genuine forgiveness, one who has suffered an unjust injury chooses to abandon his or her right to resentment and retaliation, and instead offers mercy to the offender.[149]

Dr Enright tells us:

> People, upon rationally determining that they have been unfairly treated, forgive when they wilfully abandon resentment and related responses (to which they have a right), and endeavour to respond to the wrongdoer based on the moral principle of beneficence, which may include compassion, unconditional worth, generosity, and moral love (to which the wrongdoer, by nature of the hurtful act or acts, has no right).[150]

Using both these definitions, combined with the Scriptures on forgiveness, we can accurately say that forgiveness is made up of several components:

> 1. We are aware that the offense was unfair.
> 2. We acknowledge that we have the right to respond with anger.
> 3. We give up the right to revenge and retaliation that may cause injury to the offender because God has done that for us.
> 4. We replace the feelings of resentment with compassion, benevolence and love, the way God has done for us through the death of His Son, Jesus Christ.

Dr Enright goes on to say that when people have successfully forgiven someone, they have reduced or eliminated negative feelings, thoughts and behaviours toward the offender. Instead those who forgive have developed:

- Positive *feelings* toward the offender
- Positive *behaviour* toward the offender
- Positive *thoughts* toward the offender.[151]

---

[149] Worthington, E. L., Jr. (1998). *Dimensions of forgiveness: Psychological research & theological perspectives.* Radnor, PA: Templeton Foundation Press. 140.

[150] Enright, R. D., & Fitzgibbons, R. P. (2000). *Helping clients forgive.* Washington, DC: American Psychological Association. 29.

[151] Enright, R. D. (2001). *Forgiveness is a choice.* Washington, DC: American Psychological Association. 34.

(We like to substitute the counselling words "affect" for feelings, and "cognition" for thoughts, thus giving us Affect, Behaviour, and Cognition, the ABC's of Forgiveness.)

Forgiveness vs. Reconciliation

According to Enright, forgiveness is *not* condoning the offender's actions, excusing the offender's actions, justifying the offender's actions, or just calming down.[152]

Forgiveness is also not necessarily the same thing as reconciliation. As Dr Enright has put it:

> Reconciliation is the act of two people coming together following separation. Forgiving, on the other hand, is the moral action of one individual that starts as a private act, an unseen decision within the human heart.[153]

Reconciliation involves both parties coming together, both rendering forgiveness and asking for forgiveness. Both parties are willing to still continue in a relationship with each other. However if one party feels unsafe being in a relationship with the other party who is not remorseful over his/her actions, then the injured party, after forgiving, may decide to not get reconciled and have only a limited relationship with the other party. For reconciliation to take place, there must be forgiveness beforehand. It cannot take place unless forgiveness is rendered. However, one can forgive without getting reconciled.

We may stay away from unsafe, unrepentant and unremorseful individuals or groups, even after forgiving. We may decide to never see these people again, or to limit our interaction with them. Having said that, Jesus taught clearly about what to do when we have unity problems, as seen in Matthew 5:23-26 and Matthew 18:15-18. In addition, the Bible commands that we make every effort to live at peace with all men (Romans 12:16, 18), accept one another as the Lord accepts us (Romans 15:7), and forgive and bear with one another as God bears with all of us (Colossians 3:13), so holding back from reconciling is not to be taken lightly!

---

[152] Enright, R. D. (2001). *Forgiveness is a choice*. Washington, DC: American Psychological Association. 28–30.
[153] Enright, R. D. (2001). *Forgiveness is a choice*. Washington, DC: American Psychological Association. 31.

Our point—when it comes to having a healthy, satisfying marriage that builds Love Connection, both forgiveness and reconciliation are essential. To give you encouragement, here are some findings about how forgiveness can positively affect your marriage and your mental health.

- A recent study done by Paleari, Regalia and Fincham has shown that forgiveness is directly related to marital quality. The higher the level of forgiveness, the higher the marital quality.[154]
- Fincham also concluded that forgiveness and marital satisfaction were related. He went on to show that forgiveness affects the overall behaviour of a spouse towards the partner, and that it is not independent of marital satisfaction.[155]
- Orathinkal and Vansteenwegen did studies among married couples in Belgium and concluded that forgiveness and marital satisfaction are linked.[156]
- Unforgiveness is shown to correlate highly with anger,[157] which in turn has been linked to decreased immune functioning.[158]
- Activity in the brain during unforgiveness is consistent with brain activity during stress, anger and aggression. Unforgiveness might have a neurophysical basis as an emotion.[159]
- Seybold et al. examined physical markers in patients at a Veteran Administration Medical Centre and found that people who were chronically unforgiving had blood chemistry assays that were similar to those of people under stress.[160]

---

[154] Paleari, F. G., Regalia, C., & Fincham, F. D. (2005). Marital quality, forgiveness, empathy, and rumination: A longitudinal analysis. *Journal of Social Behaviour and Personality, 3*, 368-378.

[155] Fincham, F. D. (2000). The kiss of porcupines: From attributing responsibility for forgiving. *Personal Relationships, 9*, 239-251.

[156] Orathinkal, J., & Vansteenwegen, A. (2006). The effect of forgiveness on marital satisfaction in relationship to marital stability. *Contemporary Family Therapy, 28*, 251-260.

[157] Berry, J. W., & Worthington, E. L., Jr. (2001). Forgiveness, relationship quality, stress while imagining relationship events, and physical and mental health. *Journal of Counseling Psychology, 48*, 447-455.

[158] Herbert, T., & Cohen, S. (1993). Stress and immunity in humans: a meta-analytical review. *Psychosomatic Medicine, 55*, 364-379.

[159] Pietrini, P., Guazzelli, M., Basso, G., Jaffe, K., & Grafman, J. (2000). Neural correlates of imaginal aggressive behavior assessed by positron emission tomography in healthy subjects. *The American Journal of Psychiatry, 157*, 1772-1781.

[160] Seybold, K. S., Hill, P. C., Neumann, J. K., & Chi, D. S. (2001). Physiological and psychological correlates of forgiveness. *Journal of Psychology and Christianity, 20*, 250-259.

- Testing blood pressure and heart rates, Lawler et al. found that high trait forgivers showed the least cardiovascular reactivity and best recovery patterns, whereas low trait forgivers in unforgiving states showed the highest levels of reactivity and poorest recovery patterns.[161] Unforgiving people put their health in harm's way by inducing stress and impairing heart recovery each time they are triggered by thoughts of unforgiveness. On the other hand, forgiving people quell these responses by nurturing forgiving thoughts.
- Lack of forgiveness has shown a strong correlation with anxiety in developmentally appropriate contexts of hurt (e.g., college students hurt by friends or romantic partners; parents hurt by children; spouses hurt by infidelity).[162]
- On the other hand, there is positive correlation between forgiveness and measures of well-being.[163] In other words, the more forgiving a person is, the less anxiety, depression and/or anger will remain, even after experiencing a great deal of hurt.

When we don't forgive, the stakes are high. It affects our mental health, our marriage relationships and most importantly, our salvation. When we do not forgive the party that has hurt us, we are not "punishing" them, rather, we are actually putting ourselves in harm's way.

---

[161] Lawler, K. A., Younger, J. W., Piferi, R. L., et al. (2003). A change of heart: cardiovascular correlates of forgiveness in response to interpersonal conflict. *Journal of Behavioral Medicine, 26*, 373-393.

[162] Fitzgibbons, R. P. (1986). The cognitive and emotive use of forgiveness in the treatment of anger. *Psychotherapy, 23*, 629-633; Park, Y., & Enright, R. D. (1997). The development of forgiveness in the context of adolescent friendship conflict in Korea. *Journal of Adolescence, 20*, 393-402; Subkoviak, M. J., Enright, R. D., & Wu, C. (1992, October). *Current developments related to measuring forgiveness.* Paper presented at the annual meeting of the Midwestern Educational Research Association, Chicago, IL.; Subkoviak, M. J., Enright, R. D., Wu, C., Gassin, E. A., Freedman, S., Olson, L. M., & Sarinopoulos, I. C. (1995). Measuring interpersonal forgiveness in late adolescence and middle adulthood. *Journal of Adolescence, 18*, 641-655.

[163] Coyle, C. T., & Enright, R. D. (1997). Forgiveness intervention with postabortion men. *Journal of Consulting and Clinical Psychology, 65*, 1042-1046; Sarinopoulos, I. C. (1996). *Forgiveness in adolescence and middle adulthood: Comparing the Enright Forgiveness Inventory with Wade Forgiveness Scale.* University of Wisconsin-Madison.

Process Your Anger, Guilt and Shame

We now have a working understanding of forgiveness and its importance. What could possibly stand in our way of being ready to forgive? Sometimes it is related to anger, guilt and shame. We have found that, after analysing these feelings, most people are able to start the forgiveness process..

Shame is the uncomfortable or painful feeling that we experience when we realise that a part of us is defective, bad, incomplete, rotten, phony, inadequate or a failure.[164] Enright goes on to say that shame is also the fear of what others will think when they find out what has happened to us.[165]

Guilt is when we feel bad about doing something wrong. Guilt comes from *doing* something, but shame comes from *being* something wrong or being bad.[166] Healthy guilt encompasses feeling guilty when you steal, lie, deceive or cause injury to others. Unhealthy guilt is the feeling you get when something is not actually your fault. For example, in the case of a youngster being sexually abused, just because he/she tolerated it and may have even inadvertently felt some pleasure, the child feels guilty. This is unhealthy.

In order to escape one or both kinds of guilt and shame, some people harden their consciences to the point that they do not feel any guilt. The apostle Paul wrote:

> *[1]The Spirit clearly says that in later times some will abandon the faith and follow deceiving spirits and things taught by demons. [2]Such teachings come through hypocritical liars, whose consciences have been seared as with a hot iron.* (1 Timothy 4:1-2)

In John 16:7-9, Jesus taught that the Holy Spirit helps us have the right kind of guilt:

> *[7]But I tell you the truth: It is for your good that I am going away. Unless I go away, the Counsellor will not come to you; but if I go, I will send him to you. [8]When he comes, he will convict the world of guilt in regard to sin and righteousness and judgment: [9]in regard to sin, because men do not believe in me…*

---

[164] Whitfield, C. L. (2006). *Healing the child within*. Deerfield Beach, FL: Health Communications, Inc. 44.
[165] Enright, R. D. (2001). *Forgiveness is a choice*. Washington, DC: American Psychological Association. 111.
[166] Whitfield, C. L. (2006). *Healing the child within*. Deerfield Beach, FL: Health Communications, Inc. 44.

Unhealthy guilt is often associated with people who have the surrendered coping style, who tend to think that most conflicts are usually a result of their own fault, or who feel guilty when someone does not have positive feelings towards them. For example, when they point out a wrong to a friend, and that friend becomes angry and defensive, surrendered types feel bad for having spoken up. Their self-sacrificing or subjugation lifetraps kick in and they feel guilty.

Another example of unhealthy guilt would be if someone feels guilty for not reaching a certain standard that was imposed on to him/her by others. Sometimes people with the unrelenting standards lifetrap do this to those who are close to them. In such cases, unhealthy guilt develops easily.

Healthy shame comes, for example, when someone's lies get exposed, or their deeds are exposed, or their dark side that causes harm to others is revealed. In such times, it is healthy to feel shame. Such shame is able to produce remorse and repentance. An extreme example of this is when a person is put out of fellowship from the church or disciplined appropriately, in which case he/she *should* feel ashamed, as Paul wrote to the church in Thessalonica:

> [14]*If anyone does not obey our instruction in this letter, take special note of him. Do not associate with him, in order that he may feel ashamed.* [15]*Yet do not regard him as an enemy, but warn him as a brother.* (2 Thessalonians 3:14-15)

Then there are those who do not experience any shame at all, such as those written about by the prophet Jeremiah:

> [13]*"From the least to the greatest, all are greedy for gain;*
> *prophets and priests alike, all practice deceit.*
> [14]*They dress the wound of my people as though it were not serious.*
> *'Peace, peace,' they say, when there is no peace.*
> [15]*Are they ashamed of their loathsome conduct?*
> *No, they have no shame at all;*
> *they do not even know how to blush.*
> *So they will fall among the fallen;*
> *they will be brought down when I punish them,"*
> *says the LORD.* (Jeremiah 6:13-15)

As it is with guilt and shame, anger can also be healthy and unhealthy. Not all anger is wrong. Anger can be healthy, if it is controlled and infrequent. Anger helps us to sense injustice and helps us to respond to inappropriate behaviour. It helps us to react quickly before any further harm takes place. It sends out the right signals, if harnessed properly. In Ephesians 4:26-27, Paul wisely wrote:

> [26] "In your anger do not sin"; Do not let the sun go down while you are still angry, [27] and do not give the devil a foothold.

We are taught in the Scriptures to not sin in our anger. It is how we deal with anger that determines whether it is harmful or not. In other words, anger becomes a problem when we cope with it in an unhealthy way. Usually, we cope with it in one of three ways, using one of the three coping styles, mentioned in Chapter 3, *Choose Awareness*. In processing your anger, you might find it helpful to take the following steps:

a. In the Anger Journal below, write down the significant hurts that you have experienced with which you may not have properly dealt as of yet. Write down the names of the person(s) involved and how he/she/they have hurt you. Start with the person with whom you are most angry and fill up the first two columns in the table below.

b. Write down how you coped with your anger. Which of the three coping styles do you tend to use? Surrendered, avoidant or counterattacking? Select one of the following as you fill in the table below.

Anger Journal

Who Hurt You?	How Did He/She Hurt You?	How Did You Cope With This Anger?

Take your time to do this exercise.

c. Match the level of your anger with the wrong that was committed. Rate your anger from 1-10, with 1 being "not at all forgiving" / "very angry", and 10 being "very forgiving" / "not at all angry".

Not at all forgiving / very angry	1	2	3	4	5	6	7	8	9	10	Very forgiving / not at all angry

d. Match the level of seriousness of the wrong that was committed, with 1 being "he publicly humiliated and shamed me deliberately", to 10 being "very mild", for example, "he was accidentally insensitive". For the sake of objectivity, you may need a trusted friend or a professional to help you with this.

Publicly humiliated & shamed	1	2	3	4	5	6	7	8	9	10	Very mild

e. Is there a huge gap in your ratings of the last two scales?

f. What triggered your anger? How much of it had to do with your shame (defectiveness lifetrap) being triggered? Was it a result of guilt? Think back to that event. Try and be objective about two issues—your perception of how were treated, (which may or may not have been exaggerated) and the actual reality. Use the scale below and make the comparison, with 1 being "no grace" / "full of shame & guilt", and 10 being "full of grace" / "no shame or guilt whatsoever". Again, you may need someone's help to make a better assessment of the reality of how you were shamed or abused, as often our perception can be distorted because of our lifetraps.

Your perception

No grace / full of shame or guilt	1	2	3	4	5	6	7	8	9	10	Full of grace / no shame or guilt

Reality

No grace / full of shame or guilt	1	2	3	4	5	6	7	8	9	10	Full of grace / no shame or guilt

Is there a difference between the two levels? If so, why? The larger the difference, the stronger your lifetrap is. What lifetrap(s) got triggered, in your opinion, in the above incident?

g. Begin with the incident above or an issue over which you still have resentment. Does this incident remind you of any childhood event? What is that event? What are the similarities?

_____

_____

Is there a pattern in your anger from childhood until the present time?

h. Toward whom is your anger generally directed? For example, is it towards people whom you perceived to have shamed or abused you, such as authority figures in your life?

i. Looking at the issue again, do you think you have behaved inappropriately towards the individual who has hurt you, or even to yourself? If so, how was your behaviour inappropriate? Again, to fill this out accurately, talk to a trusted friend to get an objective view.

People who tend to be overcompensators project past feelings of shame and guilt onto the person who offended them. Although there may be fault on their part, there can be an exaggeration of or an overreaction to the offender's crime. People who surrender and avoid, on the other hand, *under react* and minimise the hurts and injury. How have you acted? Have you overreacted or underreacted?

j. Do you feel guilty about your inappropriate behaviour?

k. How much energy in a given day has been channelled to this hurt? If a day is made up of 100%, what percentage of your day is taken up thinking, reflecting and ruminating about this same hurt? _____ %

l. How much bitterness and resentment do you have about this hurt? Rate it, with 1 being "no forgiveness" / "very bitter & resentful" and 10 being "totally forgiving" / "not at all bitter & resentful". Have a trusted friend help you make an objective assessment, since we sometimes deny having any resentments or bitterness towards the person who hurt us.

Not forgiving / very bitter & resentful	1	2	3	4	5	6	7	8	9	10	Very forgiving / not at all bitter & resentful

m. How happy and fulfilled are you with this level of bitterness and resentment?

n. How have you been treating the person who has angered you?
    - Unkindly?
    - Taking revenge in small ways?
    - Giving a cold shoulder?
    - Gossiping?

o. What lifetraps got triggered as a result of this hurt? For example, you may have been abused, in which case, the mistrust lifetrap may have been triggered and you are not looking at people the same way. Rather, you are now suspicious of all people and that lifetrap is very active in your life. Perhaps the defectiveness lifetrap is rearing its ugly head, because you were shamed in the past, and you are looking at yourself in a distorted and unhealthy way. So, what lifetraps have been triggered and how do you see yourself and others?

Forgiveness can *weaken* your lifetraps, and change your view of yourself and others for the better. Forgiveness can also change your coping styles, and weaken them. Forgiveness frees us from the prison of resentment and bitterness. How wonderful!

Steps to Help Couples Forgive Each Other

At the end of the day, you may identify all the needs that have not been met, gain all the insights about your lifetraps and childhood, and know how to be vulnerable instead of reacting with your unhealthy coping styles, but unless there is proper forgiveness and reconciliation, your marriage will not completely heal. Perhaps after reading the section on forgiveness, you may realise that you have not forgiven your spouse on an issue.

So it is important to go through these steps, take your time, and do this properly and thoroughly. Allowing your hurts to remain will lead to resentment and bitterness. Instead, rid your heart of all bitterness and truly forgive and get reconciled. This is challenging, no doubt. It takes putting your ego aside, and being humble. It is this step that will bring peace, tranquillity and hope back into your marriage, leading you to Love Connection.

In our experience, forgiveness begins with an understanding of God's grace. However, it doesn't always end there. Forgiving and reconciling with our spouse often involves listening and empathy as well. The first part of our explanation is centred on listening, processing, and empathising.

In attempting to sort out your unresolved conflict or an issue that you have had a hard time forgiving, remember the goal is not to *win* the argument, but to be reconciled. Do not get angry because a past issue is being brought up again. Below are the steps to help you both forgive and reconcile with each other.

1. Listen to Each Other's Pain

After processing your anger, explain your pain, in the presence of other trusted friends, to the person with whom you would like to get reconciled (for the purpose of this book, your spouse). The goal of this step is to develop empathy for each other, the foundation for forgiveness. Do this in a *vulnerable* way, as explained in Chapter 4, not by being counterattacking, or avoidant or surrendered. When we are vulnerable, healing will take place. When we use our coping styles (as explained in Chapters 3 and 4), healing will not take place. For specifics on this step, refer to Appendix 8, *Exercise to Develop Empathy*.

When we acknowledge each other's pain, it communicates understanding and empathy, and this has a way of dissolving our anger if it is done well. So saying in your own words how the other person felt, by putting yourself in his/her shoes, goes a long way in helping people to be reconciled. If you have a genuine problem showing empathy, even after doing the exercises in Appendix 8, then pastoral counselling or professional help should be sought.

2. Take Personal Responsibility

In almost all marriage counselling sessions, each spouse blames the other. Everyone thinks it is the other person's fault. While not necessarily always a 50-50 split between each marriage partner, it is fruitless to spend time analysing who is more at fault. Even if one partner is responsible for 95% of the conflict, the other must still see their 5% part in the whole process. It is also not helpful to wait for the person who contributed to the conflict more to initiate reconciliation. It takes maturity for both to work on their respective part of the conflict simultaneously. Sometimes this takes the intervention of a third party or another couple with whom both feel safe. (In the case of adultery or domestic violence, the guilty party must take 100% responsibility first for going into such forbidden territory. Only after that, at another time, can the offended or abused party be expected to even think about taking personal responsibility for his/her own issues.)

As you understand each other's viewpoint better, focus on what you did that was not helpful and how you contributed to the conflict, and acknowledge that. This takes humility, and putting your ego aside. It might help you to write in a journal about your contribution to the conflict. If you have a problem seeing what your faults are, get help from a friend. There should be a sense of remorse on your part for the contribution you made to the conflict.

3. Prepare and State Each Other's Healing Statements

Sometimes, reading out each other's pain and acknowledging personal responsibility is not enough to help the couple let go of their hurts and anger. In this case, ask each other what statements or acknowledgements would help the other person to feel healed. This may give rise to another conflict, but it is important that both sides do not label each other. Simply state what healing statements would be helpful for you to hear your spouse say. Each partner should write these things down in their journal. Then in a non-demeaning way and without any anger in the tone of voice, they should make these statements with sincerity and with gentleness.

Both sides should develop the humility needed to admit to hurting each other. Bear in mind that healing statements are not to be confused with restitution, or any condition that should be demanded before forgiveness could be rendered. Healing statements help each other feel the empathy and the personal responsibility of the other person. We need to feel that the other person takes personal responsibility and understands our pain, since in a marriage, we are moving beyond forgiveness to reconciliation. We are choosing to get reconciled, not just to forgive.

4. Prepare for Forgiveness and Reconciliation

Each partner should ask, "Am I now willing to forgive my spouse?", remembering the definition of forgiveness. Go back and read it again if necessary. If you are not ready to forgive, then ask yourself, "Why am I not willing to forgive my spouse?" Explore the following:

- My spouse has not conveyed proper understanding of his/her responsibility or was minimising.
- My spouse was too dismissive of my past childhood hurts and wounds.
- The lifetrap of punitiveness is interfering and is "asking" for some kind of punishment to be inflicted on my spouse.
- I have not had time to really deal with the pain and emotion of my childhood hurts.
- My coping style of avoidance is taking over and I do not want to feel the pain again.
- My ego is getting in the way. It is too hard for me to say, "I forgive". It may be that I want restitution first. (If this is the case, then it ceases to be forgiveness. Forgiveness is a voluntary act and is unconditional, not based on any restitution. Any act of benevolence resulting from this should be from the partner's own choice, not as a condition that is imposed.)
- I have not had time to do the homework outlined above.

5. Signs of Forgiveness and Unforgiveness

When a person is not willing to forgive, others will be able to tell. Usually their demeanour gives them away: lack of eye contact, angry expressions on the face, making demands for restitution or insisting that the other party initiate. If this is the case, then more work is needed. Some helpful books: *Forgiveness Is a Choice*[167] by Dr Robert Enright, and *Dimensions of*

---

[167] Enright, R. D. (2001). *Forgiveness is a choice*. Washington, DC: American Psychological Association.

Forgiveness[168] by Dr Everett Worthington. Remember that when forgiveness is extended, your negative feelings, thoughts and actions will be replaced by positive ones. Consider the following questions:

- Are your thoughts more positive now compared to before?
- Is there anger now when you think about the incident?
- When you tell the story, do your emotions come up like it just happened yesterday?
- Are you beginning to wish the person well? As Lewis Smede wrote, "You will know that forgiveness has begun when you recall those who hurt you and feel the power to wish them well."[169]
- If something negative happened to him/her, how would you really feel deep inside your heart?
- Are you willing to explore where you are at present in the forgiveness process? A very helpful tool is the Enright Forgiveness Inventory (EFI). The scores in the subscales will give you insight into which part of the forgiveness process needs more of your attention.[170]

If you feel that you have not forgiven or are having difficulty, then you may have your own *distorted* definition of forgiveness.

Write down your definition of forgiveness.

In my opinion, forgiveness is: _____

_____

Compare this with the definition at the beginning of this chapter. How are they different or similar?

Similar:

_____

_____

---

[168] Worthington, E. L. (1998). *Dimensions of forgiveness: Psychological research & theological perspectives.* Radnor, PA: Templeton Foundation Press.

[169] Smede, L. B. (1984). *Forgive and forget. Healing the hurts we don't deserve.* New York: Pocket Books. 29.

[170] Enright, R. D., & Rique, J. *Enright forgiveness inventory: The measurement tool of choice in forgiveness research.* Retrieved May 2, 2010, from http://www.mindgarden.com

Different:

_____

_____

Perhaps after getting hurt and having faced many injustices, your definition has changed. Perhaps your definition has been based on incorrect understanding. Either way, take stock of your previous definition and make the appropriate shift in your thinking. We need to get our definition right because God takes our unforgiveness seriously.

One exercise that might help you to be able to forgive your spouse is to reflect on a time in the past when you received forgiveness from another:

a. Who was the person offended by you?
b. What did you do to offend him/her?
c. What was your reaction initially? Did you see your contribution in the conflict?
d. What made you see your responsibility in the conflict?
e. How did the offended party react?
f. How did you apologise at that time and show empathy?
g. How did he/she feel about your apology?
h. What did they do to show that they had forgiven you?
i. Did you also get reconciled (as opposed to just stopping at forgiveness)?
j. What did that reconciliation look like to you?
k. How did that make you feel toward him/her?
l. How did being forgiven make you feel? What emotions were there?
m. Repeat this exercise thinking about someone else who forgave you.
n. Does thinking about being forgiven help you to forgive?
o. Would you like for your spouse to feel the way you felt towards the person who forgave you?
p. Are you now willing to forgive? If so, you are now able to offer the same gift to your spouse.[171] If so, proceed to Step 6 below.

---

[171] Worthington, E. L. (1999). *Hope-focused marriage counseling.* Downers Grove, IL: InterVarsity Press. 141.

6. Reconciliation Brings Love Connection
When you are ready to forgive, you and your spouse should:
- Sit facing each other
- Hold hands
- Make eye contact
- Say aloud to each other, "I forgive you"
- Record in a journal the time and place when this took place
- Record what each other said—the exact statements
- Record how you both felt when forgiveness was rendered. Jot down all the positive emotions, e.g., joy, peace, tranquillity, love, freedom.

It might also help to reassure each other that you both shall work hard to not hurt each other again, though you both will not be perfect in this area. For many of us, we do get triggered and sometimes the same issues come up again and again. In such times, and in a vulnerable way, it would be helpful to refer back to the journal to help remember when forgiveness was rendered on the same issue.

If you are not willing to let the negative thoughts go, then you are not ready to forgive. The stakes are high if you do not forgive, so make all the effort needed to get there.

Forgiveness is essential in getting reconciled. Forgiveness must come first. The rewards of forgiveness and reconciliation cannot be overestimated. People who forgive and who feel forgiven feel at peace, valued, accepted, grateful, and free. Indeed the truth does set you free, though the journey can be challenging and painful. You are to be commended for making the effort to reignite the fire of your marriage through Love Connection.

EPILOGUE

IN CONCLUSION

In conclusion, "I Choose Us" is all about Love Connection. We believe that after we have left behind the wild forest fires of the Infatuation phase, we must make the effort to constantly stoke the fires of Love Connection.

We must start with love and respect, which will involve the husbands improving in the areas of being considerate listeners, responsible leaders, and romantic lovers. Wives will try to appreciate their husbands more, initiate and enter into their husbands' worlds better, and take care to participate in the bedroom.

Of course, we will get hung up from time to time, depending on our lifetraps, and when that happens, we will need to get in touch with our child side by being vulnerable with each other, avoiding the vortex of conflict escalation! We have been honest with each other about fidelity in our relationship, even when it was painful.

At the end of the day, we know we are forgiven by God, and we will do what it takes to forgive and be reconciled with our husband or wife. And in our twilight years, after decades of Love Connection with our spouse, we will be happy that we took the time to say to each other, "I Choose Us".

APPENDIX 1
DIVORCE STATISTICS

Percentage of New Marriages which End in Divorce, in Selected Countries (2002)[172]

Country	Divorces (as % of marriages)
Sweden	54.9
Belarus	52.9
Finland	51.2
Luxembourg	47.4
Estonia	46.7
Australia	46.0
United States	45.8
Denmark	44.5
Belgium	44.0
Austria	43.4
Czech Republic	43.3
Russia	43.3
United Kingdom	42.6
Norway	40.4
Ukraine	40.0
Iceland	39.5
Germany	39.4
Lithuania	38.9

---

[172] World divorce statistics. (n.d.). *Divorce Magazine*. Retrieved January 13, 2010, from http://www.divorcemag.com/statistics/statsWorld.shtml

Country	Divorces (as % of marriages)
France	38.3
Netherlands	38.3
Hungary	37.5
Canada	37.0
Latvia	34.4
Moldova	28.1
Slovakia	26.9
Portugal	26.2
Switzerland	25.5
Bulgaria	21.1
Slovenia	20.7
Romania	19.1
Poland	17.2
Singapore	17.2
Greece	15.7
Croatia	15.5
Spain	15.2
Israel	14.8
Albania	10.9
Azerbaijan	10.3
Italy	10.0
Georgia	6.6
Armenia	6.0
Turkey	6.0
Bosnia and Herzegovina	5.0
Macedonia	5.0
Sri Lanka	1.5
India	1.1

Source: *Divorce Magazine*. Used with permission.

APPENDIX 2
DIVORCE IN SINGAPORE

As can be seen in Appendix 1, statistical figures for divorce vary significantly from country to country. While we are grateful that some countries do not have the high number of divorces that other countries do, we know that statistics can be misleading. For example, in some countries, laws make it more difficult to obtain a divorce. In other countries, the social stigma against having a divorce outweighs the pursuit of individual happiness. In other words, marriages are suffering everywhere.

Some countries have a "no-fault divorce" clause, meaning that it takes only one person to end a marriage without having to find any "fault" at all. One can simply say, "I do not want this marriage anymore", or cite any other reason, and the law will take this person's side, regardless of whether the other side objects. Thankfully, no-fault divorce has not yet been allowed in Singapore and in some other countries. Presumably, lawmakers hope that when it is difficult to obtain a divorce, couples will be inclined to take stock of their failing marriages and make more of an effort to work on them.

As for the specifics in Singapore, according to the Women's Charter in Singapore, the courts shall hold the marriage to have broken down irretrievably on one or more of the following grounds:[173]

- that the defendant has committed adultery and the plaintiff finds it intolerable to live with the defendant;
- that the defendant has behaved in such a way that the plaintiff cannot reasonably be expected to live with the defendant;
- that the defendant has deserted the plaintiff for a continuous period of at least two years immediately preceding the filing of the writ;
- that the parties to the marriage have lived apart for a continuous period of at least three years immediately preceding the filing of the writ and the defendant consents to a judgment being granted;
- that the parties to the marriage have lived apart for a continuous period of at least four years immediately preceding the filing of the writ.

---

[173] Singapore Attorney General. *Women's Charter, Part X, Chapter 1: Divorce*. Retrieved March 02, 2010, from Singapore Statutes Online: http://statutes.agc.gov.sg

APPENDIX 3
HOW WORK AFFECTS MARRIAGE

- A collaborative work by Brigham Young University and the Ministry of Community Development, Youth and Sports (2008) in Singapore saw 1,601 people being interviewed by an independent company using questionnaires that consisted of 155 items. These questions explored their family life, marriage and work conditions. A report of this research, written by Dr Blake Jones and several others, showed that flexible conditions had a positive effect not just on their job satisfaction, but also on the individual's life (physical and mental health) and on marital and familial relationships. They also found that even if the flexible work conditions are not utilised by the employees, but simply made available, the perception alone is enough for there to be a positive effect on job satisfaction, personal health, familial and marital ties. Flexibility, as defined by Dr Jones, is:

    > the ability of workers to make choices that influence when, where, and for how long they engage in work-related tasks.[174]

    Work flexibility absolutely affects our marriage in a positive way.

- The Best Buy Corporation located in Minneapolis gives its employees flexibility of time and place to work, on the condition that performance standards are reached. As a result, productivity increases have averaged 10%-20%.[175]
- Drs Sandholtz, Derr, Buckner and Carlson, showed that companies that have taken steps in creating flexibility have reaped dividends of seeing their productivity increase.[176]
- Drs Bolger, Delongis, Kessler and Schilling worked with 166 people and found a positive correlation between arguments at the workplace and

---

[174] Jones, B. L., Scoville, P., Hill, E. J., Childs, G., Leishman, J. M., & Nally, K. S. (2008). Perceived versus used workplace flexibility in Singapore: Predicting work-family fit. *Journal of Family Psychology, 22*(5), 774-783.

[175] Ressler, C., & Thompson, J. (2008). *Why work sucks and how to fix it.* New York: Penguin. 161.

[176] Sandholtz, K., Derr, B., Buckner, K., & Carlson, D. (2002). *Beyond juggling. Rebalancing your busy life.* San Francisco, CA: Berrett-Koehler. 117-121.

arguments at home.[177] The atmosphere of our workplace definitely spills over to affect the atmosphere of our homes.
- Research done by Drs Perry-Jenkins, Repetti, and Crouter showed that people who work evening shifts have higher divorce rates. Work schedule affects marriage.[178]
- Work stress and constant demands predict less marital quality.[179]
- Work-related stress has a direct influence on depression levels,[180] and depressed employees cost companies $44 billion a year in the United States.[181]
- For every $1 spent by the Federal government in the United States to promote healthy marriages and relationships, they also spend $1,000 to deal with the effects of family disintegration.[182] Isn't prevention better than cure?
- Hill et al. reports the significant way in which work affects family in cross cultural tests that were done across 48 countries.[183]
- Out of 384 Fortune 500 companies that offer paternity leave, only 9 have ever received such requests. This is because the men see taking paternity leave either as a sign of weakness or as something that would affect their promotion.[184] It goes without saying that during times such as the birth of a newborn, support from the husband would enhance Love Connection. Ask any wife if she would desire the company of her husband during such times—we would be surprised if the answer were no.

---

[177] Bolger, N., Delongis, A., Kessler, R. C., & Schilling, E. A. (1989). Effects of daily stress on negative mood. *Journal of Personality and Social Psychology, 57*, 808-818.

[178] Perry-Jenkins, M., Repetti, R., & Crouter, A. (2000). Work and family in the 1990s. *Journal of Marriage and the Family, 62*(4), 981-998.

[179] Crouter, A. C., Bumpus, M. F., Head, M. R., & McHale, S. M. (2001). Implications of overwork and overload for the quality of men's family relationships. *Journal of Marriage and the Family, 63*, 404-416.

[180] Vermulst, A., & Dubas, J. (1999). Job stress and family functioning: The mediating role for parental depression and the explaining role of emotional stability. *Tijdschrift voor Psycholigie & Gezonheid, 27*, 96-102.

[181] Stewart, W., Ricci, J., Chee, E., Hahn, S., & Morganstein, D. (2003). Cost of lost productive work time among US workers with depression. *Journal of the American Medical Association, 289*, 3135-3144.

[182] Fagan, P., & Rector, R. (2000). *The effects of divorce in America*. Washington, DC: Heritage Foundation.

[183] Hill, E. J., Yang, C. M., Hawkins, A. J., & Ferris, M. (2004). A cross-cultural test of the work-family interface in 48 countries. *Journal of Marriage and the Family, 66*, 1300-1316.

[184] Curtis, J. (2006). *The business of love*. Maitland, Florida: IOD Press.

APPENDIX 4
MARRIAGE VS. COHABITATION

We believe that God's plan for fidelity in marriage is spelled out clearly and succinctly:

> *For this reason a man will leave his father and mother and be united to his wife, and they will become one flesh.* (Genesis 2:24)
>
> *Marriage should be honored by all, and the marriage bed kept pure, for God will judge the adulterer and all the sexually immoral.* (Hebrews 13:4)

Unfortunately, marriage is getting less honoured these days, as more and more couples are opting for cohabitation over marriage. Cohabitation means that two people live together, basically as husband and wife, but without getting officially married. Many argue passionately that marriage, after all, is just a piece of paper, and that people who are in love should not need to have their love for each other witnessed formally.

However, from a logical point of view, we believe that the piece of paper argument doesn't seem to make sense. After all, when it comes to other serious agreements today, most would find it strange to not enter into a written contract. Would perspective buyers of homes simply settle with a handshake from the sellers about the price and other terms and conditions? Laws of society insist that there be a written agreement. And we believe that marriage is the most important agreement we could possibly enter into with another person during our lifetime. How much more should that sacred institution be written down in the form of a contract? In fact, by not having a formal contract, we believe, and statistics show, that the back door option to leave the partner is that much easier.

Consider the following:

- Cohabitation is not the functional equivalent of marriage. Many people opt for cohabitation because they want to test their relationship before entering into marriage. The average length of a cohabiting relationship is

two years in the UK.[185] The findings reveal that "cohabitees" resembled the less healthy state of affairs of singles more than married couples in the areas of physical health[186], emotional health and mental well-being.[187]
- Children born within an intact marriage are twice as likely to spend their entire childhood with both their parents than those born into a cohabiting union.[188] (In other words, after having children, couples who just live together without getting married are twice as likely to split up than parents who are married to each other.)
- Cohabiting men are more likely to commit infidelity than married men.[189] They are involved in unsafe sex at a slightly higher rate than single men, but at a much higher rate than married men.[190]

Looking at these statistics, one has to assume that, for some couples who are living together without getting married, one partner thinks that they are cohabiting out of a disdain for a piece of paper (why should I seek approval from an otherwise hypocritical society?), while the other partner is enjoying his/her freedom and is not loyal to the commitment that more naturally comes with marriage…

---

[185] Ermisch, J., & Francesconi, M. (1998). *Cohabitation in Great Britain: Not for long, but here to stay.* Institute for Social and Economic Research, University of Essex; Ermisch, J. (1995). *Premarital cohabitation, childbearing and the creation of one-parent families.* ESRC Research Centre on Micro-social Change, Paper Number 95-17.

[186] Pienta, A. M., Hayward, M. D., Jenkins, K. R. (2000). Health consequences of marriage for the retirement years. *Journal of Family Issues, 21*(5), 559-586.

[187] Brown, S. L. (2000). The effect of union type on psychological well-being: Depression among cohabitors versus marrieds. *Journal of Health and Social Behaviour, 41*, 241-255; Horwitz, A. V., & Raskin, H. (1998). The relationship of cohabitation and mental health: A study of a young adult cohort. *Journal of Marriage and the Family, 60*(2), 504-514; Stack, S., & Eshleman, J. R. (1998). Marital status and happiness: A 17-nation study. *Journal of Marriage and the Family, 60*, 527-536; Mastekaasa, A. (1994). The subjective well-being of the previously married: The importance of unmarried cohabitation and time since widowhood or divorce. *Social Forces, 73*, 665-692.

[188] Ermisch, J., & Francesconi, M. (2000). Patterns of household and family formation. In Berthoud, R., & Gershuny, J. (Eds.), *Seven Years in the Lives of British Families.* Bristol: The Policy Press. 21-44.

[189] Waite, L., & Gallagher, M. (2000). *The case for marriage: Why married people are happier, healthier, and better off financially.* New York: Doubleday. 91.

[190] Wellings, K., Field, J., Johnson, A. M., Wadsworth, J. (1994). Sexual behaviour in Britain. London: Penguin. 362-363.

APPENDIX 5
CORE EMOTIONAL NEEDS

Jeffrey Young's Schema Therapy is based on the idea that schemas, or lifetraps, are developed and strengthened to the extent that children's core emotional needs are not met. Schemas are kind of related to each other—they tend to come in groups or clusters. If an individual has one lifetrap, he or she will often have a related lifetrap. In research, these clusters are called "domains". Research has found that Young's schemas cluster into four domains; these four domains correspond to our four core emotional needs. Our research builds on the work of Young, Klosko & Weishaar,[191] and is explained in more detail in our parenting book, *Good Enough Parenting*.[192] We put forward the following research-based needs as a universal list of core emotional needs, applicable in all cultures:

1. Connection and Acceptance
2. Healthy Autonomy and Performance
3. Reasonable Limits
4. Realistic Expectations

We add an extra core emotional need, which we call "the plus one", based on experience and anecdotal evidence: Spiritual Values and Community.

---

[191] Young, J. E., Klosko, J. S., & Weishaar, M. E. (2003). *Schema therapy: A practitioner's guide*. New York: The Guilford Press. 9-10.

[192] Louis, J. P., & Louis, K. M. (2015). *Good enough parenting: An in-depth perspective on meeting core emotional needs and avoiding exasperation*. New York: Morgan James Publishing. 8.

APPENDIX 6
A JOURNAL FOR YOUR LIFETRAPS & COPING STYLES

Date	Who / What Triggered You?	What Lifetrap Was Triggered?	What Was Your Coping Style?

APPENDIX 7
HEALING IMAGERY EXERCISE

(This exercise is only a guide for couples and should not be considered or used as a professional tool.)

This exercise should be done after both partners have completed the lifetrap questionnaire and identified and discussed their lifetraps with each other. As you listen to your partner, it will be important to hear what lifetraps are being triggered.

First settle into a comfortable room where you have privacy and will not be distracted. Set a pleasant mood for yourselves in a way that is most relaxing for you.

Decide who will be the vulnerable partner sharing feelings and who will be the caregiver. It does not necessarily matter who takes the first turn, but one person should be the clear focus of the healing in this exercise.

If the wife goes first, then she should close her eyes and think back to a painful fight in the marriage. The husband should follow the questions in the script below. Speak slowly and softly, and allow her plenty of time to respond. This may not be easy at first, but it will be worth it in the long run.

(In the directions below we have the wife being vulnerable. This is for the purpose of example only—it could be either one of you.)

Step 1: Connecting the Past with the Present
The husband (caregiver) will ask:
- What are you remembering?
- Tell me the details of what is happening.
- Where are we?
- What were we doing before we started fighting?
- What am I saying?
- What are you saying?
- How do you feel when you remember this?
- Where is the tension in your body?

- What does it feel like for you?
- What are you thinking is true about yourself?
- What do you need that is not happening?
- What is familiar about these feelings?
- What does this remind you of?
- How is what is happening when we are in conflict similar to what happened in your childhood?

When your wife has a childhood situation in mind, have her describe what she is remembering. Ask for as much detail as possible—where she is, what the room looks like, where her parents (or siblings or teachers or whoever) are, and especially where she feels tension in her body as she remembers this earlier experience. The more detail she offers, the stronger the memory. It is important to return to the part of the brain where the memory is stored. In this way, the marital conflict fight is re-experienced and can be connected to the early life experience it triggered. This is the place where **healing** can happen.

Next you should invite your wife to share the vulnerable child part of herself, the part that holds both the pain and the capacity for creativity and love in marriage. Be patient and help your wife to feel safe. Encourage her to tune in to her feelings, which can help connect her memories.

This exercise may be most difficult for avoiders as they tend to cut themselves off from their feelings and memories. Surrenderers and overcompensators will have an easier time making the connection between what they are feeling in their marriage today and the core needs that were not met when they were younger.

Step 2: Healing the Inner Child

In the second part of this exercise, work with the childhood memory or memories that your wife has connected with present conflicts in your marriage. Remember, this is an experiential, not an intellectual, exercise. This is about being together in your heart, not in your mind. Your goal is to show empathy, understanding and caring for the hurt your wife felt as a young child.

As you listen to your wife, ask her what she needs. Reassure her that she is important to you. Tell her how much you love her, and offer messages that counteract the negative messages from her childhood. For example, if she suffers with the mistrust lifetrap, she will struggle to believe that you will be kind to her and will care about how she feels in the relationship. Tell her how much you care, how important the relationship is to you. Tell her you are sad when you see her parents (or sibling or teacher or whoever) being mean to her, yelling at her, and not caring about her feelings. Help her to see how things can be different in your marriage, and that you want to make things better for her.

When she is ready, and has finished sharing about the painful childhood experience that your fight reminds her of, thank her for allowing you to know that part of her. Remind her how much you love her, and that you are *not* the one who didn't meet her needs in childhood. Remind her that the message of her lifetrap is not reality, and that things are different (or can be different) with you.

You may repeat this exercise switching roles. You may sometimes need to allow some time before you repeat the exercise if the experience has been very emotional for one or both of you.

Understanding the power of lifetraps and the coping styles we use to respond when they are triggered is a powerful way to create healing and connection in marriage. But as with anything powerful, it is very important to be careful in how you use what you know. Always remember—understanding your partner is a tool and not a weapon. Never use this information against your partner. And please do not hesitate to go for professional help if the issues become too intense.

APPENDIX 8
EXERCISE TO DEVELOP EMPATHY

The partner who has been hurt and/or has the resentment should begin by explaining his/her hurts in a vulnerable way, just like the examples given in Chapter 4. This is why it is important to process your anger ahead of time to help you be vulnerable. After the hurting spouse finishes being vulnerable, the listening partner should provide a summary (rephrasing) of what he/she heard the other person say. The listening partner should continually say, "Is there anything else that you would like me to know?" as opposed to "Are you finished?" or "Why are you taking so long?" The listening partner should do this until the other partner has completed his/her sharing.

Do not minimise your spouse's pain or get angry because a past issue is being brought up again. Do not dismiss your spouse's issues as being trivial. Anger or other emotions may be expressed, but not in a labelling and demeaning manner, putting the other person down. There should be no raising of voices or rage.

One way to gauge this is to ask the spouse listening if the anger is appropriate or not. The partner talking needs to be vulnerable. Do not listen to the voice of your lifetraps, such as avoiding shame or guilt from being vulnerable. It is painful but this is also where the healing begins.

By the end, the listening partner should be able to give an accurate summary of the perspective of the other person. He/she may not gain new insights or may not shift in his/her emotions and develop empathy as yet, but this first step should be done. This part may take a while, especially if it involves revealing different lifetraps, and childhood experiences. This may take time if the conflict has its roots in lifetraps and the couple has never talked about this before with each other.

For some, it may take days or weeks to process your anger and painful childhood memories. Do not hurry or hasten your process unnecessarily for the sake of getting this over and done with. Until you really process your hurts and pain thoroughly, you may not be able to forgive genuinely, and then at another time in the future, you will bring this up again, and the cycle will repeat itself, except that this time it may get worse. Take your time, but work steadily towards understanding each other's situation.

The more you are able to understand and empathise, the more it will help you in the reconciliation process. When you really understand each other's childhood experiences and hurts, you will develop compassion for each other and you will be able to work towards forgiving each other.

Switch places and repeat the above with the other partner. In some situations, the act of doing the above will help each partner see their own respective faults in the conflict. For those unable to empathise or see their own fault, they should proceed with the steps below.

Read the notes of the other spouse's perspective of his/her pain. Empathising does not mean you are accepting complete responsibility. However, it does give you a window to understand your spouse's pain and hurts. Focus on your partner's viewpoint. Mull over it for a few days, if necessary. Here are some questions that may help you improve your feelings of empathy for your spouse:

- What kind of a home did he/she grow up in?
- What kind of childhood did your spouse have?
- How was your spouse treated by his/her parents?
- Are you able to write down the wounds and pains your spouse went through growing up?
- Are you able to see how these have shaped his/her worldview, particularly in the marriage?
- If you have, in anger, labelled your spouse negatively, do you think that he/she deserves that labelling when you consider the larger context of his/her life?

You should then try writing in your journal about the issue from your spouse's viewpoint. This is crucial. By entering your thoughts into a journal, you will be able to reinforce and strengthen your understanding of your spouse's viewpoint. As you do so, do not come across defensive. Simply write down his/her feelings, as if you were in your partner's shoes. When you are able to empathise with your spouse, you will then make a shift in your view of him/her. You will see your partner through a new lens.

REFERENCES

Alexander, R. (2010). *Learning to live as one: A workbook for engaged couples.* Spring Hill, TN: DPI.

Amato, P. R. (1996). Explaining the intergenerational transmission of divorce. *Journal of Marriage and the Family, 58*(3), 628-640.

Amato, P. R. (2000). Consequences of divorce for adults and children. *Journal of Marriage and the Family 62*, 1269-1287.

Amato, P. R., & Booth, A. (1997). *A generation at risk: Growing up in an era of family upheaval.* Cambridge, MA: Harvard University Press.

Amato, P. R., & Booth, A. (2001). Parental predivorce relations and offspring postdivorce well-being. *Journal of Marriage and the Family, 63*(1), 197-212.

Anthony de Mello, S. J. (1990). *Awareness.* New York: Doubleday.

Barnes, S. (1999). Immunized against infidelity: Want to avoid divorce? Then learn how to be faithful. *Chicago Tribune.* Retrieved Dec 16, 2009, from http://www.preventingaffairs.com

Barnett, R. C., Steptoe, A., & Gareis, K. C. (2005). Marital-role quality and stress-related psychobiological indicators. *Annals of Behavioral Medicine, 30*, 36-43.

Berry, J. W., & Worthington, E. L. Jr. (2001). Forgiveness, relationship quality, stress while imagining relationship events, and physical and mental health. *Journal of Counseling Psychology, 48*, 447-455.

Biblarz, T. J. (2000). Family structure and children's success: A comparison of widowed and divorced single-mother families. *Journal of Marriage and the Family, 62*(2), 533-548.

Bolger, N., Delongis, A., Kessler, R. C., & Schilling, E. A. (1989). Effects of daily stress on negative mood. *Journal of Personality and Social Psychology, 57*, 808-818.

Bradshaw, J., & Millar, J. (1991). *Lone parent families in the UK.* Department of Social Security Research Report No 6. London: HMSO.

Brown, S. L. (2000). The effect of union type on psychological well-being: Depression among cohabitors versus marrieds. *Journal of Health and Social Behaviour, 41,* 241-255.

Burghes, L., Clarke, L., & Cronin, N. (1997). *Fathers and fatherhood in Britain.* London: Family Policy Studies Centre.

Cacioppo, J. T., & William, P. (2008). *Loneliness.* New York: W. W. Norton & Company, Inc.

Cawson, P. (2002). *Child maltreatment in the family.* London: NSPCC.

Chapman, G. D. (1992). *The five love languages: The secret to love that lasts.* Chicago, IL: Northfield Publishing.

Clients, not practitioners, make therapy work - British Association for Counselling & Psychotherapy. (2008, October 17). *Medical News Today.* Retrieved May 28, 2010, from http://www.medicalnewstoday.com

Cockett, M., & Tripp, J. (1994). *The Exeter family study: Family breakdown and its impact on children.* Exeter: University of Exeter Press.

Corporate Resource Council. (2002). *Why promote healthy marriages?* [Brochure]. Retrieved January 13, 2010, from http://www.corporateresource council.org/brochures.html

Coughlin, C., & Vuchinich, S. (1996). Family experience in preadolescence and the development of male delinquency. *Journal of Marriage and the Family, 58*(2), 491-501

Coyle, C. T., & Enright, R. D. (1997). Forgiveness intervention with postabortion men. *Journal of Consulting and Clinical Psychology, 65,* 1042-1046.

Crouter, A. C., Bumpus, M. F., Head, M. R., & McHale, S. M. (2001). Implications of overwork and overload for the quality of men's family relationships. *Journal of Marriage and the Family, 63,* 404-416.

Curtis, J. (2006). *The business of love.* Maitland, Florida: IOD Press.

Daly, M., & Wilson, M. (1996). Evolutionary psychology and marital conflict: The relevance of stepchildren. In Buss, D. M., & Malamuth, N. M. (Eds.), *Sex, power, conflict: Evolutionary and feminist perspectives.* Oxford: Oxford University Press.

Deal, L., & Holt, V. (1998). Young maternal age and depressive symptoms: Results from the 1988 national maternal and infant health survey. *American Journal of Public Health, 88*(2), 266-270.

Doherty, W. J., et al. (2002). *Why marriage matters: Twenty-one conclusions from the social sciences.* New York: Institute for American Values.

Eisenberg, M. E., Olson, R. E., Neumark-Sztainer, D., Story, M., & Bearinger, L. H. (2004). Correlations between family meals and psychosocial well-being among adolescents. *Archives of Pediatrics & Adolescent Medicine, 158*(8), 792-796.

Ely, M., West, P., Sweeting, H., & Richards, M. (2000). Teenage family life, life chances, lifestyles and health: A comparison of two contemporary cohorts. *International Journal of Law, Policy and the Family, 14*, 1-30.

Enright, R. D. (2001). *Forgiveness is a choice.* Washington, DC: American Psychological Association.

Enright, R. D., & Fitzgibbons, R. P. (2000). *Helping clients forgive.* Washington, DC: American Psychological Association.

Enright, R. D., & Rique, J. *Enright forgiveness inventory: The measurement tool of choice in forgiveness research.* Retrieved May 2, 2010, from http://www.mindgarden.com

Ermisch, J. (1995). *Premarital cohabitation, childbearing and the creation of one-parent families.* ESRC Research Centre on Micro-social Change, Paper Number 95-17.

Ermisch, J., & Francesconi, M. (1998). *Cohabitation in Great Britain: Not for long, but here to stay.* Institute for Social and Economic Research, University of Essex.

Ermisch, J., & Francesconi, M. (2000). Patterns of household and family formation. In Berthoud, R., & Gershuny, J. (Eds.), *Seven Years in the Lives of British Families.* Bristol: The Policy Press.

Fagan, P., & Rector, R. (2000). *The effects of divorce in America.* Washington, DC: Heritage Foundation.

Family Policy Unit, Ministry of Community Development, Youth and Sports. (2009, October 28). *Executive summary: State of the family in Singapore*. Retrieved January 4, 2010, from http://fcd.ecitizen.gov.sg/NR/rdonlyres/2BD3B979-A48F-4C45-B29E-1CA36068585E/0/ExecutiveSummary.pdf

Fincham, F. D. (2000). The kiss of porcupines: From attributing responsibility for forgiving. *Personal Relationships, 9*, 239-251.

Fisher, H. (2004). *Why we love: The nature and chemistry of romantic love*. New York: Henry Holt and Company, LLC. 8.

Fisher, H. (2009, December 17). Real aphrodisiacs to boost desire. *O, The Oprah Magazine*. Retrieved January 18, 2010 from http://www.oprah.com/relationships/Real-Aphrodisiacs-to-Boost-Desire

Fitzgibbons, R. P. (1986). The cognitive and emotive use of forgiveness in the treatment of anger. *Psychotherapy, 23*, 629-633.

Flood-Page, C., Campbell, S., Harrington, V., & Miller. J. (2000). *Youth crime: Findings from the 1998/99 youth lifestyle survey*. London: Home Office Research, Development and Statistics Directorate, Crime and Criminal Justice Unit.

Forthofer, M. S., Markman, H. J., Cox, M., Stanley, S., & Kessler, R. C. (1996). Associations between marital distress and work loss in a national sample. *Journal of Marriage and Family, 58*, 597-605.

Glenn, N. D., & Kramer, K. B. (1987). The marriages and divorces of the children of divorce. *Journal of Marriage and the Family, 49*, 811-825.

Gottman, J. M. (1994). *Why marriages succeed or fail*. New York: Simon & Schuster.

Gottman, J. M. (1999). *The marriage clinic: A scientifically-based marital therapy*. New York: W. W. Norton & Company, Inc.

Gottman, J. M., & Silver, N. (1999). *The seven principles for making marriage work*. New York: Three Rivers Press.

Gray, J. (1997). The fall in men's return to marriage. *Journal of Human Resources, 32*(3), 481-504.

Grossbard-Schectman, S. A. (Ed.), *Marriage and the economy*. Cambridge: Cambridge University Press.

Hao, L. (1996). Family structure, private transfers, and the economic well-being of families and children. *Social Forces, 75*(1), 269-292.

Harden, B. (2001, August 12). 2-parent families rise after change in welfare laws. *The New York Times*. Retrieved on January 4, 2010, from www.nytimes.com

Harper, C., & McLanahan, S. (1998, August). *Father absence and youth incarceration*. Paper presented at the annual meeting of the American Sociological Association, San Francisco, CA.

Hatfield, E., & Walster, G. W. (1978). *A new look at love*. Reading, MA: Addison-Wesley.

Herbert, T., & Cohen, S. (1993). Stress and immunity in humans: a meta-analytical review. *Psychosomatic Medicine, 55*, 364-379.

Hetherington, E. M., & Kelly, J. (2002). *For better or for worse: Divorce reconsidered*. New York: W. W. Norton & Company, Inc.

Hill, E. J., Yang, C. M., Hawkins, A. J., & Ferris, M. (2004). A cross-cultural test of the work-family interface in 48 countries. *Journal of Marriage and the Family, 66*, 1300-1316.

Hope, S., Power, C., & Rodgers, B. (1999). Does financial hardship account for elevated psychological distress in lone mothers? *Social Science and Medicine, 49*(12), 1637-1649.

Horwitz, A. V., White, H. R., & Howell-White, S. (1996). Becoming married and mental health: A longitudinal study of a cohort of young adult. *Journal of Marriage and the Family, 58*, 895-907.

Horwitz, A. V., & Raskin, H. (1998). The relationship of cohabitation and mental health: A study of a young adult cohort. *Journal of Marriage and the Family, 60*(2), 504-514.

Horwitz, A. V., & White, H. R. (1991). Becoming married, depression, and alcohol problems among young adults. *Journal of Health and Social Behavior, 32*, 221-237.

House, J. A., Landis, K. R., & Umbertson, D. (1988). Social relationships and health. *Science, 241*, 540-545.

REFERENCES

Houston, R. (2002). *Is he cheating on you? 829 telltale signs.* New York: Lifestyle Publications.

Infatuation. (1533). In *Merriam-Webster's online dictionary.* Retrieved January 18, 2010, from http://www.merriam-webster.com/netdict.htm

Jeynes, W. H. (1999). Effects of remarriage following divorce on the academic achievement of children. *Journal of Youth and Adolescence, 28*(3), 385-393.

Johnson, G. R., Krug, E. G., & Potter, L. B. (2000). Suicide among adolescents and young adults: A cross-national comparison of 34 countries. *Suicide and Life-Threatening Behavior, 30*(1), 74-82.

Jones, B. L., Scoville, P., Hill, E. J., Childs, G., Leishman, J. M., & Nally, K. S. (2008). Perceived versus used workplace flexibility in Singapore: Predicting work-family fit. *Journal of Family Psychology, 22*(5), 774-783.

Kendrick, S., & Kendrick, A. (2008). *The love dare.* Nashville, TN: B & H Publishing Group.

Kessler, R. C., & Essex, M. (1982). Marital status and depression: The importance of coping resources. *Social Forces, 61,* 484-507.

Kessler, R. C., Borges, G., & Walters, E. E. (1999). Prevalence of and risk factors for lifetime suicide attempts in the national comorbidity survey. *Archives of General Psychiatry, 56,* 617-626.

Korenman, S., & Neumark, D. (1991). *Does marriage really make men more productive? Journal of Human Resources, 26*(2), 282-307.

Lahaye, T., & Lahaye, B. (1976). *The act of marriage.* Grand Rapids, MI: Zondervan.

Laing, S. Retrieved May 2, 2010, from http://www.SamandGeriLaing.com

Lawler, K. A., Younger, J. W., Piferi, R. L., et al. (2003). A change of heart: cardiovascular correlates of forgiveness in response to interpersonal conflict. *Journal of Behavioral Medicine, 26,* 373-393.

Lawson, A. (1988). *Adultery: An analysis of love and betrayal.* New York: Basic Books.

Lester, D. (1994). Domestic integration and suicide in 21 nations, 1950-1985. International *Journal of Comparative Sociology XXXV*(1-2), 131-137.

Lite, J. (2009, January 6). This is your brain on love: Lasting romance makes an impression--literally. *Scientific American*. Retrieved January 18, 2010, from http://www.scientificamerican.com

Louis, J. P., & Louis, K. M. (2012). *Good enough parenting: A Christian perspective on meeting core emotional needs and avoiding exasperation*. Singapore: Louis Counselling & Training Services.

Louis, J. P., & Louis, K. M. (2015). *Good enough parenting: An in-depth perspective on meeting core emotional needs and avoiding exasperation*. Singapore: Louis Counselling & Training Services.

Lupton, J., & Smith, J. P. (2002). Marriage, assets and savings. In Grossbard-Schectman, S. A. (Ed.), *Marriage and the economy*. Cambridge: Cambridge University Press.

Marks, N. F., & Lambert, J. D. (1998). Marital status continuity and change among young and midlife adults: Longitudinal effects on psychological well-being. *Journal of Family Issues, 19*, 652-686.

Marriage good for health (2009, 16 December). *The Straits Times*, A18.

Martin, T. C., & Bumpass, L. L. (1989). Recent trends in marital disruption. *Demography 26*(1), 37-51.

Massey, R. (2007, April 26). Time pressures 'leave couples only ten minutes a day to talk'. *Mail Online*. Retrieved January 13, 2010, from http://www.dailymail.co.uk/news/article-450749/

Mastekaasa, A. (1994). The subjective well-being of the previously married: The importance of unmarried cohabitation and time since widowhood or divorce. *Social Forces, 73*, 665-692.

McLanahan, S., & Sandefur, G. (1994) *Growing up with a single parent: What hurts, what helps*. Cambridge, MA: President and Fellows of Harvard College. 167-168.

McLeod, J. I. (1991). Childhood parental loss and adult depression. *Journal of Health and Social Behavior, 32*, 205-220.

Miller-Tutzauer, C., Leonard, K. E., & Windle, M. (1991). Marriage and alcohol use: A longitudinal study of maturing out. *Journal of Studies on Alcohol, 52*, 434-440.

Moore, K. A., Jekielek, S. M., & Emig, C. (2002, June). Marriage from a child's perspective: How does family structure affect children, and what can be done about it? *Child Trends Research Brief.* Washington, DC: Child Trends.

Muella, R. (2005). The effect of marital dissolution on the labour supply of males and females: Evidence from Canada. *Journal of Socio-Economics, 34,* 787-809.

Neuman, G. (2001). *Emotional infidelity.* New York: Random House Inc.

Neuman, G. (2008). The truth about cheating: *Why men stray and what you can do to prevent it.* Hoboken, NJ: John Wiley & Sons, Inc.

Neuman, G. (2009, February 12). Why Men Cheat. *The Oprah Winfrey Show.* (O. Winfrey, Interviewer). Retrieved January 16, 2010, from http://www.oprah.com/relationships/Why-Men-Cheat_2/slide_number/10#slide

Neuman, G. (2012, February 29). Saving your marriage after financial hardship. *Huffpost Weddings.* Retrieved January 31, 2015 from http://www.huffingtonpost.com/m-gary-neuman/saving-your-marriage-financial-hardship_b_1307224.html

Marriage good for health (2009, December 16). *The Straits Times,* A18.

Nolte, D. L. (1972). *Children learn what they live.* Retrieved January 15, 2010, from http://www.empowermentresources.com/info2/childrenlearn-long_version.html

O'Neill, R. (2005). *Does marriage matter?* London: Civitas, Institute for the Study of Civil Society.

Office for National Statistics. (2001). *Work and worklessness among households.* London: The Stationery Office.

Office for National Statistics. (2002). *Social trends 32.* London: The Stationery Office.

Office for National Statistics. (May 2002). *Family Resources Survey, Great Britain, 2000-01.* London: The Stationery Office.

Orathinkal, J., & Vansteenwegen, A. (2006). The effect of forgiveness on marital satisfaction in relationship to marital stability. *Contemporary Family Therapy, 28,* 251-260.

Paleari, F. G., Regalia, C., & Fincham, F. D. (2005). Marital quality, forgiveness, empathy, and rumination: A longitudinal analysis. *Journal of Social Behaviour and Personality, 3*, 368-378.

Park, Y., & Enright, R. D. (1997). The development of forgiveness in the context of adolescent friendship conflict in Korea. *Journal of Adolescence, 20*, 393-402.

Perry-Jenkins, M., Repetti, R., & Crouter, A. (2000). Work and family in the 1990s. *Journal of Marriage and the Family, 62*(4), 981-998.

Pienta, A. M., Hayward, M. D., Jenkins, K. R. (2000). Health consequences of marriage for the retirement years. *Journal of Family Issues, 21*(5), 559-586.

Pietrini, P., Guazzelli, M., Basso, G., Jaffe, K., & Grafman, J. (2000). Neural correlates of imaginal aggressive behavior assessed by positron emission tomography in healthy subjects. *The American Journal of Psychiatry, 157*, 1772-1781

Power, C., Rodgers, B., & Hope, S. (1999). Heavy alcohol consumption and marital status: Disentangling the relationship in a national study of young adults. *Addiction, 94*(10), 1477-1487.

Prime Minister Lee Hsien Loong's National Day rally speech, Sunday 22 August 2004, at the University Cultural Centre, NUS - Our future of opportunity and promise. (2004, 22 August). *National Archives of Singapore*. Retrieved May 2, 2010, from http://stars.nhb.gov.sg/stars/public/viewHTML.jsp?pdfno=2004083101

Rampell, C. (2009, May 5). As layoffs surge, women may pass men in job force. The New York Times. Retrieved January 28, 2010, from http://www.nytimes.com

Ressler, C., & Thompson, J. (2008). *Why work sucks and how to fix it*. New York: Penguin.

Rogers, S. J., & May, D. C. (2003). Spillover between marital quality and job satisfaction: Long-term patterns and gender differences. *Journal of Marriage and Family, 65*(2), 482-495.

Romantic love 'lasts just a year'. (2005, November 28). *BBC News*. Retrieved January 15, 2010, from http://news.bbc.co.uk

Ross, C. E., & Mirowsky, J. (1999). Parental divorce, life course disruption, and adult depression. *Journal of Marriage and the Family, 61*, 1034-1045.

Sampson, R. J. (1987). Urban black violence: The effect of male joblessness and family disruption. *American Journal of Sociology, 93*, 348-382.

Sampson, R. J., & Laub, J. H. (1994). Urban poverty and the family context of delinquency: A new look at structure and process in a classic study. *Child Development, 65*, 523-540.

Sandholtz, K., Derr, B., Buckner, K., & Carlson, D. (2002). *Beyond juggling. Rebalancing your busy life.* San Francisco: Berrett-Koehler.

Sarinopoulos, I. C. (1996). *Forgiveness in adolescence and middle adulthood: Comparing the Enright Forgiveness Inventory with Wade Forgiveness Scale.* University of Wisconsin-Madison.

Schoeni, R. F. (1995). Marital status and earnings in developed countries. *Journal of Population Economics, 8*, 351-359.

Scott Peck, M. (1978). *The road less travelled.* New York: Touchstone.

Seybold, K. S., Hill, P. C., Neumann, J. K., & Chi, D. S. (2001). Physiological and psychological correlates of forgiveness. *Journal of Psychology and Christianity, 20*, 250-259.

Simons, R. L., Lin, K-H., Gordon, L. C., Conger, R. D., & Lorenz, F. O. (1999). Explaining the higher incidence of adjustment problems among children of divorce compared with those in two-parent families. *Journal of Marriage and the Family, 61*(4), 1020-1033.

Singapore Attorney General. *Employment Act (Chapter 91), Part IV, Section 38(1).* Retrieved May 2, 2010, from Singapore Statutes Online: http://statutes.agc.gov.sg

Singapore Attorney General. *Women's Charter, Part X, Chapter 1: Divorce.* Retrieved March 02, 2010, from Singapore Statutes Online: http://statutes.agc.gov.sg

Singapore Department of Statistics. (2009, August 13). *Statistics Singapore - Time series on labour force participation rate.* Retrieved January 14, 2010, from http://www.singstat.gov.sg/stats/themes/economy/hist/labour.html

Smede, L. B. (1984). *Forgive and forget. Healing the hurts we don't deserve.* New York: Pocket Books.

Solomon, G. Retrieved May 2, 2010, from http://www.cinema-therapy.com

Stack, S., & Eshleman, J. R. (1998). Marital status and happiness: A 17-nation study. *Journal of Marriage and the Family, 60*, 527-536.

Sternberg, R. J. (1988). *The triangle of love: Intimacy, passion, commitment.* New York: Basic Books.

Stewart, W., Ricci, J., Chee, E., Hahn, S., & Morganstein, D. (2003). Cost of lost productive work time among US workers with depression. *Journal of the American Medical Association, 289,* 3135-3144.

Straughan, Paulin Tay. (2009). *Marriage dissolution in Singapore: Revisiting family values and ideology in marriage.* Leiden, the Netherlands: Koninklikje Brill NV.

Stress: The fight or flight response. (n.d.). *Psychologist World.* Retrieved May 2, 2010, from http://www.psychologistworld.com

Subkoviak, M. J., Enright, R. D., & Wu, C. (1992, October). *Current developments related to measuring forgiveness.* Paper presented at the annual meeting of the Midwestern Educational Research Association, Chicago, IL.

Subkoviak, M. J., Enright, R. D., Wu, C., Gassin, E. A., Freedman, S., Olson, L. M., & Sarinopoulos, I. C. (1995). Measuring interpersonal forgiveness in late adolescence and middle adulthood. *Journal of Adolescence, 18,* 641-655.

Swaminathan, N. (2007, October 23). Can a lack of sleep cause psychiatric disorders? *Scientific American.* Retrieved January 31, 2015 from http://www.scientificamerican.com/article/can-a-lack-of-sleep-cause/.

Templeton, J. (1999). *Agape love: A tradition found in eight world religions.* Radnor, PA: Templeton Foundation Press.

The Gottman Institute. *Love Maps.* Retrieved from https://itunes.apple.com/us/app/love-maps/id389288067?mt=8.

Turvey, M. D., & Olson, D. H. (2006). *Marriage & family wellness: Corporate America's business?* Roseville, MN: Life Innovation, Inc.

Vermulst, A., & Dubas, J. (1999). Job stress and family functioning: The mediating role for parental depression and the explaining role of emotional stability. *Tijdschrift voor Psycholigie & Gezonheid, 27*, 96-102.

Waite, L., & Gallagher, M. (2000). The case for marriage: *Why married people are happier, healthier, and better off financially.* New York: Doubleday.

WebMD. (n.d.) *How much sleep do children need?* Retrieved January 31, 2015 from http://www.webmd.com/parenting/guide/sleep-children.

Wellings, K., Field, J., Johnson, A. M., Wadsworth, J. (1994). *Sexual behaviour in Britain.* London: Penguin.

Whitfield, C. L. (2006). *Healing the child within.* Deerfield Beach, FL: Health Communications, Inc.

World divorce statistics. (n.d.). *Divorce Magazine.* Retrieved January 13, 2010, from http://www.divorcemag.com/statistics/statsWorld.shtml

Worthington, E. L., Jr. (1998). *Dimensions of forgiveness: Psychological research & theological perspectives.* Radnor, PA: Templeton Foundation Press.

Worthington, E. L., Jr. (1999). *Hope-focused marriage counseling.* Downers Grove, IL: InterVarsity Press.

Young, J. E., & Klosko, J. S. (1994). *Reinventing your life.* New York: Plume.

Young, J. E., Klosko, J. S., & Weishaar, M. E. (2003). *Schema therapy: A practitioner's guide.* New York: The Guilford Press.

Zill, N., Morrison, D. R., & Coiro, M. J. (1993). Long-term effects of parental divorce on parent-child relationships, adjustment, and achievement in young adulthood. *Journal of Family Psychology, 7*(1), 91-103.

INDEX

Page numbers in *italics* refer to illustrations.

A

Alexander, R., 35
Amato, P. R., 7, 8, 10, 11, 217
Anthony de Mello, S. J., 189, 190
Appreciate, see Wives

B

Barnes, S., 208
Barnett, R. C., 5
Basso, G., 222
BBC News, 19
Bearinger, L. H., 42
Berry, J. W., 222
Berthoud, R., 244
Biblarz, T. J., 10
Bolger, N., 241
Booth, A., 7, 10, 11, 217
Borges, G., 6
Bradshaw, J., 7
Brown, S. L., 244
Buckner, K., 241
Bumpus, M. F., 242
Bumpass, L. L., 1
Burghes, L., 7
Buss, D. M., 12

C

Cacioppo, J. T., 200, 201, 202
Campbell, S., 12
Carlson, D., 241
Cawson, P., 12
Chapman, G. D., 36
Cheating men
    reasons, 207
Chee, E., 242
Chi, D. S., 222
Childs, G., 241
Clarke, L., 7
Cockett, M., 7, 11
Cohen, S., 222
Coiro, M. J., 7, 10
Conger, R. D., 11
Considerate Listeners, see Husbands
Coping styles, 68–74
    avoidance, 70–72, *71*
    overcompensation, 72–74, *73*
    surrender, 68–70, *69*
Core emotional needs, 245
Corporate Resource Council, 4
Coughlin, C., 12
Cox, M., 4

Coyle, C. T., 223
Cronin, N., 7
Crouter, A. C., 242
Curtis, J., 242

D

Daly, M., 12
Deal, L., 6
Delongis, A., 241, 242
Derr, B., 241
Disintegration phase, 26–30, *28, 29*
Divorce, see also Women's Charter
   statistics, 238–239
Divorce Magazine, 1, 238
Doherty, W. J., 7
Dubas, J., 5, 242

E

Eisenberg, M. E., 42
Ely, M., 10
Emig, C., 6
Enright Forgiveness Inventory (EFI), 223, 233
Enright, R. D., 219, 220, 221, 223, 224, 232, 233
Ermisch, J., 244
Essex, M., 6
Eshleman, J. R., 252

Exercise
   anger, 226-229
   appreciate, 51
   considerate listener, 39-40
   empathy, 250-251
   imagery, 247-249
   infatuation memories, 31
   initiate, 54
   lifetraps & coping styles, 246
   participate, 57
   responsible leader, 45
   romantic lover, 48
   vortex of conflict escalation, 175

F

Fagan, P., 242
Ferris, M., 242
Field, J., 244
Fincham, F. D., 222
Fisher, H., 18, 30, 53, 56, 192
Fitzgibbons, R. P., 220, 223
Flood-Page, C., 12
Forgiveness, see also Scriptures
   definition, 218
   health, 222–223
   steps, 229–235
Forthofer, M. S., 4
Francesconi, M., 244
Freedman, S., 223

G

Gallagher, M., 5, 8, 9, 10, 244
Gareis, K. C., 5
Gassin, E. A., 223
Gershuny, J., 244
Glenn, N. D., 8
Gordon, L. C., 11
Gottman, J. M., 29, 34, 61, 174, 179
Grafman, J., 222
Gray, J., 10
Grossbard-Schectman, S. A., 9
Guazzelli, M., 222
Guilt, 224

H

Hahn, S., 242
Hao, L., 9
Harden, B., 6
Harper, C., 11
Harrington, V., 12
Hatfield, E., 17, 18, 19
Hawkins, A. J., 242
Hayward, M. D., 5, 244
Head, M. R., 242
Healing Statements, 231
Herbert, T., 222
Hetherington, E. M., 13
Hill, E. J., 241, 242
Hill, P. C., 222
Holt, V., 6

Hope, S., 5, 6
Horwitz, A. V., 6, 244
House, J. A., 201
Houston, R., 42, 205, 208, 210
Howell-White, S., 6
Husbands
   considerate listeners, 36–40
   responsible leaders, 40–45
   romantic lovers, 46–48

I

Imagery Exercise, 197–198, 247–249
Infatuation phase, 17–22, 27, 30–31, *18, 20, 29*, see also Exercise
Infidelity
   dealing with, 211–214
   definition, 206
Initiate, see Wives

J

Jaffe, K., 222
Jekielek, S. M., 6
Jenkins, K. R., 5, 244
Jeynes, W. H., 10
Johnson, A. M., 244
Johnson, G. R., 6
Jones, B. L., 241
Journal
   lifetraps, 190–191, 246

K

Kelly, J., 13
Kendrick, A., 213
Kendrick, S., 213
Kessler, R. C., 4, 6, 242
Klosko, J. S., 64, 67, 68, 76, 128, 183, 189, 198, 245
Korenman, S., 10
Kramer, K. B., 8
Krug, E. G., 6

L

Lahaye, B., 35, 56
Lahaye, T., 35, 56
Laing, S., 46
Lambert, J. D., 6
Landis, K. R., 201
Laub, J. H., 12
Lawson, A., 206
Lawler, K. A., 223
Leishman, J. M., 241
Leonard, K. E., 5
Lester, D., 6 Lifetrap, 63–173, *65*
    abandonment lifetrap, 125–130, *127*
    approval-seeking lifetrap, 152-156, *153*
    defectiveness lifetrap, 83–89, *85*
    dependence lifetrap, 115–120, *117*
    emotional deprivation lifetrap, 90–94, *91*
    emotional inhibition lifetrap, 100–104, *101*
    enmeshment lifetrap, 120–125, *121*
    entitlement lifetrap, 140–147, *142*
    failure lifetrap, 105–110, *106*
    insufficient self-control lifetrap, 147–152, *149*
    mistrust lifetrap, 78–83, *79*
    negativity lifetrap, 135–139, *137*
    punitiveness lifetrap, 162–167, *163*
    self-sacrifice lifetrap, 167–172, *168*
    social isolation lifetrap, 95–99, *96*
    subjugation lifetrap, 130–135, *132*
    unrelenting standards lifetrap, 157–162, *158*
    vulnerability lifetrap, 110–115, *112*
Lin, K-H., 12
Lite, J., 30
Lorenz, F. O., 11
Love Connection phase, 19–26, *21, 29*
Lupton, J., 9

M

Malamuth, N. M., 13
Markman, H. J., 4
Marks, N. F., 6

Marriage
- child abuse, 12
- children's performance at school, 10–11
- economics, 9–10
- health, 11
- juvenile delinquency, 11–12
- parenting, 6–12
- parents role models, 8
- relationship parents and children, 7–8
- versus cohabitation, 243–244
- work, 4

Martin, T. C., 1
Massey, R., 3
Mastekaasa, A., 244
May, D. C., 4
McHale, S. M., 242
McLanahan, S., 9, 11
McLeod, J. I., 8
Merriam-Webster's online dictionary, 17
Millar, J., 7
Miller, J., 12
Miller-Tutzauer, C., 5
Ministry of Community Development, Youth and Sports, 7, 241
Mirowsky, J., 8, 10
Moore, K. A., 6
Morganstein, D., 242
Morrison, D. R., 7, 10
Muella, R., 4
Mutual Affection phase, 26–30, *27, 29*

N

Nally, K. S., 241
Neuman, G., 42, 49, 55, 60, 205, 206, 207
Neumann, J. K., 222
Neumark, D., 10
Neumark-Sztainer, D., 42
Nolte, D. L., 182

O

O'Neill, R., 7, 8, 9, 11, 12
Office for National Statistics, 9
Olson, D. H., 4
Olson, L. M., 224
Olson, R. E., 42
Orathinkal, J., 222
Overcoming
- lifetraps, 187–202

P

Paleari, F. G., 222
Park, Y., 223
Participate, see Wives
Perry-Jenkins, M., 242
Piferi, R. L., 223

Pienta, A. M., 5, 244
Pietrini, P., 222
Potter, L. B., 6
Power, C., 5, 6
Pre-marriage counselling, 35

R

Raskin, H., 244
Rampell, C., 208
Reconciliation, *29*, 217–223
Rector, R., 242
Regalia, C., 222
Repetti, R., 242
Ressler, C., 241
Responsible Leaders, see Husbands
Ricci, J., 242
Richards, M., 10
Rique, J., 233
Rodgers, B., 5, 6
Rogers, S. J., 4
Romantic Lovers, see Husbands
Ross, C. E., 8, 10

S

Sampson, R. J., 13
Sandefur, G., 11
Sandholtz, K., 241
Sarinopoulos, I. C., 223
Schemas, see Lifetraps

Schilling, E. A., 241
Schoeni, R. F., 10
Scott Peck, M., 185
Scoville, P., 241
Scriptures
    abandonment lifetrap, 130
    approval-seeking lifetrap, 156
    child side, 180–181
    defectiveness lifetrap, 90
    dependence lifetrap, 120
    emotional deprivation lifetrap, 94
    emotional inhibition lifetrap, 104
    enmeshment lifetrap, 125
    entitlement lifetrap, 147
    failure lifetrap, 110
    forgiveness, 218–221
    infatuation, 17, 22
    insufficient self-control lifetrap, 152
    love and respect, 33–34
    mistrust lifetrap, 83
    negativity lifetrap, 139
    punitiveness lifetrap, 167
    self-sacrifice lifetrap, 172
    shame and guilt, 224–225
    sinful and spiritual side, 198–199
    social isolation lifetrap, 99
    subjugation lifetrap, 135
    unrelenting standards lifetrap, 162
    vulnerability lifetrap, 115

Seybold, K. S., 222
Shame, 224
Silver, N., 60, 174
Simons, R. L., 11
Singapore Department of Statistics, 208
Singapore Statutes Online, 38, 240
Smede, L. B., 233
Smith, J. P., 9
Solomon, G., 67
Stack, S., 244
Stanley, S., 4
Steptoe, A., 5
Sternberg, R. J., 23
    scale, 23–26
Stewart, W., 243
Story, M., 42
Straughan, Paulin Tay., 28, 38
Subkoviak, M. J., 224
Sweeting, H., 10

T

Templeton, J., 22
Thompson, J., 241
Tripp, J., 7, 11
Turvey, M. D., 4

U

Umbertson, D., 201

V

Vansteenwegen, A., 222
Vermulst, A., 5, 242
Vortex of Conflict Escalation, 172–176
    diagram, *173*
    see also Exercise
Vuchinich, S., 12
Vulnerable
    communication, 185–187
    statements, 191–197

W

Wadsworth, J., 244
Waite, L., 5, 8, 9, 10, 244
Walster, G. W., 17, 18, 19
Walters, E. E., 6
Weishaar, M. E., 75, 189, 198, 245
Wellings, K., 244
West, P., 10
White, H. R., 6
Whitfield, C. L., 181, 183, 184, 185, 224
William, P., 200, 201, 202
Wilson, M., 12
Windle, M., 5
Wives
    appreciate, 48–51
    initiate, 52–54
    participate, 54–57

Women's Charter, 240

Worthington, E. L., Jr., 220, 222, 233, 234

Wu, C., 223

Y

Yang, C. M., 242

Young, J. E., 64, 67, 68, 75, 128, 183, 189, 198, 245

Younger, J. W., 223

Youth Crime, 12

Z

Zill, N., 7, 10